WORKBOOK

CAROL NUTTALL AND DAVID EVANS

PRE-INTERMEDIATE
OUTCOMES

HEINLE
CENGAGE Learning™

Australia • Brazil • Japan • Korea • Mexico • Singapore • Spain • United Kingdom • United States

Outcomes *Pre-Intermediate Workbook*
Carol Nuttall and David Evans

Publisher: Jason Mann

Senior Commissioning Editor: John Waterman

Development Editor: Lynn Thomson

Product Manager: Ruth McAleavey

Content Project Editor: Amy Smith

Manufacturing Team Lead: Paul Herbert

Cover and text designer: Studio April

Compositor: eMC Design Ltd.

ISBN: 978-1-111-05411-3

Heinle, Cengage Learning EMEA
Cheriton House, North Way, Andover, Hampshire
SP10 5BE United Kingdom

Cengage Learning is a leading provider of customised learning solutions with office locations around the globe, including Singapore, the United Kingdom, Australia, Mexico, Brazil and Japan. Locate our local office at **international.cengage.com/region**

Cengage Learning products are represented in Canada by Nelson Education Ltd.

Visit Heinle online at **elt.heinle.com**
Visit our corporate website at **cengage.com**

CREDITS

Although every effort has been made to contact copyright holders before publication, this has not always been possible. If notified, the publisher will undertake to rectify any errors or omissions at the earliest opportunity.

Text

The publisher would like to thank the following source for permission to use their copyright protected text:

Page 43: Different Strokes is a charity set up by Younger Stroke Survivors. Different Strokes helps stroke survivors to optimise their recovery, take control of their own lives and regain as much independence as possible by offering information, advice and rehabilitation services. For more information about Different Strokes please visit www.differentstrokes.co.uk

Photos

The publisher would like to thank the following sources for permission to use their copyright protected images:

Alamy – pp7m (graham clark), 62bl (Jim Wileman), 72bl (David Wells), 90t (jeremy sutton-hibbert), 92tr (David R. Frazier Photolibrary, Inc.); Bigstockphoto – 22ml (erwinova), 22mr (iofoto.com), 22ml (CandyBoxPhoto), 22bl (crysrob), 22br (4774344sean), 44r (Perkmeup), 49ml (mountainpz), 59bl (Noam Armonn), 66bl (Nikiandr), 79ml (icholakov), 86bl (Bardofthebroch), 64br (Miri Photography); DSA – pp42tl (Simon Gross on behalf the Down's Syndrome Association DSActive Programme); Fotolia – pp16tl (Barbara Helgason), 16bml (rafer76), 16br (Digitalpress), 18tr (Rod Luey), 18mr (JJAVA), 18br (Svenja98), 22tl (Monkey Business), 22mr (Greg Pickens), 25tl (Graça Victoria), 25tl (Mustafa Ersin Kurtdal), 28ml (Arto), 29tr (Mike Thomas), 30tl (Brocreative), 30m (Georgiy Pashin), 30bl (rudybaby), 30tr (Lilja), 30br (W. Briggs), 31br (bilderbox), 32ml (forestpath), 33m (Elnur), 35tl (victor zastol'skiy), 35br (Michael Spring), 35bl (Sam Shapiro), 40br (carlosseller), 44l (Monika Adamczyk), 44m (Monika Adamczyk), 61ml (Waldo4), 64tl (easaab), 68b (Andreas Karelias), 74tl (Timothée D'arco), 96m (Mariusz Blach); Getty – pp7mr (David Levenson), 7b (Leon Neal), 29tl (isifa); iStockphoto – pp5t (Aldo Murillo), 5bl (track5), 8r (LindaYolanda), 11t (Paul Piebinga), 10l (arekmalang), 14bl (vnlit), 17t (Saso Novoselic), 20bl (webphotographeer), 22tr (Markanja), 22t (Daniel Rodriguez), 25tm (AlexStar), 28t (Anna Bryukhanova), 35t (Justin Horrocks), 37bl (ilbusca), 14t (Krzysztof Chrystowski), 47t (Robert Churchill), 49tr (lightpix), 49mr (Veni), 53t (morganl), 58bl (sjlocke), 59t (Tomaz Levstek), 61tr (monkeybusinessimages), 64tr (mbbirdy), 66t (Catherine Yeulet), 71t (Izabela Habur), 77t (Stephanie Phillips), 84t (Roman Milert), 85br (kipuxa), 88br (al_ks), 89t (Andrey Volodin), 95t (José Luis Gutiérrez), 97mr (GeorgiosArt), 98b (duncan1890); Majorityworld.com – pp90b (Shahidul Alam/Drik/Majority World); Photolibrary – pp54ml (Michael Dick); Rex Features – 84bl (Paul Grover); Shutterstock – pp12bl (Dmitriy Shironosov), 13m (Gelpi), 14mr (Jacqueline Abromeit), 16tr (Andrew Chin), 16bl (Vasiliy Koval), 16bmr (Dusan Zidar), 18mr (123stocks), 24mr (Ronen), 29bl (cjpdesigns), 29mr (Pedro Jorge Henriques Monteiro), 32tr (X.D.Luo), 38bl (Itinerant Lens), 46br (Michal Kowalski), 48m (Chad McDermott), 49br (BedoMedo), 56b (Paul Prescott), 60br (ene), 64bl (Roman Sika), 72tr (Aga & Miko), 79mr (Creations), 81bl (AVAVA), 87m (Kenneth William Caleno), 94bl (Lynne Carpenter); Little, Brown Book Group – pp7bl (Illustrator: Hannah Firman).

Illustrations by Mark Draisey and Clive Goddard

Printed by Seng Lee Press, Singapore
2 3 4 5 6 7 8 9 10 – 15 14 13 12 11

CONTENTS

01   FAMILY AND FRIENDS   P.4

02   SHOPS   P.10

03   EAT   P.16

04   JOBS   P.22

05   RELAX   P.28

06   HOME   P.34

07   MIND AND BODY   P.40

08   GETTING THERE   P.46

09   SCIENCE AND NATURE   P.52

10   EDUCATION   P.58

11   PLACES TO STAY   P.64

12   PHONE   P.70

13   CULTURE   P.76

14   THINGS   P.82

15   THE ECONOMY AND MONEY   P.88

16   DATES AND HISTORY   P.94

AUDIOSCRIPT   P.101

ANSWER KEY   P.113

01 FAMILY AND FRIENDS

VOCABULARY People you know

A Choose a word from the box below to complete each sentence.

aunt	boyfriend	brother	businessman
colleague	cousin	dad	flatmate
friend	gran	housewife	neighbour
sister	teenager	uncle	waiter

1 My little .... is very annoying, but I love him!
2 I share my apartment with another girl. My .... is Spanish, and her name is Carla.
3 My parents are both from Delhi, in India. My .... is a doctor.
4 My mum is a .... and doesn't work.
5 I don't have any brothers or sisters but my aunt has two children. I'm very close to my ....
6 James and I work together. We're ....

B Place the following words with their opposites in the box below. There are some examples to help you.

impatient	mean	plain	stupid
unfit	uncaring	~~strict~~	~~untidy~~

patient	1	....
clever	2	....
attractive	3	....
fit	4	....
generous	5	....
easy-going		*strict*
neat		*untidy*
caring	6	....

> **Learner tip**
>
> Build up a list of words and phrases to describe people's character and appearance. Putting them next to their opposites is a good way to remember them!

C Complete the sentences with an adjective from exercise B.

1 Don't worry. I can wait for you. I'm ....
2 She plays football and tennis, and she swims. She's so ....
3 My uncle never gives me anything. He's so ....
4 My sister is five and she is fantastic at maths. She's so ....
5 You're not interested in me. You are so ....
6 Kelly's an .... girl, with long hair and lovely eyes, but Jane's a bit .... However, Jane is very .... , and looks after her friends.

Language note *fit* versus *healthy*

You are *fit* when you exercise a lot, play sport regularly or train hard. *Fit* means your body is in very good condition.
When you are *healthy*, you eat well, sleep well and do not get sick easily.

GRAMMAR Question formation

A Complete the questions with the question words. Then answer them about yourself.

How	Why	When	How long
Is	What	How old	Do

1 Q: .... did you start learning English?
   A: ....
2 Q: .... have you known your best friend?
   A: ....
3 Q: .... is your favourite food?
   A: ....
4 Q: .... you like Madonna?
   A: ....
5 Q: .... much do you pay to go to the cinema in your country?
   A: ....
6 Q: .... your hair dark or fair?
   A: ....
7 Q: .... do you like your best friend?
   A: Because ....
8 Q: .... are you? Do you still go to school or college? Or do you work?
   A: ....

B Correct the mistakes in the following questions.

1 Why you like him?
   ....
2 You have been waiting how long?
   ....
3 You did like Kerry's new boyfriend?
   ....
4 When you met your wife?
   ....
5 How you make that delicious spaghetti dish?
   ....
6 From where you are?
   ....

DEVELOPING CONVERSATIONS
Responding naturally

A Make the responses to the following questions more natural. There is an example to help you.

A: Do you get on with your boss?
B: No, I don't get on with my boss. My boss is very strict, and not at all friendly.
B: No, I don't. He's very strict, and not at all friendly.

1 A: Where are you from?
   B: I come from Bangalore, in India.
   ....

2 A: How long have you been in London?
   B: I have been in London for two weeks.
   ....

3 A: Have you got any brothers or sisters?
   B: I have got brothers and sisters. I have got one brother and two sisters.
   ....

4 A: Are you studying here?
   B: I am studying Business Studies at the university.
   ....

5 A: Do you live near the university?
   B: I live quite near to the university. I share a flat with another student.
   ....

6 A: Do you get on with your flatmate?
   B: I do not get on with my flatmate. He is really untidy and mean.
   ....

B Give your own short answers to the following questions.

1 Where are you from?   ....
2 How long have you been studying English?
   ....
3 Do you like the language?   ....
4 Do you get on with your classmates?
   ....
5 Do you live near your language school?   ....

LISTENING

A Match the following words with the definitions and then check your answers.

1 immigrant   ....
2 primary school   ....
3 secondary school   ....
4 field   ....
5 harvest   ....

a piece of land used for farming
b school for 12–18 year-olds
c person who comes to live in a country from another country
d time when farmers collect the foods they grow on the land
e school for 5–11 year-olds

B 🔊 1.1 Listen to three people talk about where they spent their childhood. Decide where each person grew up: A in the country, B by the sea, C in different countries, D in a city.

Speaker 1   A B C D
Speaker 2   A B C D
Speaker 3   A B C D

C Match the sentence halves.

1 Babur Wahidi went to a multicultural   ....
2 Babur enjoyed being at the school   ....
3 Babur's situation improved at secondary school ....
4 Joe remembers sometimes feeling lonely   ....
5 Carrie found it difficult to   ....
6 Carrie now has no problem   ....

a on the farm where he grew up.
b because the teachers understood their students' needs.
c moving to a different town and starting a new job.
d primary school in Bradford.
e change school all the time.
f after classmates learnt he was good at football.

D 🔊 1.1 Listen again and check your answers.

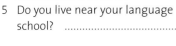

> **Learner tip**
>
> If a listening task asks you to complete a sentence, read through the questions carefully before you listen. Think about what you are going to hear. Listen carefully to the audioscript. Then choose your answers.

GRAMMAR Present simple

A **Put the number of each sentence into the correct part of the table below.**

1 My brother works in Zurich.
2 The sun rises in the East.
3 I walk the dog twice a day.
4 Do you see your old school friends much?
5 Does a pentagon have four sides, or five?
6 Kelly and I go to the cinema every week.

fact	regular occurrence / habit

B **Put the adverbs in the box into the correct place on the line below. The first two are done for you.**

always	never	quite often	usually
sometimes	hardly ever	not very often	

never .... always

0%   100%

....

C **Now add these adverb phrases to the diagrams.**

every day	two or three times a week
once a month	four or five times a year

never .... always

0%   100%

....

D **Make sentences and questions using the words in brackets.**

1 (go / I / to the cinema / often) at the weekend.
....

2 (you / often / how / visit / do) your grandparents?
....

3 (go / twice a week / they / to the local gym)
....

4 (two or three times a year / meet up with / I / my old school friends)
....

5 (you / need to speak English / sometimes / do) at work?
....

6 (quite often / visits / David / his sister) in Toronto.
....

7 (hear / I / Rachel / sometimes / arguing) with her flatmate.
....

8 (hardly ever / Wendy / see / I) any more.
....

Language note spelling rules

Look at the spelling rules for *he / she / it* in the present tense.
When a verb ends in *-s, -sh, -ch, -o*, add *-es* to the ending, e.g. *She goes to a primary school. She finishes school at 3.15.*
When a verb ends in a consonant + *-y*, change the ending to *-ies*, e.g. *He studies French and Chinese. He never tidies his bedroom.*

E **Read the text about three places where people live a very long life. Complete the gaps with the correct present simple form of the verb in brackets.**

Okinawa in Japan, Ovodda in Sardinia and Loma Linda in California share something interesting. They are all good places to live. In all of them, people live a long life, many reaching 100. Scientists are studying the communities in these areas to find out why this happens.

Okinawans [1] .... (grow) old more slowly than people in other parts of the world. Scientists say that most of them [2] .... (stay) healthy for longer, too. A major reason for this [3] .... (seem) to be their diet. The Okinawans eat a lot of tofu and soya, and a wide range of vegetables and fruit. They [4] .... (believe) that it is not healthy to fill your stomach completely, and so they [5] .... (not eat) big meals. Their simple lifestyle includes daily exercise, and their stress levels [6] .... (be) lower than those of people living in cities.

In the mountain village of Ovodda, Sardinia, people also [7] .... (live) long lives, but Professor Luca Deiana, who [8] .... (study) the community, believes there is another reason for the Sardinians' longevity. An Ovoddan man usually [9] .... (marry) a woman from the same community. Professor Deiana believes that the local people pass on their good health to their children.

Dr Gary Fraser is researching the people of Loma Linda, in California, and he [10] .... (have) a different theory about their long lives. This community is a very religious one, and most of the people are Seventh-Day Adventists. They lead healthy lives, and an important part of their life is the belief in something. Dr Fraser believes this reduces their levels of stress.

There are several possible reasons why the people in these communities live so long, but they do have certain characteristics in common. Their communities are fairly small, family is very important, their diet is a healthy one and they get plenty of exercise. Perhaps the rest of us can learn something from them!

READING

A **Read the two texts below quickly and answer the questions.**

1 The title of the article is:
   a Book of the month
   b My favourite book
   c This week's top two writers
2 The article comes from:
   a a magazine
   b a book
   c a science journal
3 The writers come from:
   a Scotland and Australia
   b Zimbabwe and India
   c Botswana and India
4 The two writers write books about:
   a sport
   b people
   c studying

B **Read the article again. Decide whether the statements are true (T) or false (F).**

1 Alexander McCall Smith grew up in Scotland.   ....
2 He taught at the University of Botswana.   ....
3 He thinks the people of Botswana are mean.   ....
4 Aravind Adiga lives and works in America.   ....
5 His book has won an award.   ....
6 Both writers write about the goodness in people.   ....

C **Choose a suitable word from the box below to complete the sentences.**

spend	human	keeps	plays	paints	family

1 Laura .... a diary of all the important things that happen to her each day.
2 Everyone is selfish sometimes; it's part of .... nature!
3 The newspaper report .... an awful picture of children's behaviour in the classroom, but this is not always true.
4 I often .... time fishing with my grandfather at the weekend.
5 Mandy and John are both musical. Mandy .... the piano and John the bassoon.
6 At weekends, I enjoy walking in the mountains with friends and ....

This week's top two
writers

The writer, Alexander McCall Smith was born to Scottish parents in Rhodesia, now Zimbabwe, in 1948. He grew up there, and then moved to Scotland to study law at the University of Edinburgh. Returning to Africa, he taught law at the University of Botswana for a number of years. During this time, he noticed the warmth and kindness of the people of Botswana. He now lives in Scotland with his wife, Elizabeth, and two daughters, Lucy and Emily. Although he travels widely as a writer, his favourite activities include spending time at home with his family, cooking for family and friends and playing the bassoon in the Really Terrible Orchestra.

McCall Smith has written many books, including children's stories, but is best-known for his books about  a lady detective in Botswana. Mma Ramotswe, a lady 'of traditional build', likes drinking bush tea and helping people. So, she opens the 'Number One Ladies' Detective Agency', and does just that. There have been several books about her, and each one shows the gentle, funny, and mostly good side of human nature; the side the writer sees in the people of Botswana.

Aravind Adiga was born in southeastern India, the son of a doctor, and grew up in Mangalore and Australia. He studied English Literature at Columbia University in New York and Magdalen College, Oxford. After that Adiga became a journalist with the *Financial Times*. He also worked for *Time* magazine in India and other parts of Asia. After deciding to stay in Mumbai, he wrote a book called *The White Tiger*, which won an important literary award, the Man Booker prize, in 2008.

The book follows the story of its main character, Balram Halwai, who starts life as a servant in modern India, and finally becomes a successful businessman. As he tells his story, Balram shows the reader a part of India that we don't usually see, and the reality of life for the Indian poor. The book paints a picture that is both shocking and powerful. It shows us how difficult it is for many poor people to find a better life in modern India.

 How did Adiga, who is from a comfortable middle-class family, create such a realistic story about the poor? He says that as a journalist he travelled widely, and spent a lot of time talking with poor people at railway stations. He kept a diary of those conversations, and used his notes to build the character of Balram.

GRAMMAR Similarities and contrasts

Complete the sentences with *both*, *neither*, *all*, *none*, *whereas* or *but*.

1 Sally and Ginny .... enjoy going to the cinema.
2 Sally's favourite actor is Brad Pitt, ... Ginny prefers Clive Owen.
3 Ralph and I .... like playing sport, but .... of us likes watching it on TV!
4 .... of my friends are Linkin Park fans. We're going to their concert in September!
5 Jane and I are a little lazy. .... of us likes tidying up our room!
6 .... of us is very patient. We .... get frustrated easily and shout a lot!
7 The two are very different. Zach is very outgoing and friendly, ... Kevin is rather shy.
8 My gran's very practical and makes things, ... Grandad's rather careless and breaks them!

LISTENING

A 🔊 **1.2 Listen to a mother talking about her teenage son and daughter. Write down two similarities and two differences between them.**

Similarities: ....
....
....
....

Differences: ....
....
....
....

B 🔊 **1.2 Listen again and check your answers.**

VOCABULARY Character and habits

A **Complete the following character adjective collocations with a suitable word from the box below.**

neat	clever	friendly	kind	calm	honest

1 .... and outgoing
2 .... and tidy
3 .... and patient
4 .... and wise
5 .... and open
6 .... and caring

B **Match the adjectives (1–6) with the definitions (a–f).**

1 determined
2 patient
3 wise
4 soft
5 open
6 strict

a always says what he / she thinks
b able to think carefully and make good decisions
c not strict
d doesn't get angry easily
e expects people to do what he / she says
f tries very hard to do something well

C **Complete the sentences with a suitable word or phrase from exercise B.**

1 Steve's very .... , and doesn't allow his children much freedom.
2 My uncle's .... I always go to him for advice when I have a problem.
3 Dad's really .... , and I can always get what I want from him.
4 Joe's .... to pass his exam this time, and is working really hard.
5 Tina's .... She always tells you what she really thinks.
6 Helen's a really .... teacher. I've never seen her shout at her students.

PRONUNCIATION The weak form *of*

A 🔊 **1.3 Listen to the following sentences from Listening exercise B. Notice how *of* is pronounced in the sentences below.**

1 Ralph and I both like playing sport, but neither **of** us likes watching it on TV!
2 All **of** my friends are Linkin Park fans.
3 None **of** us is very patient.

B **The word *of* is often pronounced as a weak form so you hear /əv/. Practise saying the following phrases using the weak form /əv/.**

1 Both of us
2 All of them
3 Neither of them
4 None of us
5 Many of you

C 🔊 **1.4 Listen, then repeat exercise B.**

DEVELOPING WRITING
An email – a character reference

A Holly is a teacher at a secondary school. One of her students is going to study in France, and wants to stay with a family. Fill the gaps with words or phrases from the box to complete the email.

also	Thank you for	any more information
Dear	In her spare time	I am sure

⬤⬤⬤

From	Holly Dibble
To	Mme Juliette Baton
Subject	Reference for Sue Brown

A ¹ .... Madame Baton,

B ² .... your letter, asking me about Sue Brown. I am Sue's French teacher and I have known her for three years. Sue studies hard and her French is good. She wants to go to France because she is keen to practise the language and learn more about life in France.

C Sue is outgoing and makes friends easily. She is ³ .... kind and caring and popular with her classmates. In fact, she is never mean or selfish.

D ⁴ .... she plays tennis, and when she's at home, she likes reading books and watching films. Her mother tells me she helps around the house although she doesn't like cooking much! ⁵ .... you will find her a pleasant and helpful guest.

E Please write back to me if you need ⁶ .... or have any questions.

F Yours sincerely,

Holly Dibble

B Match the paragraphs in the email to the descriptions.

1 Introduce yourself and talk about your student and why they want to visit the country. ....
2 Close the letter. ....
3 Tell the reader about the person's character. ....
4 Say hello to the reader. ....
5 Talk about what the student likes. ....
6 Offer more help. ....

C You are a teacher. Your student is studying Polish. He is going to study in Poland for a month and wants to stay with a family. Write an email about him to Mrs Mojewski.

1 Rashid Kirijian, age 17
2 My student for 3 years – wants to be a translator
3 Clever, hardworking, friendly, polite, good company
4 likes basketball and swimming, plays water polo

Vocabulary Builder Quiz 1 (OVB pp2–5)

Try the *OVB* quiz for Unit 1. Write your answers in your notebook. Then check them and record your score.

A Choose the correct word.
1 I really hate my *colleague / cousin* Luigi. He's nothing like the rest of my family.
2 My father was a *liberal / strict* man, and allowed us a lot of freedom when we were kids.
3 Usama is quite *annoying / generous*, and often brings me presents.
4 Sylvie gets on with her *neighbour / flatmate*, who lives in the flat above her.
5 A *wise / confident* woman once told me, 'We cannot all do great things, but we can do small things with great love.'

B Complete the sentences with the correct form of the word in CAPITALS.
1 I believe in eating a .... diet.   HEALTH
2 Yalda was sorry for her bad .... at the party.   BEHAVE
3 Ana Maria, your room is really .... ! Tidy it up!   MESS
4 I come from Mexico, so I like a lot of .... in my food.   SPICY
5 Jamal, go and wash those .... hands before dinner!   DIRT
6 Bjorn worked very hard to make his business ....   SUCCESS
7 I've won €500! It's my .... day!   LUCK
8 Sherine and her sister had a really big .... yesterday.   ARGUE

C Cross out the adjectives that don't go with the nouns.
1 good / happy / bad / useful   advice
2 happy / unhappy / difficult / enthusiastic   childhood
3 bad / violent / beautiful / good   behaviour
4 lucky / low / annual / monthly / high   income
5 sports / hotel / fresh / health   facilities

D Complete the sentences with the correct words.
1 According .... Alana, Uri's got no cousins.
2 Pedro was in trouble .... being late to work this morning.
3 Isabella is doing some research .... her family history.
4 It is difficult for families .... low incomes to pay their bills.
5 My gran played a big part .... my childhood development.
6 I'm going .... Bristol next week.
7 François is not very patient .... people.

Score ____/25

Wait a couple of weeks and try the quiz again.
Compare your scores.

02 SHOPS

VOCABULARY

A Match words in the box to items in the picture.

tie	shirt	watch	camera	hat
suit	skirt	coat	laptop	mobile phone

B Complete the text with a suitable word or phrase.

good value	reliable	suit	bright
complicated	good quality	last	thick
smart	wide selection		

I always buy my clothes in the sales, and this weekend I found some real bargains! I wanted to buy a couple of shirts, so I went into M&S. My local branch has got a ¹.................... of different styles and colours. They're generally well made and of ².................... . Anyway, I found these packs of two for £20, which I thought was pretty ³.................... , as you normally pay that for one. Unfortunately, the only ones they had in my size were green and brown. Green isn't my colour; it just doesn't ⁴.................... me at all! Then I found a lovely ⁵.................... coat that I bought for visiting clients, and a ⁶.................... woollen sweater to keep me warm in winter. It's red, which will be ⁷.................... and cheerful on those cold grey mornings!
Well, I was feeling pretty pleased with myself, so I thought I'd have a look in the Mobile Shop next, to see what offers there were on mobiles. I really fancied the new Ericsson model. They're usually a ⁸.................... brand, and ⁹.................... longer than a lot of others. However, when the guy in the shop started telling me about all the extra features on it, it seemed really ¹⁰.................... . I couldn't understand what he was talking about, so I decided I'd bought enough for one day!

C Cross out the word which does not usually form a collocation with the key word.

1. conduct — *research / a study / a survey / children / an orchestra*
2. cause — *a problem / a meal / arguments / harm / pain*
3. compulsive — *school / shopping / gambling / theft / lying*
4. spend — *time / money / your life / an effort*
5. addict — *drug ~ / play ~ / TV ~ / shopping ~*
6. luxury — *items / goods / meal / hotel*

> **Learner tip**
>
> Record vocabulary connected with a topic together on the same page in your vocabulary notebook. For example, make a list of the words connected with shopping that you already know and add the new words from the unit as you learn them. This will help you remember them.

LISTENING

A 🔊 2.1 You are going to hear a radio programme in which three people talk about the problem of compulsive shopping. Decide whether the statements are true (T) or false (F).

1. 20% of British people are compulsive shoppers. ....
2. Maria's husband was worried that she was spending too much money. ....
3. Maria says she has got 135 bags in her wardrobe. ....
4. Compulsive shopping disorder only affects women. ....
5. Keith's wife left him. ....
6. Keith says that men don't usually buy the same things as women. ....

B 🎧 **2.1 Listen again and answer the questions.**

1 What did Maria's husband tell her to do about her problem?

....

....

2 How has the problem affected Keith's relationship with his wife?

....

....

Learner tip

When you do a listening task, try to gain a general understanding, or the 'gist' of what you listen to the first time you hear it. Don't worry about answering all the questions. The second time you listen, you can complete the exercise.

DEVELOPING CONVERSATIONS
Complimenting

Use the words and phrases from the box to complete the dialogue below.

they have	Cool	love	much was it
good value	good	great	did you get it
Did they have it in any other colours			

S: Jane! You look ¹ .... !
   I ² .... that skirt!
   Where ³ .... ?

J: Oh, hi, Sally! Yeah, er, I got it in Top Shop, actually.

S: Really? ⁴ .... ! How
   ⁵ .... ?

J: It was only £15.

S: ⁶ .... ?

J: Yeah ... red, green and ... blue, I think. You look
   ⁷ .... , too. Is that a new top?

S: Yes, it is. I got it in the sale at Primark for £5.

J: That's ⁸ .... ! Did
   ⁹ .... any cheap trousers?

S: I'm not sure. Why don't you go and see? I'll go with you, if you like.

GRAMMAR Past simple

A **Match the questions (1–5) with the answers (a–e) to complete the dialogue.**

1 Did you do anything interesting this morning? ....
2 Really? Was it any good? ....
3 Oh. Did you buy anything nice? ....
4 Oh, right. Are they the ones you're wearing? They're lovely! ....
5 You're joking! They look really good quality. Did they have any other colours? ....

a I think I saw some in blue and brown. Why don't you go and have a look?

b Well, I wanted to get a dress to wear to my cousin's wedding, but I didn't find anything I liked. I bought some nice shoes, though.

c Yeah. I went to that new shopping centre in Bracknell.

d Nice, aren't they? They were reasonable, too. I only paid €15 for them.

e It was OK. There were some nice clothes shops, but there wasn't much else.

B **Choose the correct words in italics to complete the sentences.**

1 I *buy / bought* a new watch in town yesterday.
2 We *selled / sold* our old car last month.
3 I *went / go* to the market this morning and *find / found* all sorts of bargains! Leather bags for £15!
4 Mum and Dad are *giving / gave* me a new mobile for my birthday last week, so do you want my old one?
5 There's a nice laptop in that shop. It only *cost / costs* £99.
6 I'm fed up! I *was spending / spent* £80 on this dress and then ten minutes later I *see / saw* the same one for just £40 in another shop!

C **Complete the conversation. Use the correct forms of the verbs in brackets.**

Dave: Oh, you're back, darling! ¹ .... (you go) to IKEA?

Sally: Yeah, it ² .... (be) great! It was packed, though. There are always too many people there.

D: ³ .... (find) what you wanted?

S: Well, they ⁴ .... (not have) the table, but I ⁵ .... (get) these really nice cups. Do you like them?

D: Yes, they're really nice! And ⁶ .... (you get) that lovely lamp there, too?

S: Oh no! I ⁷ .... (buy) that from Heavenly Homes.

D: I love it! ⁸ .... (do) they have any others like it?

S: Well, not exactly the same, but there was one that was similar. I ⁹ .... (find) it hard to choose between them.

D: Why ¹⁰ .... (you not buy) both of them? We really need two.

S: Well, they were too expensive, to be honest.

DEVELOPING CONVERSATIONS
Making offers and checking

A Match the phrases in the box to their function.

Not at all	Would you like a
Thanks a lot	Are you sure
Thanks!	Of course
You don't mind	Do you want to
Do you want me to	

1 Making offers:..

....

2 Checking:...
3 Responding:...
4 Accepting the offer:..

B Fill the gaps with a suitable phrase from the box in exercise A.

A: I'd like this please.

B: Have you tried it out?

A: Yes. It works fine. Could you pack it for me? It's going to travel on a plane.

B: ¹....................................... bag?

A: Hmm, have you got anything stronger? I don't want it to break.

B: Well, we may have a box in the store room.
²....................................... have a look?

A: ³....................................... ?

B: Yes, ⁴....................................... . I'll just be a minute.

A: Great. ⁵....................................... .

C: Oh, no! Only one changing room!

D: Is that all you want to try on?

C: Yeah, it is.

D: ⁶....................................... go first, then? I'll wait.

C: Really? ⁷....................................... ?

D: ⁸....................................... . I'm trying on all these. Go on.

C: ⁹....................................... .

GRAMMAR Comparatives

A Choose the most suitable phrase to complete the sentences.

1 They're a bit tight. Have you .... size?
  a   got them in a more bigger
  b   any in a smaller
  c   got some in a bigger

2 This chair's very hard. Do you .... ?
  a   got anything less
  b   have anything more comfortable
  c   have a more soft one

3 I'm afraid we don't have that style any more, Madam. Would you like to try .... ?
  a   something a little more modern
  b   a moderner one
  c   less modern one

4 This MP3 player doesn't work very well. Can I have ...., please?
  a   worse than this
  b   one better
  c   a better one

5 You'll break a leg wearing roller skates, Tim! Why don't you try an activity that is .... ?
  a   more safe
  b   less dangerous
  c   more comfortable

B Write questions using the words in brackets.

1 I'm afraid it's too small! .... (large)?

2 I'm afraid it's too expensive.
.... (cheap)?

4 It looks rather old fashioned!
.... (modern)?

3 It doesn't look very strong.
.... (good quality)?

5 It's too hard. ....
(comfortable)?

READING

A Place the following items in the correct group in the table.

shirt	hairdryer	toothbrush
face cream	wine	trousers
cheese	lipstick	vacuum cleaner
chicken	skirt	dishwasher

food and drink	clothing
toiletries and cosmetics	electrical goods

B Read the following newspaper article and choose the most suitable headline.

1 **The changing face of men's shopping**

2 **Men buy face cream and women buy drills!?**

3 **Women still best shoppers**

C Choose the best ending to each of the statements.

1 The report says that:
  a 70% of women in the UK shop in supermarkets
  b women do most of the food shopping in the UK.

2 Cheap fashion imports from China and the rest of the Far East mean:
  a women buy more clothes
  b an increase in prices.

3 The report says that:
  a more men are buying toiletries
  b men are interested in their appearance.

4 Supermarkets now sell electrical goods to:
  a get men to shop there
  b get women to buy them.

D Underline eight comparative words and phrases in the text.

A recent report on the differences between men and women's shopping habits found changes in the balance of buying activity between the sexes. The report, published last month by the market research company, Street Trends, focused on the areas of food and drink, toiletries and cosmetics, clothing and electrical goods.

Little change was found in food and drink shopping habits. Over 70% of supermarket shopping in the UK is done by the women of the household, and they generally control how much is spent on food. The report suggests that women show a greater ability to find special offers, and are more interested than men in getting good value when they shop. Similarly, in the area of clothing, women are still greater consumers than men. There has been a general increase in the purchase of clothes over the last few years, due to the introduction to the UK of cheap fashion from China and the rest of the Far East. Discount clothing has become more popular, as retailers have become skilled in reproducing fashion designs at lower costs. This is most noticeable in women's fashion, where purchases have increased significantly in the last year.

Interesting changes were seen, however, in the purchase of toiletries and electrical goods. Approximately 80% of British women do most of the shopping for cosmetics and toiletries, but the men's toiletry market is growing, as younger men are more interested in their physical appearance than they were five years ago. Well-known cosmetics companies are now targeting men with new skincare products. In the case of electrical goods, men have traditionally been regarded as the main buyers in the household. However, women are now taking a more active role in the purchase of these items. Several major supermarkets are expanding into this area and targeting female customers, so further changes are expected in these areas in the future.

PRONUNCIATION Stress in collocations

A Look at the following phrases from the reading text. Practise saying them. Stress the underlined syllable in each phrase.

food and <u>drink</u>   toiletries and cos<u>me</u>tics
e<u>lec</u>trical goods   market re<u>search</u>
special <u>offer</u>   good <u>value</u>   Far <u>East</u>

B ⟳ **2.2** Listen and repeat the phrases.

GRAMMAR Passives

A Rewrite the following sentences in the active voice.

1 Little change was found in food and drink shopping habits.
The report ....

2 Interesting changes were seen, however, in the purchase of toiletries and electrical goods.
However, the report ....
....

3 Men are now being targeted by cosmetics companies.
Cosmetic companies ....

4 Electrical goods are now bought more often by women.
Women ....

5 Cheap clothing is being imported to the UK from China and the Far East.
The UK ....

6 Many purchasing decisions are affected by children.
Children ....

B Rewrite the following sentences with the correct form of the passive.

1 The store is selling men's suits at half price.
Men's suits are being sold at half price.

2 A shop assistant caught a man stealing ladies' perfume yesterday.
A man ....

3 Many shop owners use pleasant aromas to encourage customers to buy more.
Pleasant aromas ....

4 Many small shop owners are firing their staff due to the economic problems. The staff of many small shops ....
....

5 Two businessmen opened the store in 1947.
The store ....

6 The shop encourages customers to buy its products over the Internet.
The shop's customers ....
....

C Choose the correct form of the following words in italics.

Many customers were very upset when the British chain store, Woolworths, [1] *is forced / was forced* to close at the beginning of the year. However, the brand [2] *was bought / bought* by Shop Direct in February, and recently, it [3] *introduces / has been introduced* to the market once more as an online business.

The new website offers toys, children's clothes, electrical goods and themed parties. It also [4] *is sold / sells* CDs, DVDs and video games. People are delighted that the brand name [5] *has been kept / is kept* by the Shop Direct Group, and believe that the online business will be a huge success.

Learner tip

Newspaper articles and formal reports often use the passive voice to emphasise an important piece of information. Look out for the passive whenever you read this kind of text, and see how it is used.

DEVELOPING WRITING An email – informal writing

A Read the email and answer the questions.

1 Are Elena and Enrique:
  a colleagues?
  b uncle and niece?
  c friends?

2 Why is Elena writing to Enrique?
....

3 What did Elena do this morning?
....

4 What are Elena and Enrique's plans for next month?
....

Vocabulary Builder Quiz 2 (OVB pp6–9)

Try the OVB quiz for Unit 2. Write your answers in your notebook. Then check them and record your score.

A Write the opposites of these words.
1 reliable ....
2 silly ....
3 plain ....
4 loose ....
5 comfortable ....
6 shut ....

B Complete the sentences with the correct noun.

fine	quality	brand	designs
guide	temple	receipt	

1 Anil will only wear one .... of athletic shoes.
2 I want to visit an ancient Hindu .... when I go to Khulna.
3 I really like some of Zara's fashion .... this year.
4 When I paid for my new phone I didn't get a ....
5 Pierre paid a .... for smoking on the train.
6 Dina is a tour .... and takes people on coach tours around her city.
7 I want some of your best .... meat, please.

C Match the sentence halves.
1 That meal was really good
2 Boris spread false
3 That shop offers very reliable
4 They've got a wide
5 I got a 25%
6 I asked for a medium size but they were out

a selection of children's shoes.
b service to its customers.
c discount on this new dress.
d value at only £20 for the two of us.
e of stock.
f rumours about Haris and Jolanda.

D Decide whether the statements are true (T) or false (F).
1 If a dress *suits* you, it's the right size for your body. ....
2 If you *employ* someone, you give them a job. ....
3 You *damage* things, but *injure* a person. ....
4 Someone who is *bright* is not very intelligent. ....
5 We say a car *lasts* when it is not very fast. ....
6 Workers are *exploited* if they are treated unfairly. ....

Score ___/25

Wait a couple of weeks and try the quiz again. Compare your scores.

Hi Enrique

How are you? Thanks for your card and present. I'm wearing the top, and the card is standing on my desk as I write.

On my birthday, some friends and I ¹ .... (go) out dancing, and the DJ at the club ² .... (play) a lot of Latin music. I ³ .... (think) of you in Argentina, and ⁴ .... (wish) you were here! In Italy, we don't dance in cafeterias like you do over there, but we have some great night clubs. You'll see when you come next month.

My uncle ⁵ .... (give) me some money for my birthday, so I ⁶ .... (decide) to go shopping this morning. There's a new shop in the centre that sells discount clothes and equipment for outdoor sports. It's a lot cheaper than other sports shops in Milan. I ⁷ .... (buy) a new sleeping bag for our camping trip, some shorts, a T-shirt and some climbing gloves and only ⁸ .... (pay) 60 euros! Have you got everything ready for our trip? Remember to bring your climbing shoes!

See you very soon now!

Take care,

Elena

B Write the past simple of the verbs in brackets to complete the email above.

C Underline the eight phrases that we can use when we write to a friend.

Hi, James!
Thank you very much for your letter, dated 15th March.
Dear Julie
How are you?
Dear Mr Hanson
I'm writing to ask for some information about St Petersburg.
It was great to hear from you again.
I wanted to ask you something.
I look forward to hearing from you.
Write soon
Take care
Best wishes
Yours sincerely

D Imagine you are Enrique. Write a reply to Elena. Use the plan below to help you.
Paragraph 1: Thank her for her email, and say something about her birthday.
Paragraph 2: Comment on her shopping news, and say something about things you have bought for the camping trip.
Paragraph 3: Ask her some questions about your plans for the trip.

03 EAT

VOCABULARY Restaurants

A Write the correct type of food under each photo.

seafood	Italian	fast food	Chinese	Japanese	Mexican

1 ....

2 ....

3 ....

4 ....

5 ....

6 ....

B Match the sentence halves.

1 That Turkish café is really good value
2 I'm not fond of fast
3 I love all kinds of spicy
4 I've decided to stop eating red
5 I'm going to try out that new sushi

a food, but sometimes you need something quick and easy.
b dishes, especially Mexican food.
c meat, as it's not good for you.
d bar in Camden. I've heard it's really good.
e for money. You can eat well for under £20.

C Place the following words and phrases under the correct heading below.

choice	friendly and polite	busy	disgusting
dishes	good selection	helpful	crowded
slow	fast and efficient	terrace	delicious
view	portions		

food	staff and service	describing the restaurant

D Complete the sentences below with words or phrases from exercise C.

1 I like that new restaurant down the road. It's got a great .... of food, and there's a .... of different wines, too.

2 I'm not going back to that Mexican place again! When I asked the waiter for advice he wasn't very .... , and the food was ....!

3 I tried to call the waitress but she was .... serving another customer. It was ten minutes before she was free.

4 We sat outside on the .... , and the .... from up there was amazing! We could see all over the city.

5 The staff were very .... at that French restaurant, and always served us with a smile, but the .... were really small, so we were still hungry afterwards!

6 The good thing about that Italian place is that the service is .... , so you can have your meal and leave in an hour.

7 Mm! This churrasco is really ....! Can you pass me the chimichurri? I'd quite like some more!

8 This restaurant really is international! They serve .... from all over the world. It's rather .... , though! You can't move in here, and it's really noisy!

DEVELOPING CONVERSATIONS
Suggestions and deciding where to go

A Unscramble the suggestions.

1 A: that Thai / the corner / how / round / place / about / ?

....

   B: To be honest, I don't really feel like spicy food today.

   A: could / we / instead / well / that vegetarian / in the square / go / restaurant / to

....

2 C: sushi bar / how / new / about / on Samson Street / the / ?

....

   D: To be honest, I don't really feel like Japanese food.

   C: we / that Greek / well / instead / restaurant / could / to / go / down the road

....

3 E: seafood / in / about / restaurant / how / that / the centre / ?

....

   F: To be honest, I don't really feel like fish today.

   E: instead / go / could / The Cooking Pot / well / to / we / on James Street

....

B Complete the conversation with the responses (a–f).

a Great idea! I love their curries.
b Yes, but they haven't got enough vegetarian dishes on the menu. I don't want to eat spaghetti with tomato sauce again!
c It'll be too noisy to talk in there, then! I fancy going somewhere quiet, so we can chat.
d I'm not sure. Have you been to La Vita Bella yet?
e Yes, I do.
f We'll have to book though.

A: Where do you want to go tonight?
B: ¹ ....
A: Oh, I went there last week. We waited an hour to get a table! That's too long to wait in a restaurant that doesn't take bookings. I'm not going there again! How about Neil's Kitchen? There have been good reviews of that.
B: ² ....
A: Oh, yes! I forgot you don't eat meat! Do you like seafood?
B: ³ ....
A: Well, there's a nice little fish restaurant in the centre. ⁴ .... It gets busy.
B: ⁵ ....
A: Well, then we could go to the Indian down the road instead. That doesn't get busy until the pubs close.
B: ⁶ ....

GRAMMAR Present perfect simple

A Match the sentences (1–6) with the correct response (a–f).

1 I've never eaten grilled squid before. ....
2 Have you read *Great Cooking At Home*? ....
3 Have you tried that recipe for vindaloo curry yet? ....
4 Have you been to that Chinese restaurant, The Lantern? ....
5 I've only eaten ekmek in a restaurant. Is it easy to make? ....
6 I've never been to the city centre. ....

a Well, I can show you how to make it, if you like.
b Oh, don't bother! It's too crowded and polluted!
c No, I've never heard of it, to be honest. Is it good?
d Why don't you try some? It's delicious!
e Yes, I found some really great recipes in there!
f Yes, but I'm afraid it wasn't spicy enough for Kevin!

B Put the words in brackets into the correct form of the present perfect simple.

1 .... (you ever eat) snails?
2 .... (you be) to that Italian restaurant on the corner yet? It's great. I .... (be) there three times!
3 .... (you ever try) falafel? They're a kind of vegetarian meatball, made with chick-peas.
4 This is the first time I .... (make) Thai food. I hope you like it!
5 Bob .... (never eat) curry before. He doesn't eat much spicy food.
6 .... (you read) that cookbook I gave you yet?

Language note

When we talk about travel experiences, we use 'be'. e.g. *Have you ever **been** to Niagara Falls? I've **been** to Alaska twice. I've never **been** abroad.*

C Complete the mini-dialogues with the correct form of the present perfect simple or the past simple.

1 Kate: .... (you be) to Edinburgh before?
   Gunter: Yes, I .... two years ago. How about you?
   Kate: I .... (never be) here before! It's really cold!
   Gunter: .... (you visit) the castle yet?
   Kate: No, I .... I must go. How about you?
   Gunter: I .... (go) yesterday. It was amazing!
2 Yuri: .... (you be) to any good restaurants yet?
   Xavier: Well, I .... (go) to The Apple last night.
   Yuri: Oh, that famous chef's place? .... (he be) there?

READING

A Read the blog about sandwiches around the world. Match each blog entry with the correct country below.

Vietnam	Ireland	Austria	France

A ....   B ....   C ....   D ....

B In which description(s) does the writer mention that:
1 the sandwiches are not expensive?   ....
2 the bread is made in the shop?   ....
3 the place gets very busy?   ....
4 the restaurant is very old?   ....
5 the ingredients used are local?   ....

Learner tip

When you answer questions about a text, do not worry about unknown words. In the text opposite, a lot of words refer to ingredients for making food. You can understand from the context that they are ingredients, but it is not necessary to know exactly what they are.

C Match the words from the blog (1–10) with the definitions (a–j).

1 recipe (line 1)
2 falafel (line 8)
3 the premises (line 19)
4 variety (line 20)
5 ingredient (line 20)
6 discount (line 32)
7 reasonable (prices) (line 34)
8 trendy (line 42)
9 filling (line 43)
10 logo (line 48)

a fashionable and modern
b one food item which is used with others to make a dish
c what is placed inside a sandwich
d not very expensive
e the restaurant/shop building
f instructions for making a dish
g a special design which a shop or business uses
h chickpea balls
i special low price
j a number of different things

D Underline the words that can go with these phrases.

1 freshly made   *coffee / orange juice / newspaper / ice cream*
2 extremely popular   *football team / restaurant / person / Mexican*
3 a variety of   *food / ingredients / dishes / colours*
4 fresh   *fruit / fish / water / table / vegetables / bread*
5 food   *fast / spicy / health / fruit / junk / frozen*
6 price   *reasonable / discount / full / half*

Pete's Eats Blog

I travel a lot in my search for new and exciting recipes, and I suddenly realised that the one thing I haven't talked about is one of the most common lunchtime foods in the world. Yes, you guessed it: the sandwich!

A L'As du Fallafel – Paris

If you're looking for a cheap but tasty meal in Paris, then make this your first choice. Be prepared to wait in line at lunchtime, however, as it's extremely popular! The falafel sandwich here is unbeatable, with grilled aubergine, cabbage, hummus,
10 tahini and hot sauce accompanying the delicious chickpea balls. You can either buy to take away or choose to sit in the small space available for diners.

Falafel sandwich

B Banhmibistro – Ho Chi Minh City

Banh mi sandwiches, pronounced bun mee, are Vietnamese sandwiches served in a French baguette. One of the best places that serves them is the Banhmibistro in Ho Chi Minh City.

The bread is freshly baked on the premises, and you can choose from
20 a variety of native Vietnamese ingredients, such as coriander, fish sauce, pickled carrots, radishes and hot peppers, to fill your banh mi. A personal favourite is the Bistro Special, which contains a delicious variety of meats such as barbecue pork, ham and pâté.

Bahn mi sandwich

C O'Briens Sandwich Bar – Dublin

These people have mastered the art of sandwich-making! They use wonderfully thick slices of fresh bread, and fill them with a wide
30 variety of tasty ingredients. The turkey and brie sandwich with cranberry is excellent!

The good news is they offer discount prices for students, and their full prices are reasonable, too! The business is growing fast, with sandwich bars in several different countries, so I hope this doesn't mean that their quality will suffer!

Turkey and brie sandwich

D The Black Camel – Vienna

40 This is actually a famous family-owned restaurant, which has existed since 1618. Many Viennese eat here regularly. The restaurant food is expensive, but the trendy delicatessen sells deliciously fresh sandwiches at reasonable prices. Popular fillings include minced blood sausage, herring salad, mushroom salad and ham and lentils.

Tourists can pay a bit extra, and buy a packed lunch in a souvenir box decorated with the restaurant's logo of a black camel wearing a headdress.

Herring salad sandwich

GRAMMAR *too / not enough*

A Complete the sentences with *too* or *not ... enough* and the adjectives in the box.

hard	cooked	expensive	big	spicy	chilled

1 I can't eat this soup. It's ....! Bring me some cold water, please!
2 This bread isn't very fresh. It's .... to eat!
3 This fish is not .... It's still raw!
4 This wine isn't .... Could you bring us another bottle?
5 This is .... ! You've overcharged us!
6 Waiter! This table is .... for six people. Could you give us another, please?

B Complete the following dialogue with a suitable phrase from the box.

wasn't hot enough	haven't been	has had
too slow	I've never heard	have you tried

A: Where shall we go then?
B: How about Joe's Place? We [1] .... there for ages!
A: I know, but the service was [2] .... the last time we went, remember. Let's go somewhere new. [3] .... that Mexican restaurant on Keene Street?
B: No, [4] .... of it. What's it like?
A: Well, the chilli [5] .... for me, but you'll like it. And they do really nice tacos.
B: Mm, you know I don't like spicy food! The new fish restaurant in Hooton [6] .... some good reviews. We could go there.
A: OK, then. Let's go there.

C Say what is wrong with this kitchen. Write sentences using the words below.

dirty	room	untidy	staff	work

Language note

Not ... enough + noun: When the phrase is followed by a noun, *'not'* comes before the verb. e.g. We do**n't have** enough food to eat. You have**n't made** enough paella. We don't say 'We have not enough food.'

LISTENING

A 🔊 3.1 Listen to two people having a meal in a restaurant. What kind of restaurant are they in?

....

B Listen again.

1 What do the couple order to eat? Underline the dishes.

moussaka	tzatziki	gazpacho
	spetsofai	souvlaki

2 What do they decide to drink? Underline the correct answer.

water	beer	wine

C 🔊 3.2 Listen to the rest of their conversation, and answer the questions.

1 Why doesn't Claire want to eat the spetsofai?
....
2 Does Claire like the tzatziki? Why (not)?
....
3 Do they order a dessert?
....

D How do Socrates and Claire feel about the food? Tick (✓) the best answer.

	is enthusiastic	likes some of it	doesn't like it
Socrates			
Claire			

E Match the descriptions (a–d) in the menu below with the correct dish (1–4).

1 *Greek salad*   a *yoghurt and cucumber salad, flavoured with garlic*
2 *tzatziki*   b *spicy sausage with green peppers*
3 *souvlaki*   c *tomatoes, cucumber, peppers and olives, with goat's cheese*
4 *spetsofai*   d *small pieces of grilled pork served on a stick*

Learner tip

When you listen to two or more speakers, notice how each speaker feels, and their opinion.

GRAMMAR

Offers, requests, permission, suggestions

A Match the following questions with their function.
  a offer   b request   c asking permission   d suggestion
  1 Could I have the day off, please, Mr Brown? ....
  2 Shall I take your coat, Madam? ....
  3 Could I have my steak well done, please? ....
  4 Shall we order drinks first? ....
  5 Shall I bring you some water, Sir? ....
  6 Shall we order a dessert? ....
  7 Could I borrow your phone to call the babysitter? ....
  8 Could you bring us the bill, please? ....

Language note

- -

We usually make a request when we want somebody to do
something for us. e.g. *Could you make me a coffee, please?*
We ask permission when we want to do something but are not
sure if it's acceptable. e.g. *Could I open the window, please?*

B Use the prompts to complete the mini-dialogues.
  1 Waiter: Would you like me to bring you some wine, Sir?
     Guest: (don't drink alcohol / bottle of sparkling water, please?)
     ....
  2 Manager: Right, Juan. Could you clear those tables, and set them
              for tomorrow, please?
     Juan: Er ... Mrs Kent (leave early, please?)
     ....
              My mother has asked me to collect my brother from his
              judo lesson.
  3 Man: Shall we go for a Chinese meal, then?
     Woman: (don't feel like / pizza, instead?)
     ....
  4 Man: Oh! I can't find my car keys.
     Waiter: They fell on the floor. (help you / look / them, Sir?)
     ....

VOCABULARY Describing food

A Match the types of food (1–6) with the descriptions
   (a–f).
   1 potato   ....   4 mango   ....
   2 courgette ....   5 garlic   ....
   3 squid   ....   6 mushroom ....

   a It's a kind of fruit. It's large and yellow, almost orange
      in colour. It's got a sweet taste. You usually eat it raw.
   b It's a small, brownish grey fungus. It grows in the
      ground. It's quite soft. You usually eat it fried or
      grilled. It is often used in salads or on pizzas.
   c It's a kind of seafood. It has a long, soft body, and ten
      small arms, called tentacles. It has a mild taste, and
      you usually eat it fried or grilled. You sometimes cook
      it in a sauce.
   d It's a kind of vegetable. It's hard, and white on the
      inside with a thin, brown skin. It has a mild taste, and
      you can eat it fried, boiled or roasted. It accompanies
      most meat and fish dishes.
   e It's small, white and hard. It has a very strong taste.
      You usually add it to cooked food to give it more
      flavour, but some people eat it raw in salads, or on a
      piece of bread and butter.
   f It's a kind of vegetable. It's long, with a green skin. It's
      not very hard, and has a mild taste. You usually eat
      it fried or boiled. You can add it to most vegetable
      dishes and salads.

PRONUNCIATION

A 🔊 **3.3 Listen to the words on the left. Then choose the
words in the line with the same sound.**

1 would	/ʊ/	count	could	book
2 shall	/æ/	champagne	chant	pancake
3 enough	/ʌ/	rough	cough	hungry
4 juice	/uː/	root	boil	fruit

B 🔊 **3.4 Listen to all the words and check your answers.**

C **Practise saying the words.**

DEVELOPING WRITING

A review – a restaurant

A **Holly writes a food and eating blog for her local
newspaper's website. Read Holly's reviews of two
restaurants below.**
   1 Which restaurant did she think was good?
      ....
   2 Which restaurant did she think was poor?
      ....

B Read the reviews again. What does Holly say about...
1 the quality of the food
   (A) .... (B) ....
2 the service
   (A) .... (B) ....
3 the design of the restaurant
   (A) .... (B) ....
4 the price
   (A) .... (B) ....

● ● ○

Holly's hungry blogspot

Here are my views on two more restaurants:

Ⓐ I had a lovely meal at the Flying Fish restaurant in Wade Street last week. The food was delicious. I had grilled squid which was soft and juicy. Cooked perfectly. The service was also good, and the staff were extremely helpful. The only disappointment was the interior design. The room was too dark, and we couldn't see what we were eating. Apart from that it was an enjoyable evening. The prices were reasonable, too! Overall, it was really good value for money.

Ⓑ The Taj Mahal restaurant in Park Road had a pleasant atmosphere and was nicely decorated. The food was tasty and well-prepared. I had a chicken vindaloo that was really spicy, and full of flavour! Unfortunately, the service wasn't as good. The staff were rather unfriendly and never smiled, and our waiter was too slow. We waited for twenty minutes before he came to take our order, and another half an hour before he served our food. The restaurant wasn't even busy! It was very expensive, too. Indian restaurants are usually reasonable, so I found this one very disappointing!

C Plan a review of a restaurant. Think about what you liked and didn't like. Choose the words and phrases you want to use to describe each part of your experience.

friendly and polite	modern	reasonable	cheap
good value for money	delicious	full of flavour	fast
unfriendly and rude	well-lit	well-prepared	slow
tastefully decorated	tasteless	unwelcoming	dark
too expensive	helpful	overcooked	

Name of restaurant: ....
1 quality of food: ....
....
2 the service: ....
....
3 the interior design: ....
....
4 the price: ....

D Write your review in 80–100 words.

Vocabulary Builder Quiz 3 (*OVB* pp10–13)

Try the *OVB* quiz for Unit 3. Write your answers in your notebook. Then check them and record your score.

A Match the sentence halves.
1 A salad is included   a for meat pie?
2 I want a jug   b to shellfish.
3 I'm allergic   c of the mountain from here.
4 All meals are served   d of potatoes, carrots and
5 Can I have the recipe   onions.
6 There's a wonderful   e in the price.
  view   f on the terrace, please?
7 The soup consists   g of water, please.
8 Can I sit outside   h with a side salad.

B Complete the sentences with the correct form of the word in CAPITALS.
1 Have you made the .... for the
  chicken yet?   STUFF
2 My favourite .... is Monet's
  'Water Lilies'.   PAINT
3 We complained about the poor ....   SERVE
4 I have a milk ....   ALLERGIC
5 The restaurant accepts party ....
  of up to 30.   BOOK
6 There's a good .... of vegetarian
  dishes.   CHOICE

C Choose the correct word.
1 I prefer eating *raw / bitter* vegetables to cooked ones.
2 This soup's *disgusting / delicious*! Can I have some more?
3 Leave the potato *shells / skins* on and bake them in the oven.
4 The food was *incredible / reasonable*! We really enjoyed it.
5 The service was very good, so I left a *tip / option*.
6 They have several fish *recipes / dishes* on the menu.

D Complete the sentences with a suitable word.
1 Hello, there! Come .... I'll be with you in two seconds.
2 In Vietnam, you can often buy banh mi sandwiches at a street ....
3 The stew's really hot, so wait a minute for it to cool ....
4 That restaurant's very popular, so it's a good idea to book in ....
5 We sat .... at 7pm but the waiter didn't take our order until 8!

Score ____/25

Wait a couple of weeks and try the quiz again. Compare your scores.

04 JOBS

VOCABULARY
Jobs and experiences at work

A Match the job with the photograph.

1 architect ....   5 builder ....
2 care   6 sales
   assistant ....   manager ....
3 secretary ....   7 teacher ....
4 pilot ....   8 chef ....

B Who does what? Complete the descriptions with a job from exercise A.

Jobs Quiz

1 A .... works in the local home for the elderly. Their duties are as follows: they work shifts, doing a night shift once a month. They need to be fit, because they may have to help lift patients, and sometimes work on their feet for long hours. Because they work with people they sometimes need patience and kindness.

2 A primary school .... works with children between the ages of five and 11. They need to be energetic and fairly active and also to be patient. They work about 20 hours a week in the classroom and write reports on their students at the end of each week.

3 A .... has several duties. They plan the menu at the beginning of each week, and order food. They give instructions to a team of people who prepare, cook and serve food for their guests. It's hard work and they work long hours.

4 Every .... does a long and difficult training course to learn their job. When they pass all the tests, they are ready to start the job. Most of them start with short trips. More experienced ones work away from home for days at a time. They travel all over the world and sometimes do several flights in a day.

5 A .... job involves a lot of different things in any one day. Their main duties include reading and answering emails and making appointments for their boss. They also help their boss organise the work he or she has to do in a typical day like meetings, visits, and phone calls.

6 Because a .... manages a sales team it is important that they like working with people. It is important to encourage and motivate the team to do well, and to discuss ways to market a new product so that it sells well. Travel is an important part of their job. They usually meet old and new clients to talk about the products and services they sell.

7 An .... is a highly-trained professional. They need to know about new building materials and how to use technology. They talk to their clients, do research and then draw up plans. If the client likes the plans, the builders start their job and what was a picture on paper becomes a new house, a bridge, a factory or a park..

8 .... often work outside but can work inside too. The work is hard and most of them are men. They need to understand architectural plans and be able to use different kinds of building material. They are sometimes called in to do repairs when a house is damaged after a storm, or a fire.

Language note

In English we use *they* or *their* a lot when the sex of the person we talk about is not important.
A doctor has a hard job. They work long hours and their job often involves making difficult decisions.

DEVELOPING CONVERSATIONS Questions about jobs

A Match the questions (1–7) with the answers (a–g).

1 How long have you worked there?
2 Do you travel much?
3 Is the money good, then?
4 So, do you get on with the people you work with?
5 What do you do?
6 So, do you enjoy it?
7 What're the hours like?

a I work in a travel agency.
b Three years now.
c Quite a lot. I get free air tickets, and discounts on some of the holidays I sell.
d During the week, we work nine till five thirty, but we always finish late on Fridays.
e It's not bad. There's a good bonus system, where you get paid extra if you sell over a certain number of holidays in a month.
f Well, the manager can be a bit difficult, but the rest of the staff are fine.
g Yes, I do. I like meeting people, and helping them make the right choice about where they want to go.

B **Write the questions in the correct order.**

1 do / what / do / you?

.... ?

I'm a chemist. I work for a company that makes perfumes.

2 it / enjoy / you / do?

.... ?

Yes, it can be fun. We try to create different aromas, and it's exciting when you find something new.

3 the / what / like / are / hours?

.... ?

OK. I usually work from eight until four.

4 money / good / is / the?

.... ?

Yes, I'm the head of department, so my salary's quite high.

5 people / you / with / get on / do / the / work / you / with?

.... ?

Generally, yes, but we do occasionally have disagreements.

LISTENING

A **You are going to listen to an interview with firefighter. Before you listen, read these statements. Decide whether they are true (T) or false (F).**

1 There are over 300 women firefighters in London. ....
2 Most of the work is about fighting fires. ....
3 Firefighters do a lot of first aid. ....
4 Firefighters need to be in good physical condition. ....
5 A small part of the job is about educating people. ....
6 Firefighters give a lot of talks. ....

B ✹ **4.1 Listen to the first part of the interview and check your answers.**

C **Listen again and tick (✓) the activities that Megan mentions.**

rescue people and animals	write reports on accidents
go to fires	deal with bombs
check equipment	make appointments
give first aid	make visits to schools
do fitness training	clean the fire station

D ✹ **4.2 Listen to the second part of the interview and complete the sentences below.**

1 Megan enjoys ....
2 She also likes giving ....
3 The most difficult part of the job is when
   ....
4 Megan really doesn't like ....

GRAMMAR

Present continuous and present simple

A **Choose the correct form of the verb in each sentence.**

A: So, Enrique, what [1] *do you do / are you doing*?

E: I'm an architect.

A: [2] *Do you work / Are you working* alone, or with a team?

E: I [3] *run / am running* my own office with a partner.

A: Oh, I see. And [4] *do you work / are you working* long hours?

E: Sometimes, yes. Right now, we're busy, so we [5] *work / are working* 10–12 hours a day. But it's not always like that.

A: What [6] *do you work / are you working* on at the moment? Anything interesting?

E: Yes, we [7] *design / are designing* a sports and leisure centre, and it's very exciting.

A: [8] *Do you ever get / Are you ever getting* stressed out?

E: Very rarely. I [9] *don't work / am not working* alone, so we [10] *share / are sharing* the worry!

B **Put the verbs in brackets in the correct form, present continuous or present simple.**

A DAY IN THE LIFE OF A

Wedding Co-ordinator

I work as a wedding co-ordinator. That means I [1] .... (organise) wedding receptions. I have a great team who work together well, so we almost never [2] .... (experience) problems. When a couple book, we [3] .... (have) several meetings to talk about anything special they would like to do. Today, for example, our couple is of mixed nationality. The bride is British Indian and the groom's Scottish. He wanted bagpipes; she wanted Indian food on the menu.

Nine o'clock

So, right now, I [4] .... (check) the final details with the head chef. He and his staff [5] .... (prepare) a wonderful menu. They're very busy, so I'm leaving them in peace.

Ten o'clock

The first problem of the day. Two members of the bar staff are ill and can't come in, so the bar manager [6] .... (look) for replacements.

Two o'clock

The reception room is almost ready, and looks fabulous. The waitresses [7] .... (place) the final flower decorations on the tables, and we're nearly ready! What can I say? This [8] .... (be) a typical day at work!

VOCABULARY Activities at work

A Complete the dialogues below with the present continuous form of the verbs in the box.

do	attend	study	install
advertise	gain	cause	

1 A: So, Meena, how's work?
   M: Oh, don't ask! We .... some new software in the office at the moment, and it .... all sorts of problems. So my boss is not a happy man!

2 B: So, are you doing anything interesting at the moment, Pavlo?
   P: Yes, I am, actually! As part of my nurse's training, I .... some voluntary work in an old people's home. I've met some wonderful people, and I .... some valuable work experience! I've discovered I really enjoy working with the elderly!

3 C: Fiona, how are you getting on with your research?
   F: Fine. I .... ways to deal with stress in the office, and it's very interesting.

4 E: So, how are things at work, Malik?
   M: OK. I .... an exhibition this week. We .... our new photocopying equipment.

B Choose the correct verb to complete the following conversation with a sales manager from a large company.

A: So, Rashid, what are you [1] *working on / organising* at the moment?
R: Well, a lot's happening at work at the moment, actually! I'm [2] *teaching / learning* the sales team all about the company's new product.
A: Oh! Is that on the market already?
R: No, the company's going to launch it next month, but we want to be ready to sell it. I'm [3] *negotiating / advising* them on how to approach their clients. Fortunately, they're a good group, and are [4] *learning / teaching* fast.
A: Right! So, why are you so excited about it, then?
R: I've just made contact with a really big company, and am trying to [5] *organise / advise* a meeting with them. They're interested in the new product, and I'm hoping to [6] *work on / negotiate* a deal.

C Match each verb below with the group of words (1–4). One word is wrong in each group. Underline it.

do	run	make	negotiate

1 .... the price / a deal / an agreement / an evening
2 .... an offer / some research / a presentation / a training course
3 .... a business / a negotiation / the sales team / a restaurant
4 .... an offer / a presentation / some research / a proposal

GRAMMAR Plans and wishes for the future

A Match the sentence halves.

1 I've started guitar lessons and I'm hoping
2 I'm interested in the Far East, so I'm thinking
3 I studied History, and I'd like
4 I got good results in my exams, so I'm going
5 I want to see the world, so I'm planning
6 I've worked hard, so I'm expecting

a to work in a museum.
b to study medicine.
c to work here, save some money and then travel.
d to play in a band when I'm older.
e to get good results
f of teaching English in Thailand next year.

B Make the following sentences negative.

1 I'm going to go and live abroad.
   ....
2 I'd like to work with animals.
   ....
3 I'm thinking of becoming a firefighter.
   ....
4 I'm planning to stay in my present job.
   ....
5 I'd like to become a doctor.
   ....
6 I'm expecting to continue studying next year.
   ....

C Read this interview from a newspaper and complete the gaps using *going to*, *planning to*, *would like to* or *hoping to*.

A number of students choose to take a gap year between leaving school and going to university. They usually travel, or gain some work experience during this time. Some go and do voluntary work. Alice Ter Haar, our reporter, interviewed Kami Smith, a school leaver who is planning to take a gap year.

Alice: So, Kami, you've finished school! What are you [1] .... do next?

Kami: Well, first of all, I [2] .... do some voluntary work in East Africa. I [3] .... work there for six months. I [4] .... study environmental science at university, so I [5] .... gain some experience of working in a different climate.

Alice: Wow! That sounds amazing!

Kami: Well, I hope so. I [6] .... study climate change, and so I [7] .... travel to places where the climate's changing. I [8] .... go to Antarctica next year.

READING

A Read the job advertisements below. Match the items in the photographs with the jobs (A–C).

1 ....   2 ....   3 ....

A

Volunteer Hosts

Are you a science student, or someone who <u>cares</u> about the oceans? Perhaps <u>you are planning to become</u> a marine biologist. If so, would you like to get some useful work experience?

The National Marine Aquarium <u>is looking for</u> volunteer hosts to give educational talks and answer visitors' questions. Working days and hours can be arranged to suit you.

For further information, email Sally Dunn at *sdunn@national-aquarium.com*

B

Groomer required – West London

A smart pet boutique and salon based in West London is looking for an experienced dog groomer. Duties include bathing and drying dogs, as well as grooming their coats.

If you are interested, please contact Julian on 07780 624 356 to arrange an interview.

C

NANNY NEEDED – GENEVA, SWITZERLAND

A British family living in Geneva is looking for an experienced nanny to help look after two children aged eight and five years old. The mother is a restaurant owner and the father is the head chef. The family lives close to the city centre, and owns a dog and a cat. They would like the nanny to work mainly in the evenings, with Mondays completely free. This position is suitable for anyone who speaks very good English and French.

For further details, please contact Mrs Blake on 0041 22 578 390.

Glossary

host: person who looks after visitors or guests
marine biologist: person who studies life in the sea
groomer: person who washes and brushes pets' coats
aquarium: place where people go to see fish and underwater plants.

Learner tip

Every time you read a text, practise looking for examples of grammatical structures you have learnt. This will help you understand how they work in a natural context. Look back at the <u>underlined</u> verb phrases in the text and check why they are used there. Do this regularly as you follow this course.

B Which job(s) require(s) someone who:
1 speaks a foreign language?   ....
2 has previous work experience?   ....and.......
3 will work for no money?   ....
4 likes working with dogs and cats? ....and.......
5 is happy to work six days a week?   ....
6 is happy working with the public?   ....

C Complete the sentences with one of the phrases from the box.

my work experience	night shift
job advertisement	team
marketing department	long hours

1 I work very .... in a busy department store.
2 I'm training to be a computer technician, and I'm doing .... in a large company.
3 I saw your .... in the local paper, and I'd like to apply for the position.
4 I work in the ...., and we develop ways to advertise the company's new products.
5 I enjoy being a nurse, but I hate doing the .... I prefer working in the day.
6 My .... works very hard.

VOCABULARY Forming words

A Six of the words below can be verbs and nouns. The others are only verbs. Put them in the correct column.

		verb / noun	verb
volunteer	research		
interview	experience		
manage	offer		
advertise	negotiate		
apply	work		

B Now write the noun form of the four verbs above.

employ → *employment*
1 .... → ....
2 .... → ....
3 .... → ....
4 .... → ....

Language note *job* versus *work*

Use *job* to talk specifically about what a person does. *I have a new job as an accountant.*
Use *work* to talk in general about something you are doing. *I'm doing some work at the moment, so we'll talk later.*

GRAMMAR Past continuous and past simple

A Complete the sentences with the correct form of the verb in brackets.

1 Someone threw a brick through my window while I
.... (work)

2 While he was doing the presentation, a mouse
.... (run across the room)

3 What .... (you do) when the
fire started in the office?

4 His boss came in while he ....
(buy) Christmas presents for his friends online.

5 I .... (not notice) that she was
photocopying important documents.

6 She received the job offer while she
.... (travel) around Europe.

B Complete the story with the correct past continuous or past simple form of the verb in brackets.

I was really excited when this big computer software company
asked me to go for an interview. So, I ¹ .... (go) shopping
and ² .... (buy) a new suit. When I ³ .... (wake) up
on the day of the interview, it ⁴ .... (rain). I ⁵ ....
(not want) to get wet, so I ⁶ .... (call) a taxi. As I
⁷ .... (get) out of the taxi, a bus ⁸ .... (go) past
and splashed water all over me! I went to the bathroom to clean
myself up. While I ⁹ .... (clean) my skirt, another woman
came in. She was also wet, and tried to dry herself. We laughed
about it together, and then I left and went to wait outside the
interview room. Five minutes later they called me in. A woman
¹⁰ .... (sit) behind a desk, and when she looked up, I saw it
was the woman from the bathroom! I'm happy to say I got the job!

LISTENING

🎧 **4.3 Listen to an interview with two teleworkers. Then, write down:**

1 why they decided to work from home.
Viktor was ....
Yoko was ....

2 when they made their decision.
Viktor made his decision while ....
Yoko made her decision while ....

PRONUNCIATION

was and *were* in past continuous

A 🎧 4.4 Listen to how *was* and *were* are said in the sentences.

1 I was working an eight-hour day.

2 My kids were coming home from school alone.

B 🎧 4.5 Listen and repeat what you hear.

C Practise saying the sentences.

1 We were discussing marketing plans when the lights
went out.

2 Sam was writing his report when his boss called.

D 🎧 4.6 Listen and repeat.

DEVELOPING WRITING

A formal email – asking for information

A Read the advert. Does the job interest you?

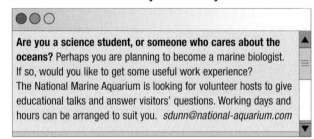

Are you a science student, or someone who cares about the oceans? Perhaps you are planning to become a marine biologist. If so, would you like to get some useful work experience? The National Marine Aquarium is looking for volunteer hosts to give educational talks and answer visitors' questions. Working days and hours can be arranged to suit you. *sdunn@national-aquarium.com*

B Read Chad's email. What does he ask for?

....

From	Chad Duffy [cduffy@tiscali.com]
To	sdunn@national-aquarium.com
Subject	volunteer host vacancy

Dear Ms Dunn,

A) I saw your advertisement for volunteer hosts on the National Marine Aquarium's website, and I am writing to ask for further information about the position.

B) At present, I am studying Marine Biology at Southampton University, and am in my third year. I visited the Aquarium last month and saw your amazing shark population. I am planning to specialise in the study of sharks in my future career, and am hoping to gain work experience in this area.

C) I am very interested in the post. Could you send me more information about the job and an application form, please?

D) I look forward to hearing from you.

Yours sincerely,

Chad Duffy

C Match the paragraphs (A–D) in the email to the descriptions (1–4) below.

1 give information about yourself ....
2 ask for information ....
3 say politely that you expect a reply ....
4 explain why you are writing ....

D A formal email is organised like an informal email but the language is different. Write the formal language from Chad's email next to the informal language in Charlie's email.

informal email	formal email
Hi Gill	
I'm working in a pub at the moment.	
Can you send me the photos from your party?	
Thanks a lot.	
Can't wait to hear from you!	
Lots of love	
Charlie	

E Write a formal email applying for this job. Use the advert and the notes below. Write about 120 words.

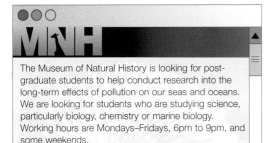

MNH

The Museum of Natural History is looking for post-graduate students to help conduct research into the long-term effects of pollution on our seas and oceans. We are looking for students who are studying science, particularly biology, chemistry or marine biology. Working hours are Mondays–Fridays, 6pm to 9pm, and some weekends.
For further information, email Greg Norman at
gregnorm@mnh.com

introduce myself
* *2nd year post-graduate - PhD in Marine Biology*
* *special interest in endangered sea plants*

questions to ask
* *which seas/oceans are they studying?*
* *will we go on study trips?*
* *ask for application form*

Vocabulary Builder Quiz 4 (*OVB* pp14–17)

Try the *OVB* quiz for Unit 2. Write your answers in your notebook. Then check them and record your score.

A Use the verbs in the box to make nouns that end in *-ment* or *-tion*.

install	present	advertise	negotiate	manage
apply	develop	contribute		

1 I made a .... to a group of about 200 people and I was really nervous.
2 Have you seen the latest Volkswagen .... on TV? It's very good.
3 The .... of our new telephone only took ten minutes.
4 I've just filled in a job .... form and sent it off to that company.
5 Sayid, thank you! You have made an important .... to this project.
6 The company has been sold and is under new ....
7 The government refused to enter into .... with the transport workers.
8 The company is growing because the .... of new products is extremely important to the company.

B Decide whether the statements are true (T) or false (F).

1 You make an *appointment* to see the doctor at a particular time. ....
2 A *product* is a piece of work that you do over a long period of time. ....
3 A large meeting where people talk about their work is a *conference*. ....
4 If you *rent* a house, you own it. ....
5 When you keep *accounts*, you write down how much money you make and spend. ....

C Complete the sentences with one of the words in the box.

fight	click	forward	make	form	skills

1 Put .... a proposal at the next meeting.
2 Fill in an application .... online and send it with a short letter.
3 She's got good management ....
4 They will .... for equal rights at work.
5 Go to the website and .... on the link to Japan.
6 It's important to .... a good impression at a job interview.

D Cross out the words that don't go with the following.

1 *social / weight / foreign / management* policy
2 *part-time / voluntary / pension / shift* work
3 *fixed / basic / low / depressing* salary
4 *computer / security / unemployed / heating* system
5 *marketing / studio / business / design* consultant
6 *competitive / night / eight-hour / early* shift

Score ___ /25

Wait a couple of weeks and try the quiz again.
Compare your scores.

05 RELAX

VOCABULARY
Activities, places and equipment

A Put the following activities into the correct columns below.

| fishing | exercise | swimming | cards | golf |
| Pilates | cycling | gymnastics | football | walking |

play	go	do

B Read the text below and answer the questions.

The Two-Minute Test

This isn't difficult but can you do the anagrams and answer the questions in two minutes?

Ready!
Steady!
Go!

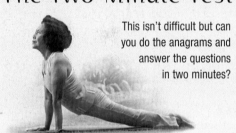

ceand   nnteiy tuesnim   net ot ffneeti

obotflla   ntneis   eamg   siceerex

ptssor qupeiemtn   llbvoeylla   ketbbllasa

1   You play this sport outside, with two or four players. You hit a ball over a net with a racket.

2   How long is a normal football match?

3   Salsa, tango and waltz are all kinds of ...

4   Is Pilates a sport, a game or a form of exercise?

5   You play this sport inside or outside, in teams of six. You hit a ball over a net with your hands.

6   Rackets, bats and golf clubs are all types of ...

7   Which sport do you play on a court?

8   How many players are there in a basketball team?

9   Which sport do you play on a pitch?

10 Which word can you *not* use to describe gear?
    equipment   kit   game   clothes

DEVELOPING CONVERSATIONS
Introducing negative comments

A Complete the negative comments.

1   A: Did you enjoy the film?
    B: I have to say, ... (acting / not good)

2   A: What did you think of the match?
    B: To be honest, ...
       (I / be / disappointed / Chelsea / not / win)

3   A: What was the book like?
    B: I must admit, ...
       (I / not / like / romantic novels)

4   A: Do you want to go swimming?
    B: To be honest, ...
       (I / can't stand / swim)

5   A: We could play tennis on Saturday.
    B I have to say, ... (I / useless at tennis)

6   A: I know, how about playing golf?
    B: I must admit, ...
       (think / golf / boring)

B Read the conversation. Write *to be honest*, *I have to say* or *I must admit* in each gap 1–3. For gaps 4–6, complete the phrases.

Anil: Phew! I'm exhausted! I've just been to my first Tai Chi lesson. It's the strangest form of exercise I've ever tried!

Henny: Did you enjoy it, then?

Anil: I'm not sure, really. ¹ ...., it was more difficult than I expected. It's actually quite hard to do the exercises slowly and correctly.

Henny: So, are you going to continue doing it?

Anil: Well, ² ...., I think I prefer team sports. I think I'm going to join a football club instead.

Henny: ³ ...., I'm not surprised. I didn't think you'd like it!

Anil: So, what about you, Henny? Did you go with Dae to play tennis?

Henny: Yes, I did, actually.

Anil: And did you like it?

Henny: To be honest, ⁴ .... (too difficult). I couldn't hit the ball well. Dae is good at it, but she's very fit, and she's taken lessons.

Anil: So, what are you going to do?

Henny: Well, I have to say, ⁵ ....
         (prefer / dancing). I must admit,
         ⁶ .... (not / like / sport much any more). I want to get fit, though, so I might join a dance class and learn the tango.

C 🔊 5.1 Listen and check your ideas for exercise B.

GRAMMAR

Might, present continuous, *be going to* + verb

A **Match the sentence halves.**

1 I'm thinking of going to
2 If the weather's good tomorrow,
3 I'm exhausted! I'm
4 Nontos phoned earlier.
5 I'm going to go to the gym this afternoon,
6 That's a good idea! If I'm free,

a not going to do anything this evening.
b to join a Pilates class.
c the cinema this evening. Do you want to come?
d I might come with you.
e I might go shopping.
f Ann and I are meeting him at the pub later.

B **Choose the correct form to complete the following sentences. In some cases, both forms are possible.**

1 *We're meeting / We might meet* at the cinema at 7 o'clock. The film starts at 7.15. Do you want to come?
2 *I'm going / I'm thinking of going* to Paris at the weekend. Do you think I should?
3 A: What *are you doing / might you do* at the weekend?
   B: I don't know. *I'm going / I might go* to see my grandmother.
4 A: Kimbo, I won't come shopping with you today. The weather's so nice, *I might do / I'm going to do* some gardening. It might rain tomorrow!
   B: Oh! OK, then. I don't fancy going on my own, so *I might do / I'm doing* some work instead.
5 A: *Might you come / Are you going to come* for a meal with us later?
   B: I might. What time *are you meeting / are you going to meet*?
6 *I'm watching / I'm going to watch* a DVD tonight.

C **Complete the mini-dialogues. Use a suitable form – *might*, present continuous or *going to* – with the verb in brackets.**

1 A: Right, Ken! We .... Anil at 5 o'clock outside the stadium. The match starts at 5.30, so don't be late! (meet)
2 A: Jorge! .... for a drink after work? (you come)
   B: I don't know, Dae. I .... home and have an early night. I'm exhausted. (go)
3 A: Aneli, you haven't worn those for ten years! What .... ? (you / do)
   B: I .... running, and lose weight before our holiday! (go)
4 We .... a barbecue this evening and look at those clouds! It's going to rain! (have) What .... ? The house is too small for 20 people! (we/do)

LISTENING

A **Match the sports with the photographs above.**

1 sepak takraw ......   3 badminton ......
2 underwater rugby ......   4 tennis ......

B 🔊 **5.1 Listen to three friends talking about their plans to get fit. What sport does each person decide to do?**

Dave: ....
Beret: ....
Heidi: ....

C **Listen again and answer the questions.**

1 What type of sport does Heidi like?
....
2 Why is Heidi not happy with Dave?
....
3 Why doesn't Beret want to try Heidi's sport?
....
4 Why isn't underwater rugby a violent sport?
....
5 Do you play sepak takraw with your legs and feet or your arms and legs?
....
6 Why does Beret decide to go with David?
....

05

VOCABULARY Sports and games verbs

A Choose the correct verb in italics in the following sentences:

1 Liverpool *won* / *beat* Juventus 2–0 yesterday.
2 Gerrard *scored* / *kicked* both goals.
3 In the Chelsea–Manchester City match last night, Chelsea *drew* / *won* 3–2.
4 When I last *scored* / *timed* myself running, I ran three miles in ten minutes.
5 My dad has always *beaten* / *supported* Liverpool, but to be honest, I prefer Arsenal.
6 In rugby, players *throw* / *kick* the ball when they pass it to their team mates.

B Match words from boxes A and B to write a list of ten sporting collocations. Some words in A are used more than once.

| A | football | running | tennis | golf |
| | swimming | dance | sports | |

B	pool	event	racket	pitch
	course	class	track	gear
	clubs	court		

C Label the items from exercise B in the photographs.

D Match the sentence halves.

1 I'm going to try out the new 18-hole golf
2 Jim, have you got your swimming
3 Are there any good sports
4 Alice, haven't you got a dance
5 Mum, I can't find my tennis
6 Is there a good running

a events on in the area this weekend?
b racket, and I'm playing in a tournament in half an hour!
c class at 7.30 this evening?
d course at Bagshot this afternoon.
e track near here? I've brought my trainers.
f gear ready? It's time to go.

GRAMMAR Superlatives

A Look at the spelling rules in the Language note. Complete the sentences with the superlative form of the adjectives in brackets:

1 The .... (exciting) thing I've ever done was jump from an aeroplane with a parachute.
2 The .... (big) party I've ever had was for my 21st birthday, when I invited 100 people.
3 The .... (easy) exam I've ever taken was my driving test. I passed first time!
4 The .... (good) holiday I've ever had was in Thailand two years ago. I met my girlfriend there and fell in love!
5 The .... (expensive) car I've ever bought was my BMW.
6 The .... (hard) thing I've ever had to do was break up with my last boyfriend. He was really upset, and I felt guilty.
7 The .... (bad) thing I've ever done was cheat in an exam at school. I got 80%, but I'd copied from my neighbour's paper.
8 The .... (popular) football team in my country is Juventus.
9 The .... (fit) guy I know is my break-dance instructor.
10 The .... (successful) woman I know is my mum. She runs her own business, goes to the gym twice a week, and still finds time for us!

Language note

Remember how to form superlative adjectives:
1 words of one syllable take *-est* e.g. *old – the oldest*
2 words of three syllables or more take *the most*, or *the least* before them e.g. *intelligent – the most intelligent*
3 Some words of two syllables take *the + -est*. e.g. *pretty – the prettiest*. Others take *the most; the least*. e.g. *aware – the most aware*

Always check the comparative and superlative forms of two-syllable adjectives as you learn them.

B Write sentences with a superlative + the present perfect.

    e.g. It / bad / film / we / ever see.
    It's the worst film we've ever seen.

1 This / expensive / car / I / ever buy.

....

2 This / exciting / sport / I / ever try.

....

3 That / big / pizza / I / ever see.

....

4 That / good / game / he / ever play.

....

5 She / successful / tennis player / I / ever know.

....

6 That / easy / game / I / ever / win.

....

C Complete the sentences in the factsheet with the superlative of the adjectives in brackets.

D Complete the factsheet with the missing information (a–g) from the box below.

98,772 people	594	3,000 miles
31 hours	$132 million	24 hours
8 days		

PRONUNCIATION

A Place the groups of words under the correct symbols.

/ɪ/	/eɪ/	/æ/	/ɪst/	/iː/

1 larg**est**   cycl**ist**   fast**est**
2 ch**a**llenging   m**a**rathon   b**a**dminton
3 sk**i**   **ea**sy   t**ea**m
4 w**i**n   **i**nstruct   b**u**siness
5 pl**ay**   br**ea**k   r**a**ce

B 🔊 5.2 Listen and check.

C Practise saying the words. Then, add the following words to the table.

stadium	**i**nteresting	long**est**	compl**e**te
g**a**me	pr**e**tty	ex**a**m	achi**e**ve

SPORTS FACTSHEET

◀**1** The ¹ .... (long) aerobics class lasted for ª .... and took place in a shopping centre car park in Colombia.

◀**2** The world's ² .... (large) football stadium is Camp Nou in Barcelona, Spain. It can seat ᵇ ....

◀**3** The world's ³ .... (challenging) bicycle race is Race Across America (RAAM). It covers about ᶜ ....

◀**4** The ⁴ .... (fast) cyclist ever to complete the RAAM is Pete Penseyres. He covered 3,107 miles in ᵈ .... , 9 hours and 47 minutes in 1986.

◀**5** Cristiano Ronaldo became the world's ⁵ .... (expensive) football player after his Real Madrid transfer of ᵉ ....

◀**6** The ⁶ .... (large) ski lesson was attended by ᶠ .... skiers, who were instructed by Hansjürg Gredig (Switzerland) of the Swiss-Snowsport School at Sarn-Heinzenberg (Graubünden), Switzerland, on 23 February 2008.

◀**7** The ⁷ .... (long) marathon playing tennis (singles) was ᵍ .... 35 minutes and 30 seconds and was achieved by George L. Bolter and Athos Rostan III (both USA), in Hickory, NC, USA, on 8–9 November 2008.

VOCABULARY Word families

A Write the noun forms of the adjectives below. Check your spelling.

adjective	noun	adjective	noun
tired	*tiredness*	homeless	
happy		weak	
aware		ill	
conscious		lazy	
fit		mad	

B Complete the text with the correct adjective or noun form of the words from the box.

aware	mad	weak	lazy	population	homeless

Many cities are over-populated, and one of the biggest problems facing them is ¹ .... There are just not enough homes for everyone. London, for example, is the most heavily-² .... city in Europe, with almost 5,000 people per square kilometre.

Some people believe that homeless people are ³ ...., and that they don't work. This is a simplistic view, because many homeless people have jobs, but the high cost of living in major cities means that they can't afford the rent.

Shelter, the charity for the homeless, is trying to raise people's ⁴ .... of the problem. 'Nobody wants to be on the streets,' says one spokesman. 'It's complete ⁵ .... to think that these people are lazy and ⁶ .... There are whole families that need help. The government must provide more homes, with rents that people can afford to pay.'

READING

A Read the blog entry about three ways to relax. Match one of the techniques with the photograph.

B Decide whether the statements are true (T) or false (F).

1 All three relaxation techniques ask you to breathe correctly. ....
2 The most complicated technique is the yoga technique. ....
3 The yoga technique works best if you are alone and sitting down. ....
4 The guided imagery technique asks you to look at a picture. ....
5 The guided imagery technique does not work in a crowded room. ....
6 The progressive muscle technique asks you to focus on your body. ....

●○○

Feeling Stressed Out?

Today I'm going to look at stress. Most people have some basic strategies for dealing with stress: they might go for a walk, sit and listen to some relaxing music, have a hot bath, or take a nap. These all help. But today here are my top three tips that will really relax your mind and your body. So here we go.

Tip number 1: Yoga breathing technique
This is one of the easiest ways to relax. The yoga breathing technique is most effective when you are in a quiet place, and sitting in the well-known 'lotus position'. But you can also do it at the office, on the bus or in the park. Sit up or stand up straight. Choose a point to look at, and focus on it while you are breathing. Close your mouth and breathe in through your nose slowly and deeply, counting up to four. Hold your breath for four seconds, and then breathe out slowly, with your mouth closed. Again, count to four, and imagine all the stress and tension of the day leaving your body. Repeat the exercise up to ten times.

Tip number 2: Guided imagery relaxation technique
Another simple way to relax is to use the guided imagery technique. Find a quiet place and get into a comfortable position. Breathe deeply and slowly, and imagine you are breathing in peace and breathing out stress. Once you feel more relaxed, think of a picture of the most relaxing place you can imagine. Perhaps it's a beach on a tropical island, or a cosy armchair by an open fire. Allow yourself to daydream. When you feel relaxed, count down from ten, and tell yourself that when you get to 'one' you'll feel calm and refreshed. It really works!

Tip number 3: Progressive muscle relaxation technique
This is one of my personal favourites. You tense and then relax the muscles in different parts of your body. This really helps ease tension and makes you relax. You might find that the most enjoyable time to do this is in the evening. Sit down or lie down in a quiet place. Start with the feet. Tense up the muscle group in the feet, and hold for five seconds. Breathe in as you tense up. Then, release the tension all at once, and breathe out. Stay relaxed for ten seconds. Work your way up the body from one muscle group to the next. Repeat the exercise. Continue doing this until you have completed the whole body.

Right! Go ahead and try one of them! Enjoy yourself!
Then let me know what you think by posting a comment below …

DEVELOPING WRITING
A blog – your favourite game

An online games magazine has invited readers to send a description of their favourite game or sport to their weekly blog. They want to know how and why they started the game, if they play with others, when and where, and what future plans they have for this game.

A Read one reader's blog entry.

1 What's the name of his favourite game?
....

2 How did he start playing the game?
....

3 How long has he been a club member?
....

4 What's he going to do in the future?
....

B Match the headings with the paragraphs.

1 Where, when and who I play with ....
2 Future plans for the game ....
3 How I started playing the game ....

C Underline any useful language about a game or a sport.

a My favourite game is chess. I started playing this game with my dad when I was five years old. Then I joined the local chess club. I've been a member for 12 years now, and I still enjoy it.

b I like chess because it's the most exciting game I've ever played. Although it's not a team game, chess can help you meet people. Several of my friends are members of my club. Now I've joined chess.com on the internet, and I play against people from all over the world.

c Next month I'm going to play in my first local tournament, so I'm practising hard. If I do well in that, I might take part in a larger tournament next May. Then ... who knows?!

D Write your own entry for the blog. Use the notes below to help you, and write three paragraphs, like the model above.

Favourite game blog entry:
My favourite game/sport is ...
I started playing ... when I ...

I like ... because ...
I've joined a ... club.
I play every ... with my friends / partner, etc.

I'm hoping to / thinking of / going to ...
I might ...

1 When and how you started.
2 The rules of the game / sport.
3 Why you like it.

Remember to check your grammar and spelling!

Vocabulary Builder Quiz 5 (*OVB* pp18–21)

Try the *OVB* quiz for Unit 5. Write your answers in your notebook. Then check them and record your score.

A Choose the correct word.
1 Hannah *beat / won* Xavier at table tennis last night.
2 Which golf *bat / club* are you going to use?
3 The team walked onto the football *court / pitch* and everyone cheered.
4 Avaaz and Greenpeace have launched a major *campaign / survey* against climate change.
5 *Spectators / Supporters* of the team gathered in the streets to welcome their players home.

B Complete the sentences with the correct preposition.
1 I have a real weakness .... shellfish.
2 Boris often cheats .... cards.
3 I suffer .... a nut allergy.
4 Some illnesses are related .... poor diet.
5 They informed us .... the accident two hours later.

C Complete the sentences with the correct form of the word in CAPITALS.
1 They want to raise .... of the problems caused by alcohol. AWARE
2 The .... of the Internet has helped businesses everywhere. INVENT
3 I lost .... after the car hit a tree. CONSCIOUS
4 We go .... every Sunday morning. CYCLE
5 Mental .... affects many people at some time in their life. ILL

D Match the sentence halves.
1 She walks at a brisk
2 There is a ban
3 Julios ran three laps of the race
4 In the final, Keira faced
5 They're conducting

a track yesterday evening.
b pace every morning.
c a difficult opponent, but managed to beat her.
d a survey of people's sleeping habits.
e on smoking in the gym.

E Cross out the word that does not collocate with the key word.
1 basketball *match / court / bat / team*
2 attract *a crowd / scores / attention / large audiences*
3 golf *club / course / ball / racket*
4 win *an opponent / a match / money / a medal*
5 stay *awake / calm / full / friends*

Score ___ /25

Wait a couple of weeks and try the quiz again. Compare your scores.

DEVELOPING CONVERSATIONS
Explaining where places are

A Complete this conversation with the questions in the box.

So what's it like?	Where's it near?
How big is it?	So where are you from?
Really? Whereabouts?	Have you always lived there?
What do you like most about living there?	
And is there anything you don't like about it?	

A: [1] ....

B: I'm from Italy, the south of Italy actually.

A: [2] ....

B: I don't think you'll know it. It's a place called Ravello.

A: No, never heard of it.

[3] ....

B: It's just south of Naples.

A: Oh, right. I know Naples.

[4] ....

B: Well, lovely. It's a beautiful place, very near the sea.

A: Sounds wonderful.

[5] ....

B: Oh, it's just a little village.

A: It must be great.

[6] ....

B: I love the countryside and the mountains.

A: [7] ....

B: Yes, all my life.

A: [8] ....

B: Yes. There are too many tourists!

VOCABULARY Cities and areas

A Choose the word which forms a collocation with the key word.

1 car   *area / bank / plant / trees*
2 town   *village / square / circle / border*
3 agricultural   *boat / traffic / wall / area*
4 transport   *system / climate / factories / place*
5 Atlantic   *plant / country / coast / forest*
6 river   *coast / bank / church / shop*
7 24-hour   *culture / system / crime / fields*
8 cold   *square / climate / museum / port*

B Complete the sentences with the words in the box.

murders	factories	24-hour culture	beach	rural
parks	desert	industrial	historic	bank

1 I live in an .... area right next to a huge car plant.
2 This is a very .... town. There are lots of old churches and you can even see parts of the old city wall.
3 Our village is very .... It is surrounded by farms and fields.
4 This is a very green city because we have a lot of ....
5 I live near the ocean, so I spend all my time on the ....
6 We have a .... in our town. The bars and shops are open all night.
7 Some people live in boats tied to the .... of the river.
8 The pollution is really bad where we live because there are so many ....
9 I live in quite a dangerous area. There were two .... in my street last year.
10 It's always very dry and very hot where I live because it's in the middle of the ....

PRONUNCIATION /s/ or /z/?

Look at the underlined sounds. Write /s/ or /z/ next to each word. Check your answers using a learner's dictionary.

tree<u>s</u>	/z/	<u>s</u>ystem	....
park<u>s</u>	/s/	mu<u>s</u>eum	....
de<u>s</u>ert	....	fore<u>s</u>t	....
indu<u>s</u>trial	....	bar<u>s</u>	....
hi<u>s</u>toric	....	boat<u>s</u>	....
factorie<u>s</u>	....	pla<u>c</u>e	....
<u>s</u>quare	....	<u>c</u>ircle	....
coa<u>s</u>t	....	dangerou<u>s</u>	....

Learner tip

You can find a guide to phonemic symbols such as /s/ and /z/ in the inside front cover of the Vocabulary Builder (in the back of the Student's Book) or in any good learner's dictionary.

READING

A Read this newspaper article quickly. Which home is best for:

1 a young professional couple? ....
2 a family with young children? ....
3 a single person? ....

B Read the article again, then answer the questions.

1 Which property is the biggest? ....
2 Which is closest to the shops? ....
3 Which has the best access to green space? ....
4 Which has the best security? ....
5 Which is the best for public transport? ....
6 Which is the noisiest? ....

HOMES *For You*

Buying a new home is one of the most important decisions in everyone's life, so don't miss our weekly guide to the best properties currently on the market in the area.

A This bright spacious studio is in the heart of the historic city centre, just a few minutes from the main square and very close to the main railway and bus stations. The large studio room has spectacular views over one of the city's main shopping streets. There is also a separate kitchen and a modern bathroom.

B This one bedroom luxury flat is situated in the north of the city close to the main business district. It is arranged over two floors: the bedroom and living room are on the upper floor with stairs leading down to the fully fitted kitchen and bathroom. The flat is in a modern block with its own car park, gym, burglar alarm and 24-hour porter.

C This elegant four bedroom house has a living room, dining room and kitchen, as well as a large garden and a garage with space for two cars. It is located in a quiet street in the western suburbs of the city. There is a park at the end of the road and an excellent local school just five minutes' walk away.

Glossary

studio: a flat with one main room for sleeping and living
burglar alarm: a system that gives a warning when a thief enters a building
porter: a person who watches the entrance to a building
suburbs: an area of houses and flats outside the centre of a city

GRAMMAR *have to / don't have to / can*

A **Choose the correct forms to complete these sentences.**

1 The bus stop is only five minutes away, so you *can / have to* walk there easily.
2 He *has to / doesn't have to* pay rent because he owns the flat.
3 There's a gym in the building, so you *can / have to* keep fit.
4 The heating has an automatic switch, so you *have to / don't have to* turn it off at night.
5 This building has a car park, so you *don't have to / can* park in the street.
6 They *have to / don't have to* go home early because there are no buses after ten o'clock.
7 We have a gardener who comes every week, so we *can / don't have to* worry about the garden.
8 They live in the suburbs, so they *can / have to* drive to the countryside easily.

B **Complete this email from a foreign student living with a family in Wales to a friend in the USA. Use *have to*, *don't have to*, or *can*.**

To	Klara Bunnenberg
From	Pia Cambiaghi
Subject	Life with my new 'family'

Hi Klara

Just a quick email to tell you about the family I'm living with. The Keen family are very friendly and in some ways life is very easy. Back home I
¹ .... wash my own clothes and do some cooking and cleaning. But it's very easy here – I ² .... do anything! I ³ .... use the kitchen to have breakfast, make a drink and stuff. I ⁴ ....also use the living room to watch TV. But there's one problem.

When I go out to see friends I ⁵ .... be back at 10 pm! Can you believe it? I'm 18!!! At home I ⁶ .... come home when I want. OK, I ⁷ .... phone my parents and tell them where I am but that's normal, right? They need to know where I am. Anyway, I'm not happy here and I have to look for another place to live – the family are really nice but I just can't stay here.

OK, I ⁸ .... go. I have an exam tomorrow and I need to study.
Mail me back soon!

Lots of love
Pia

LISTENING

A **6.1 Listen to the conversation between a landlady and a tenant. Which of these sentences best describes the situation?**

a The tenant is complaining to the landlady about his room.
b The landlady is unhappy because the tenant hasn't paid his rent.
c The landlady is showing the room to the tenant for the first time.
d The tenant is leaving his room after several years.

Language note renting a flat

The person who rents a flat *to* someone is the landlord or landlady.
The person who rents a flat *from* the landlord or landlady is a tenant

B **Tick (✓) the subjects the landlady and tenant talk about.**

1 the room
2 the house rules
3 transport
4 heating in the house
5 the rent
6 the dog

C **Listen again. Decide whether the statements are true (T) or false (F).**

1 There's a nice view out of the bedroom window. ....
2 There's a TV in the room. ....
3 The man has his own bathroom. ....
4 The man is a non-smoker. ....
5 The man can use her kitchen before eight o'clock. ....
6 He has to pay extra for heating. ....
7 The heating comes on at six in the morning. ....
8 The man has to pay three months' rent in advance. ....

DEVELOPING WRITING
A letter – describing where you live

A Look at the letter quickly. Is it:
a   an informal letter to parents?
b   an informal formal letter to a company or an institution?
c   a letter to a friend?

B Match the descriptions of the paragraphs (1–4) with the paragraphs (A–D).
1   Talks about the family and house rules   ....
2   Asks his friend to write back to him.   ....
3   Gives information about where his room is.   ....
4   Describes his room.   ....

> 32 Ship Way
> Portsmouth
> PO16 4TY
>
> 15 October
>
> Dear Mahdi,
>
> A   I'm writing to give you my new address because I've finally found somewhere to live. It's a small room at the top of a big family house about two kilometres from the centre of Portsmouth. Here's a photo of the place. You can see it's very different from the houses at home. It's a good location for me because it's only five minutes' walk to the university and I can also get to the beach easily.
>
> B   There's not much furniture in the room — only a bed, a chair and a desk, as well as a kettle so I can make some tea. There's also no TV in my room but I don't mind because it means I'll have more time to do my course work.
>
> C   The family who own the house are friendly but quite strict. They have two young children who go to bed early, so I have to be quiet in the evenings. I also can't invite guests to my room during the week. But the best thing about the room is that the rent is very cheap, so I hope to have a little bit of extra money this term.
>
> D   Now that you know my address, please write and tell me all the news from home.
>
> Best wishes,
>
> Ibrahim

C Read the letter and answer these questions.
1   Why is Ibrahim writing to his friend?
....
2   Where is he living?
....
3   What does he like about the location?
....
4   What furniture does he have in his room?
....
5   What is missing from the room?
....
6   Why does Ibrahim have to be quiet in the evenings?
....
7   What other house rules are there?
....
8   What is the best thing about the room?
....

> **Language note**
> -
>
> You can close informal emails and letters in different ways.
> Use *Best wishes* for a person you know but are not close to.
> Use *Love* or *Lots of love* for family or close friends.

D Read the statements. Decide whether they are true (T) or false (F).
1   Ibrahim is living in Manchester.   ....
2   His room is in a big house.   ....
3   The house he is staying in is similar to houses at home.   ....
4   He can study more because there's no TV in his room.   ....
5   Ibrahim doesn't like the family.   ....
6   Because the rent isn't expensive, he has more money.   ....

E Now write a letter. Describe your new home. Use the four paragraphs in Ibrahim's letter to help you. Include the following:
- Put the address and date at the top.
- Begin 'Dear, ...'
- Give a reason for writing: 'I'm writing to ...', or 'I'm writing because ...'
- Describe the building and the location and say what you like about it.
- Describe the room and its furniture.
- Talk about the people that you live with and any rules that you have to follow.
- Ask the other person to write to you with news.
- Sign off with 'Best wishes'.

VOCABULARY Staying with people

A Match the sentence halves.

1 Would you like to hang   ....
2 There's a lot of crime in this area, so always lock   ....
3 If you're feeling hungry please help   ....
4 The carpets are very valuable, so please take   ....
5 My hair is wet, so can I   ....
6 I couldn't find a bank, so can you   ....
7 Follow me and I'll show   ....
8 Why don't you sit   ....

a yourself to the food in the fridge.
b the door when you go out.
c lend me some money until this evening?
d your coat in this wardrobe?
e down in this armchair and relax?
f you the guest bedroom.
g off your shoes in the porch.
h borrow a hair dryer?

B Mark each sentence G for guest or H for host.

1 Would you like to sit down and I'll make you some tea?   ....
2 Can I borrow you hairdryer, please? I left mine at home.   ....
3 Of course. In Japan we always take off our shoes too.   ....
4 When are your other guests leaving?   ....
5 Please help yourself to a drink if you're thirsty.   ....
6 Why don't you have dinner with us tonight?   ....
7 Could I use the phone for a minute? I need to phone a friend.   ....
8 Please make sure you turn down your music after eight because the children go to bed then.   ....

DEVELOPING CONVERSATIONS
Asking for permission

A Use the prompts to ask permission to do the following.

1 It's raining. Ask to borrow an umbrella.
   Do you ....?
2 You're bored. Ask to switch on the TV.
   Is it ....?
3 You want to check your emails. Ask to use the computer.
   Do you ....?
4 You're hungry. Ask to take food from the fridge.
   Is it ....?
5 You want a friend to stay the night. Ask your flatmate if that's OK.
   Do you ....?
6 You have no credit on your mobile. Ask to borrow the phone to make a call.
   May I ....?

B Choose the best answer to the four requests above.

1 Give permission:
   a Please do!
   b Yes, I do.
2 Refuse permission:
   a Well, actually, I'd rather you didn't.
   b Of course.
3 Refuse permission:
   a Yes, I do.
   b No, I'm sorry but that's not possible.
4 Give permission:
   a Please help yourself.
   b No, of course not.
5 Refuse permission:
   a No, of course not!
   b Well, actually, I'd rather you didn't.
6 Give permission:
   a No, I'm sorry but that's not possible.
   b Of course. Please help yourself.

C Complete this conversation between a guest and a host.

G: Oh, it's 7.30. Do [1] .... switch on the TV to watch the football?
H: Well, [2] .... I'm sorry but I don't like football.
G: Oh, OK. No problem. Is [3] .... I borrow your radio and take it up to my bedroom?
H: Yes, [4] .... Please [5] ....
  Are you going to listen to the football then?
G: Yes. It's a big game for Croatia. We're playing Brazil.
H: Oh, right. I've got a better idea. I'll take the radio and you watch the TV.
G: Really? That's very kind. Are you sure?
H: Yes, of course. [6] .... It's an important game.
G: Thank you very much! That is very kind of you.
H: You're welcome!

GRAMMAR Future

A Use the prompts in brackets to write responses, using *will* or *won't*.

1 A: You're late for class for the third time this week!
   B: I'm sorry. I promise (do it again)
   ....

2 A: You've borrowed £10 from me already this month.
   B: I know, but (pay you back)
   ....

3 A: My train has been cancelled.
   B: Oh, no! Poor you. (pick you up in the car)
   ....

4 A: The phone's ringing again.
   B: Don't worry. (get it)
   ....

5 A: There seems to be a problem with the computer.
   B: Really? (look into it)
   ....

6 A: Can you buy me a ticket for the concert this evening?
   B: I haven't got any money, so (be able to)
   ....

7 A: These bags are really heavy.
   B: Give them to me. (carry them for you)
   ....

8 A: There's someone at the front door.
   B: Don't get up. (see who it is)
   ....

B Look at the answers in 1–8 from exercise A again. Mark each one immediate response (IR), offer (O), or promise (P). Some sentences can have more than one answer.

C Fill the gaps in this dialogue with *will*, *'ll* or *won't*.

A: Is that your phone?
B: Yeah. I [1] .... just answer it. Hello? Oh, hi, Mum! You're coming back early? In about two hours! Oh, OK. Yeah, love you too. Bye.
A: Was that your parents?
B: Yeah. And this place is in a terrible mess.
A: Don't panic. I [2] .... help you. I'll do the kitchen.
B: Great! Thanks. And I [3] .... clean the living room. I [4] .... do my room – there's not enough time.
A: Hey, I've got an idea. I [5] .... call my brother. He can come over and help us.
B: Good thinking. One thing is for sure.
A: What's that?
B: I [6] .... have a party again when my parents aren't here. And that's a promise!
A: Yeah, yeah, yeah.

Vocabulary Builder Quiz 6 (*OVB* pp22–25)

Try the *OVB* quiz for Unit 6. Write your answers in your notebook. Then check them and record your score.

A Match the sentence halves.
1 My sister left   ....
2 The bank lent   ....
3 I borrowed   ....
4 The story spread   ....
5 Their kids are allowed   ....
6 He took off   ....

a her bag in the restaurant.
b his coat because it was so hot.
c to stay out late on Saturday nights.
d him $1000 to start a business.
e through the village very quickly.
f his car for the weekend.

B Choose the correct word.
1 I'm ready for bed. I've had a very *tired / tiring* day.
2 I couldn't do my maths homework. It was much too *hard / dry*.
3 I can't hear you. It's much too *noisy / exciting* in here.
4 You can stay at my house tonight. We've got a *spare / set* room.
5 He doesn't pay any rent for his flat. It's *free / freedom*.
6 You'll like the view. It's very *rural / countryside*.

C Choose the word that does not form a collocation with the key word.
1 overnight   *stay / flight / wall*
2 alarm   *square / clock / bell*
3 steel   *plant / takeaway / tool*
4 bank   *balance / show / account*
5 TV   *company / advert / basin*
6 kitchen   *wood / table / knife*
7 house   *mate / alarm / rules*

D Decide whether the statements are true (T) or false (F)?
1 A *border* separates two countries.   ....
2 A *port* is a factory where things are made.   ....
3 A *pint* is a unit for measuring weight.   ....
4 A *budget* is an amount of money that you can spend.   ....
5 A *corner* is a place where two lines or walls meet.   ....
6 A *guest* is a person who invites you to his or her home.   ....

Score ___ /25

Wait a couple of weeks and try the quiz again. Compare your scores.

07 MIND AND BODY

VOCABULARY
Illnesses and health problems

A Read the clues. Then write the health problems in the grid.

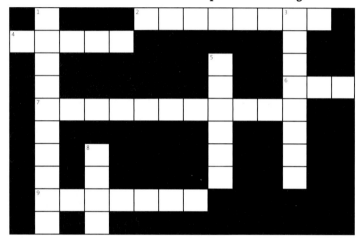

ACROSS →
2 A sore head (8)
4 A loud noise you make when your throat is sore or uncomfortable, and you want to clear it (5)
6 An illness with a high fever, aching body, cold, etc. (3)
7 When body heat is higher than normal (11)
9 A negative reaction of the body to something that is normally harmless (7)

DOWN ↓
1 A pain, when you can't swallow or speak easily (4, 6)
3 An allergy which appears in springtime, rather like a bad cold (8)
5 A medical condition that makes it difficult to breathe (6)
8 An illness with a running nose, sneezing, etc. (4)

B Choose the correct verb in each sentence.
1 When I get hay fever, my eyes *wash / water* all the time.
2 I've got a sore throat and I can't *sneeze / swallow*.
3 I feel hot and cold and I'm *sweating / swallowing* a lot.
4 If I go near a cat, I start *sneezing / hurting* and I can't breathe.
5 I've lost my appetite and my whole body *coughs / aches*.
6 I get these awful headaches that sometimes *last / make* up to an hour!
7 The pain's so bad that I can't *concentrate / swallow* on my work.
8 Have you got any throat sweets? My throat hurts when I *sweat / cough*.

GRAMMAR Giving advice
(*should, ought to, why don't you*)

A Choose the correct phrase – *why don't you, ought to* or *should* – to complete the sentences.
1 A: I've got a bad back.
   B: I don't think you .... lift that heavy box, then.
2 Look, you've been working all day. .... take a break?
3 I know you don't want to upset him, but you .... tell him how you feel.
4 A: Ow! I've cut myself!
   B: You .... put a plaster on that.
5 What .... I do about my nosebleed? It won't stop!
6 .... put some lavender oil on that burn? It's good for the pain, and helps it get better.
7 You .... go to the doctor's about that rash. You've had it for a week now.
8 You .... complain! You've waited an hour for your soup.

Language note

1 *Should, ought to* and *why don't you* are all fairly polite ways of giving advice, but *should* and *ought to* are slightly more forceful. The speaker is certain that this is what the other person should do, e.g. *You ought to finish your work before you leave.*
2 *Why don't you* introduces a more gentle suggestion, as a possibility, e.g. *If you're worried, why don't you talk to the teacher about it?*

B Correct the mistakes in the following sentences.
1 I think you shouldn't come to work if you're not well.
2 Maybe you should to put something on that cut.
3 He's got an awful cough. He oughts to stop smoking!
4 Katie looks awful! Why not you take her to see the doctor?
5 You ought stay in bed with that high temperature.
6 You don't ought eat chocolate when you've got an upset stomach.

DEVELOPING CONVERSATIONS
Common questions about illness

A **Complete the conversations with the questions in the box.**

> Are you OK?
> Are you taking anything for it?
> Have you been to the doctor's about it?

1 A: ....?
   B: No, not really. I've got an upset stomach.
2 A: ....?
   B: No, not yet. I've got an appointment tomorrow, and I'll see what she says.
3 A: ....?
   B: Well, I'm taking these tablets, but they make me sleepy.
4 A: ....?
   B: Yes, I went this morning, and she told me to get some rest.
5 A: ....?
   B: No, I'm not. I've had this terrible headache all morning.
6 A: ....?
   B: Well, I've got this cough mixture and some throat sweets.

B **Match the conversations (1–6) with the correct advice (a–f).**

1 A: So what did the doctor say about your hay fever?
   B: ....
2 A: Good news. My leg isn't broken! But it really hurts.
   B: Fantastic! So what did the doctor say?
   A: ....
3 A: What did the doctor say about the rash on your arm?
   B: ....
4 A: So, did the doctor say you weigh too much?
   B: Yes, she did! No surprise to me.
   A: And what advice did she give you?
   B: ....
5 A: What did the doctor tell you to do about your upset stomach?
   B: ....
6 A: The doctor told me my cough's got worse.
   B: Really? And what did she tell you to do about it?
   A: ....

a 'You should go to bed, drink lots of water and eat nothing but rice with some lemon in it.'
b 'Why don't you start jogging?'
c 'Why don't you take some throat sweets and gargle with salt water three times a day?'
d 'You ought to take it easy, put your leg up and rest for a few days.'
e 'You should take these tablets, and put some drops in your eyes three times a day.'
f 'You should wear cotton clothes and use this cream three times a day.'

LISTENING

A 🔊 **7.1 You are going to hear two conversations. In each case, one speaker has a problem. Listen, and decide what problem they have.**

1 ....
2 ....

B **What advice does the other speaker give them?**

1 ....
2 ....

C **In conversation 2, what does the man tell the woman to do at the end?**

....

D **Match each conversation with one of the pictures.**

LISTENING

Reproduced with the permission of the Down's Syndrome Association

A The children in the photo have Down's Syndrome (DS). How much do you know about DS? Tick (✓) the best answer to complete the sentences.

1 DS is:
   a mental illness
   b a condition babies are born with
   c a disease.
2 People with DS:
   a are usually physically disabled
   b cannot speak
   c can learn to read and write.
3 People with DS:
   a never have learning difficulties
   b have learning difficulties
   c sometimes have learning difficulties.
4 Many people with the condition lead:
   a active, semi-independent lives
   b inactive, dependent lives
   c inactive, semi-dependent lives.

B 🔊 7.2 Listen to the first part of an interview with a doctor talking about people with DS and check your answers.

C Read the statements and tick (✓) the sentences that are true. Listen and check your answers.

1 In the UK one in every 1,000 babies is born with DS.
2 The general public now understands a lot about this condition.
3 DS occurs after a child is born.
4 A person with DS does not suffer from the condition.
5 People with DS are unable to play team games.
6 There are three football teams for children with DS.

D 🔊 7.3 In part two of the interview Dr Aziz talks about a woman with DS who has done a lot in her life. Complete these notes as you listen.

Ruth Cromer is an example of someone with DS who attended
¹.................. .
She succeeded in learning to ².................. , and taught herself to
³.................. .
She became ⁴.................. , and has appeared on TV several times.
She also writes articles and gives ⁵.................. about DS.

VOCABULARY Forming words

A Form adjectives from the following words and place them in the correct list in the table below.

afford	finance	compare	industry
occasion	centre	enjoy	music
believe	emotion	culture	accept
rely	cure		

-able	-al
inevitable	physical

B Use a dictionary to check your answers, especially your spelling.

C Complete the sentences below with some of the adjectives from exercise A.

1 I like going out for an .... meal, but not all the time.
2 George works in a large factory in the .... area. It's over the other side of town.
3 Sometimes a person's .... problems can develop into mental illness.
4 Jack had to work in a restaurant when he was at university because he had almost no .... help from his parents.
5 The car I wanted was too expensive. So I bought a smaller, more .... one.
6 The flat's in a .... location near the High Street, so shops, the cinema and the college are close by.
7 Vienna is a city with a strong .... background in music and visual arts.
8 I had a very .... evening with your family, Hannah. They're lovely people.

D Choose the correct adjective to complete the following sentences.

1 Julios plays the guitar, drums and piano. He's very *musical / enjoyable*.
2 This house is not expensive. It's *financial / affordable*.
3 Umberto gets upset very easily, and screams and shouts. He's quite *emotional / reliable*.
4 One area of London is called the City. It is full of banks and is the *industrial / financial* centre.
5 Kylie is a good friend, and is always willing to help me when I have a problem. She's very *reliable / believable*.
6 We had a very pleasant day out by the river. It was very *cultural / enjoyable*.

PRONUNCIATION

A **Underline** the stress on these words.

<u>cen</u>tral	musical	industrial	physical
unbelievable	enjoyable	reliable	curable

B 🔊 **7.4 Listen and check your answers. Notice that the last syllable in each word is unstressed.**

C 🔊 **7.5 Practise saying these sentences. Then listen and repeat.**
1 The flat is really central.
2 Most kids are pretty musical.
3 That part of town is really industrial.
4 Rugby's a very physical game.
5 That's unbelievable!
6 The course was enjoyable.
7 The cars they make are very reliable.
8 A lot of diseases are curable.

DEVELOPING WRITING A webpage – fundraising

Language note

A *charity* is an organisation which collects money to help people or projects that need support, e.g. UNICEF, WWF, etc.
To *raise money for charity* is to do something in order to collect money for a particular organisation, e.g. *Andre is going to cycle from London to Paris to raise money for Greenpeace.* This is also known as *fundraising*.

A Read the fundraising webpage and answer the questions.
1 Who is Marianna going to raise money for?
....
2 Why is she raising money for this charity?
....
3 What is she going to do?
....
4 How much money is she hoping to raise?
....

B Match the headings (1–6) to the parts of the webpage (a–f).
1 What I am going to do ....
2 How much money I'm hoping to raise ....
3 Why I'm interested in helping this charity ....
4 Thanks ....
5 Information about the health problem ....
6 How much money I've raised until now ....

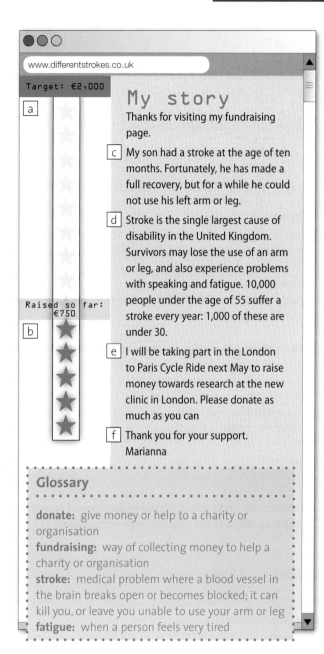

www.differentstrokes.co.uk

Target: €2,000

My story

Thanks for visiting my fundraising page.

[c] My son had a stroke at the age of ten months. Fortunately, he has made a full recovery, but for a while he could not use his left arm or leg.

[d] Stroke is the single largest cause of disability in the United Kingdom. Survivors may lose the use of an arm or leg, and also experience problems with speaking and fatigue. 10,000 people under the age of 55 suffer a stroke every year: 1,000 of these are under 30.

[e] I will be taking part in the London to Paris Cycle Ride next May to raise money towards research at the new clinic in London. Please donate as much as you can

[f] Thank you for your support.
Marianna

Raised so far:
€750

Glossary

donate: give money or help to a charity or organisation
fundraising: way of collecting money to help a charity or organisation
stroke: medical problem where a blood vessel in the brain breaks open or becomes blocked; it can kill you, or leave you unable to use your arm or leg
fatigue: when a person feels very tired

C Raoul has decided to do something to raise money for the charity Speakability. He is going to write a fundraising webpage, and has written some notes. Read Raoul's notes and write a webpage like Marianna's above.

1 *Target: to raise* €*5,000*
2 *My reason for helping: accident in 2005, head injury, aphasia for two years. Speakability helped me speak again*
3 *Charity: Speakability UK.*
4 *Description: they help people who cannot speak, read or write after suffering a stroke, head injury, etc. Medical name for this problem – aphasia*
5 *What I'm going to do: walk from Edinburgh to Brighton*

VOCABULARY Parts of the body

A Complete the sentences with one of the words from the box.

legs	face	stomach	feet	finger	lips	ear	hair

1 After working on the computer for four hours, he went for a walk to stretch his ....
2 Tom threw the ball at me and it hit me in the .... My nose and mouth are still sore!
3 I hurt my hand playing volleyball, and I can't get my ring off my .... !
4 She's got really long, blond ....
5 Wear sunglasses when you ski and don't forget your .... can crack from the dry wind, so put sun protection on them.
6 While we were boxing, Jorge hit me on the left side of my head and my .... 's all red now!
7 You shouldn't swim on a full .... , so don't go after lunch.
8 Peter, your .... smell after wearing those football boots!

B Choose the words or phrases that are not used in English.

1 have a black eye / an eyeball / eye hair / have good eyesight
2 hair style / yellow hair / a hairdryer / a hairdresser
3 broken arm / armband / armchair / armstand
4 backache / back arm / backside / back pain / back bone
5 have a mouthful / mouthwash / mouth ache / have a sore mouth

GRAMMAR Imperatives

A Complete the sentences with the imperative of one of the verbs in the box. Make them negative where necessary.

eat	leave	drink	take	let	put	touch	call

1 If you're not sure, ... the doctor.
2 .... the milk bottle back in the fridge after breakfast.
3 .... your shoes there! Someone will fall over them! Put them in the cupboard.
4 It says you should take these after a meal, so .... something first.
5 .... more than four tablets a day.
6 Here! You've got a bad back. .... me take those bags.
7 .... this juice, Katie. Go on, it's good for you.
8 .... that iron! It's hot! You'll burn yourself!

B Match the sentences (1–8) in exercise A with their function (a–f).

a encouragement ....   d instruction ....
b order ....   e offer ....
c warning ....   f advice ....

Language note

We use the imperative more frequently when we are giving advice or instructions to friends and family.
We don't use the imperative in formal situations. We use the more polite form of *should, ought to* and *why don't you*.

C You are the doctor looking at the people in the picture. You have just walked into the waiting room. Tell your patients what to do. Use the phrases below to help you, and use negative forms where necessary.

eat	go to bed	put on some cream
take some painkillers		drink hot drinks and fruit juice

1 ....
2 ....
3 ....
4 ....
5 ....

READING

A Read the webpage opposite, and match the three types of therapy with the photographs.

1 ....   2 ....   3 ....

B Match the words in bold in the text with their meaning below.

1 move your hand over a part of your body, pressing down slightly ....
2 machine that heats a room in a house ....
3 wash your mouth and throat with a liquid, without swallowing it ....
4 methods for curing a health problem ....
5 place a mixture over heat ....
6 gas rising from hot water ....
7 signs of an illness ....
8 a small living thing that causes an illness that can be passed to other people ....

C Read the text again. Which remedy / remedies ...

1 fights the virus? ....
2 fight the symptoms? ....
3 do you swallow? ....
4 advise you to rub part of your body? ....
5 helps stop the virus affecting other people? ....

Holistic Health Answers Your Questions

Q Can you give me some advice about alternative remedies for the flu?

A There are several ways to treat the flu. The best method is to take echinacea as soon as you feel slightly unwell. This will stop the **virus** from developing. If the **symptoms** have already appeared, then you should try one or more of the following remedies.

a) Aromatherapy for colds and flu

Several essential oils help fight the virus. Mix basil, eucalyptus and pine in some almond oil and **rub** it on your chest to clear your blocked nose. If you have a chesty cough, put some basil, pine and tea tree in a bowl of hot water and breathe in the **steam**. Don't do this if you suffer from asthma. If you have a sore throat, try putting one drop of tea tree and one drop of lemon in a small glass of water and **gargle**. Don't swallow it, though! For children, you should add some honey. Finally, **burn** a mixture of the oils to keep the home atmosphere healthy, and stop other family members catching the virus. At night, place a slightly wet towel on the **radiator** in each bedroom, and put two drops of eucalyptus and tea tree on it. This helps sleepers' noses stay clear.

b) Nutrition for flu and colds

For a couple of days, you should swallow only liquids – water, juices, teas and soups. Freshly made juices and homemade soups are the most effective **remedy** for flu symptoms. Make chicken and rice soup, and add some garlic and ginger. Freshly-made fruit juice also helps lower a high temperature. Drink at least six to eight glasses of liquid a day, to make it easier for the body to fight the virus. Don't drink milk because it blocks the nose.

c) Hydrotherapy for flu

As well as following the advice above, why don't you take hot baths, or hot foot-baths followed by a 'cold mitten rub'? Keep your feet warm at all times. To warm your feet, sit them in a hot mustard bath for five to ten minutes. Put one large spoonful of mustard powder in four cups of hot water. After a hot bath, try the cold mitten rub. Wet a small towel or washcloth with cold water. Wrap this round your hand and rub your other arm hard, beginning with the fingers and finishing at the shoulder. Do this again, and then dry your arm with the towel. Repeat the action on your other arm, and then do your legs, feet and body.

Glossary

holistic health: health advice that includes diet and exercise as well as helping the particular health problem
alternative (medicine, therapy, treatment, remedy, etc.): different forms of treating health problems, which use plants, diet, massage, etc.
mitten: a kind of glove that covers the whole hand

Vocabulary Builder Quiz 7 (*OVB* pp26–29)

Try the *OVB* quiz for Unit 7. Write your answers in your notebook. Then check them and record your score.

A Complete the sentences with the correct form of the word in CAPITALS.

1	I get .... easily.	ANXIETY
2	His behaviour was not .... !	ACCEPT
3	She is physically	DISABILITY
4	They're a very .... family.	RELIGION
5	I want to learn more about Ivan's .... background.	CULTURE
6	She felt .... after he left her.	DEPRESSION
7	Thank you for your .... gift.	GENEROSITY

B Correct the errors in the collocations.

1 I've got a sad stomach ache.
2 Take a deep muscle through your nose.
3 She's made a speedy diarrhoea from the flu.
4 He broke out in a burn after touching the cat.
5 Don't forget to brush your hair after eating sweets.

C Decide whether the statements are true (T) or false (F).

1 A *dose* of medicine is the amount you take. ....
2 If an injury *heals*, it gets worse. ....
3 If you *exceed* the correct amount of medicine, you take too much. ....
4 We say something is *inevitable* when it may happen. ....
5 A *prescription* is when your body is very hot. ....
6 A *scar* is a mark on your skin from an old wound or injury. ....
7 You have a *physical* disability when part of your mind does not work properly. ....

D Cross out the word that does not go with the word on the right.

1 healthy / put on an / lose your / work up an — appetite
2 head / back / throat / stomach — ache
3 wise / severe / bouts of / mild — depression
4 heart / cold / panic / asthma — attack
5 unwanted / allergic / first / back — reaction
6 take a deep / hold your / suffer from / get out of — breath

Score ____ /25

Wait a couple of weeks and try the quiz again. Compare your scores.

VOCABULARY Places in town

A Read the clues (1–8) and write the words in the spaces on the grid.

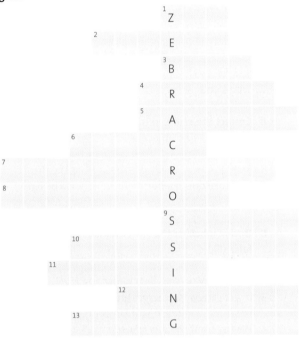

```
1  Z
2  E
3  B
4  R
5  A
6  C
7  R
8  O
9  S
10 S
11 I
12 N
13 G
```

1 A place where you can see wild animals, eg. lions, tigers and bears.
2 A building where you can see interesting historical or scientific objects.
3 A place where you can pay money in or take it out.
4 A way to cross a river on foot or by car.
5 You go to this station to catch a train.
6 You go to this station to report a crime.
7 A place where you can play games like football or tennis.
8 Cars drive round this.
9 An underground train system in American English.
10 A place where two roads meet.
11 Cars stop at these lights.
12 A famous building or statue.
13 A place where you find swings and slides for children.

B Underline the word which does not make a compound word with the key word.

1 sports	*ground*	*TV*	*programme*
2 police	*station*	*woman*	*day*
3 town	*hall*	*centre*	*shop*
4 cross	*road*	*shirt*	*word*
5 traffic	*lights*	*warden*	*car*
6 play	*ground*	*room*	*person*
7 bus	*drink*	*station*	*stop*
8 church	*hall*	*person*	*meeting*

Language note

Compound nouns are made up of two words. Sometimes the words form a single word, e.g. a *roundabout*, a *crossroads*. Sometimes they are two words, e.g. *traffic lights*, a *sports ground*.

PRONUNCIATION
Stress on compound nouns

Learner tip

In compound nouns the main stress is usually on the first word.
'*traffic lights*
When you don't know, check in a good learner's dictionary. They have marks to show where the main stress is. Remember to mark the stress on new words in your vocabulary book.

A 🔊 **8.1 Mark the stress on the following compound nouns.**
1 crossroads
2 roundabout
3 underground
4 playground
5 traffic lights
6 sports ground
7 town hall
8 police station
9 traffic warden
10 sports programme
11 town centre
12 police woman

B Listen and check your answers.

DEVELOPING CONVERSATIONS
Giving directions

A Complete the sentences with one of the phrases in the box.

near here	I get to	you tell me
the way to	know where	the nearest

1 Excuse me. How do .... the sports ground?
2 Excuse me. Is there a tube station .... ,
  please?
3 Excuse me. Do you .... the police station is?
4 Excuse me. Do you know .... the town hall,
  please?
5 Excuse me. .... how to get to the museum,
  please?
6 Excuse me. Where's .... bank?

B Look at this map and give directions from the railway station to the police station by numbering these sentences in the right order.

a At the roundabout, go straight on.   ....
b Go down the road past the town hall.   ....
c Come out of the railway station and turn left.   ....
d Go past the church.   ....
e You'll find the police station on the next corner on the left. ....
f Turn left.   ....
g Take the first turning on the right.   ....
h At the end of the road you'll see a monument   ....

LISTENING

A 🔊 8.2 Listen to the directions and follow the route on the map starting at the railway station. Where does the route finish? ....

B Which of these things were mentioned in the directions? Tick (✓) the ones you hear. Then listen again to check.

1 crossroads
2 playground
3 sports ground
4 corner
5 traffic lights
6 bridge
7 church
8 railway station
9 monument
10 roundabout
11 river
12 police station

C 🔊 8.3 Listen to a man giving a woman directions. They are in the park. Follow the route on the map and answer these questions.

1 Where does the woman want to go?
....
2 What mistake does the man make?
....
3 Where do the man's directions take the woman?
....

READING

A Read this magazine article quickly and choose the best description.

a A description of a journey that the writer has made

b Advice for people who are planning a holiday

c An advertisement for a holiday in the USA

d Advice for business travellers

Many people dream of travelling across the USA. It's one of the world's great journeys and it's surprisingly easy to make that dream come true, as our travel expert explains.

You can travel across the USA by bus, train or plane, but for the real experience, you have to drive. There's no need to buy a car, because renting a car is easy. There are car hire offices at all major airports and most companies will offer one-way rental, which means that you don't have to return the car to the same office.

When you're driving, remember that the distances between cities can be very long, so choose a comfortable car with air conditioning and make sure you take lots of your favourite music with you.

You'll probably start your journey in New York on the east coast or in Los Angeles on the west coast. They are both fascinating cities but don't spend too long there – get out on the road! That's where you'll experience the real USA.

Most people agree that the south west of the USA is the most interesting part of the country. That's where you'll find the mountains of Utah and the deserts of Arizona with world-famous sights such as the Grand Canyon and Monument Valley.

As for accommodation, there are lots of motels everywhere and you don't normally need to book in advance, so you don't have to plan your journey in too much detail. You'll also find plenty of diners serving good American food like hamburgers, hot dogs and pizza. But be careful! Americans are big eaters, so you can expect to return home a few kilos heavier than you arrived!

Glossary

air conditioning: a system that controls the temperature inside a car
fascinating: very interesting
motels: hotels for drivers
diners: cheap restaurants

ROAD TRIP USA

B Read the article again. What are the writer's opinions? Decide whether the statements are true (T) or false (F).

1 It's very difficult to make the trip across the USA. ....

2 It's a good idea to drive. ....

3 It's a good idea to buy a car. ....

4 It's a long way between cities. ....

5 You should spend a lot of time in New York and Los Angeles. ....

6 The north east is the most interesting area. ....

7 American hotels cost a lot of money. ....

8 It's a good idea to book hotels in advance. ....

GRAMMAR Articles (*a, an, the* and no article)

A Choose the right articles to complete these sentences.
1 He was late but he had *a / an* good excuse.
2 Is this *a / the* right bus stop for Oxford Street?
3 Can you recommend *a / the* restaurant in this town?
4 We are hoping to have *a / the* holiday in *a / the* USA this year.
5 I got lost in *a / the* city yesterday, so I asked *a / the* policeman for directions.
6 We took *a / the* taxi to *an / the* airport.
7 I wanted to rent *a / the* car but *a / the* car rental office was closed.
8 We had *a / the* cup of coffee when we got to *a / the* hotel.

B Complete these sentences with *a, an, the* or *0* (for no article).
1 I normally like .... pasta but I didn't like .... pasta we had yesterday.
2 He doesn't like .... animals but he bought .... pet dog for his daughter.
3 I'm very interested in .... cars, but I don't have .... car at the moment.
4 He works with .... computers all the time but he's never found .... computer he really likes.
5 She travels around .... world all the time, but she doesn't have .... driving licence.
6 I've just bought .... new tennis racquet although I don't really play .... tennis.

C Fill the gaps in this text with *a, an, the* or *0* (for no article).

ECOTOURISM

Ecotourism is for ¹ .... people who care about ² .... environment. It often involves ³ .... travel to poor counties where plants and animals are ⁴ .... main attractions. Ecotourism helps people in poor countries to make money and helps people in rich countries to think about ⁵ .... effect that human beings have on ⁶ .... world around them.

D Find and correct the eight mistakes in the use of articles in this text. Then check by looking again at paragraph 2 of the magazine article on page 48.

You can travel across USA by a bus, train or plane, but for real experience, you have to drive. There's no need to buy a car, because renting car is easy. There are the car hire offices at all major airports and most companies will offer an one-way rental which means that you don't have to return a car to same office.

LISTENING

A ◈ 8.4 Listen to the first part of a conversation between Greg and his friend Anna about Greg's road trip on Route 66. Tick (✓) the correct answer.
1 Greg had a:
 a great time b terrible time.
2 Route 66 is:
 a 4,248 miles long b 2,448 miles long.
3 Each day, Greg travelled:
 a 116 miles b 150 miles.
4 Route 66 is:
 a a normal road b a modern six-lane motorway.

B Match these words in the box to the photos. There are two words for each photo.

| valley | Cadillac | arch |
| river | monument | National park |

....

....

....

C ◈ 8.5 Listen to the second part of the conversation. Number the photos 1–3 in the order you hear them.

VOCABULARY Transport

A Complete the table with the words in the box.

cycle lane	traffic jam	station	walk
motorway	helmet	airport	zebra crossing
umbrella	flight	ride	platform
park	check-in	underground	

car	bike	train	plane	foot

B Use the words in the table to complete these conversations.

1. A: Do you think that it's dangerous to .... a bike in the city?

   B: No, not really. I always wear a .... and there are lots of ...., so I can avoid the cars.

2. A: What time is your plane to Brussels?

   B: Well, the .... leaves at ten o'clock and I have to .... an hour before, so I'll try to arrive at the .... at half past eight.

3. A: Excuse me, can you tell me which train goes to the Tower of London?

   B: Yes. It's probably best to take the train to Tower Hill .... You can get it at .... number three.

4. I'm sorry I'm late. My car was stuck in a huge .... because there was a crash on the .... Then when I got here I couldn't find a place to ....

5. A: Does it take a long time to get there on foot?

   B: No, you can .... there in ten minutes. Cross the road at the .... and take the first turning on the right. But take an .... because it's raining!

C Underline the word or phrase that does not complete the sentence.

1	We got off ...	the bus / the train / the car
2	Our flight was ...	delayed / crashed / cancelled
3	The car stopped at ...	the licence / the service station / the traffic lights
4	We gave a tip to ...	the waiter / the policeman / the taxi driver
5	I took ...	the underground / the website / the coach
6	It caused ...	a traffic jam / an airport / terrible delays

GRAMMAR Quantifiers

A Which of these sentences talk about the most cars and which talks about the fewest? Rank them from 1 to 3.

a There aren't many cars on the road. ....

b There are a lot of cars on the road. ....

c There aren't any cars on the road. ....

B Rewrite the sentences from exercise A but use 'traffic' instead of 'cars'.

1 ....

2 ....

3 ....

Language note

Uncountable nouns have no plural form and are not used with a / an. In the exercise above, remember that 'cars' are countable but 'traffic' is uncountable. Other common uncountable nouns include *transport, money, information, homework* and *food*.

C Rewrite these sentences, replacing the underlined word with the word in brackets.

1 There isn't much parking in this part of town. (car parks)

....

2 There's a strike today, so there are no buses or trains. (public transport)

....

3 It's very polluted here because there are a lot of factories in this area. (industry)

....

4 I can't lend you anything because I've only got a few coins on me. (money)

....

5 She's in a terrible hurry because she only has a little time before her bus arrives. (minutes)

....

D Choose the correct words in this conversation.

A: How *many / much* times have you been to Japan?

B: I've only been there once.

A: How *many / much* time did you spend there?

B: I was there for a week.

A: Did you enjoy it there?

B: I had a great time but I don't speak *any / no* Japanese so I had a *few / little* problems communicating.

A: Did you eat *much / many* Japanese food?

B: Oh, yes. I ate *a lot of / much* fish.

DEVELOPING WRITING
An email – giving directions

A Read the email and answer these questions.

1 What has Peter invited Raj to?

2 What's the best way of getting to Peter's home?

3 What is the route from Scott's Park tube station to Peter's home? Draw it on the map.

4 What is Peter's address?

5 What should Raj do when he gets to the house?

6 What should Raj do if he has a problem?

Email window:

From	Peter Sainsbury
Subject	Dinner on Saturday
Date	14 November
To	Raj Ramakrishnan

Hi Raj,

I'm pleased to hear that you can come round for dinner on Saturday. We are only five minutes' walk away from Scott's Park station, so it's probably best to come by tube. When you come out of the station, turn left and go down the road until you come to the traffic lights. Then, turn right, go past the town hall and take the first turning on the left. This is Avenue Road and we are at number 23, opposite the church. When you get to the house, ring the top bell, marked P. Sainsbury.

Give me a call on 0736727887 if you have any problems.

Look forward to seeing you at about 8.00 on Saturday.

Best wishes,

Peter

B **You live at 15 High Street, opposite the cinema. Invite a friend called Martine Kovacs to lunch at 1.00 on Friday and use the map to give her directions from the tube station to your house. Include the following:**
- From, Subject, Date, To
- A greeting (e.g. *Hi Martine*, or *Dear Martine*,)
- A short sentence to introduce the email
- The directions
- Information about your address and the time of the lunch
- Say what to do if there's a problem
- Closing (e.g. *Best wishes*, *Love from*, etc.)

Vocabulary Builder Quiz 8 (*OVB* pp30–33)

Try the *OVB* quiz for Unit 8. Write your answers in your notebook. Then check them and record your score.

A **Complete the sentences with the words in the box.**

| pray | couple | hard-working | trust | exit | licence |

1 Have you noticed the married .... across the road?
2 I know he'll succeed because he's very ....
3 You should leave the roundabout at the third ....
4 They are going to the mosque to ....
5 The policeman stopped him and asked to see his driving ....
6 I lent him some money because I .... him.

B **Match the sentence halves.**
1 He saw what happened, so he reported   ....
2 The car hit him as he was crossing   ....
3 The government is holding   ....
4 They were lost, so they consulted   ....
5 He was angry because they charged   ....
6 She stayed late to clear up   ....

a a map of the area.
b him a lot of money.
c the mess that the children had made.
d an election early next year.
e the accident to the police.
f the road outside the police station.

C **Complete the sentences with the correct form of the word in CAPITALS.**
1 Traffic is now moving .... after the earlier accident.   FREE
2 The Prime Minister is going to the conference on .... warming.   GLOBE
3 We had to wait an hour because the plane was ....   DELAY
4 They had a holiday on a beautiful .... boat.   SAIL
5 I'm sorry the train to Dover has been ....   CANCELLATION
6 There was complete .... on the roads this morning.   CHAOTIC

D **Decide whether the statements are true (T) or false (F).**
1 A *reputation* is an official document that gives permission to do something.   ....
2 A *service station* is a building near a motorway where you can buy petrol and food.   ....
3 A *coach* is something that is built to remind people of something important.   ....
4 An *adventure* is something exciting or dangerous that you do.   ....
5 A *landmark* is something that you can recognise easily.   ....
6 A *lorry* is a bus that is used for long journeys.   ....
7 When you *hire* something, you buy it.   ....

Score ___ /25

Wait a couple of weeks and try the quiz again. Compare your scores.

VOCABULARY Science and nature

A Choose the correct word in italics to complete the sentences.

1 Scientists are *exploring / investigating* the Amazon Jungle in search of new plants.
2 Dian Fossey *experimented on / studied* mountain gorillas in Rwanda.
3 Biologists are *investigating / observing* the causes of cancer.
4 A scientist has *invented / discovered* the skeleton of a Tyrannosaurus Rex in Spain.
5 Charles Babbage *invented / discovered* the 'analytical engine', which was the first computer.
6 Many animals are in danger of becoming *rare / extinct*.

Language note

When you *discover* something, you
1 find something that you didn't know existed.
2 learn how to make something new.
Invent: use your own ideas to create something new

B Match the sentence halves.

1 The French chemist L. J. Gay-Lussac (1778–1850) did ....
2 The World Wildlife Fund is an organisation that tries to ....
3 Environmentalist groups try to persuade governments to ....
4 Many larger animals, such as the blue whale, are in ....
5 Marie Curie (1867–1934) discovered radium and conducted ....

a protect wild animals and plants.
b danger of becoming extinct.
c research into radioactivity.
d experiments on air pressure and temperature while flying in balloons over Paris.
e fund research into climate change.

C Complete the collocations in the sentences with the words below.

research	resources	experiments	shortage	pollution	extinct

1 Water .... is a major international problem. We should stop using so much water.
2 There aren't many great white sharks left. In fact, they are becoming ....
3 The government should fund .... into the causes of Alzheimer's disease, so that it can be treated.
4 In cities most noise .... is caused by traffic.
5 We should try to save the earth's natural .... , as there is not much water and natural gas left.
6 Scientists are conducting .... on chimpanzees to study their behaviour when frightened or angry.

LISTENING

A ✎ 9.1 You are going to hear three news stories. Before you listen, talk to a partner about the cartoons. Then listen and match each story to a picture.

B Listen again and choose the best answer.

1 The first story is about a student who has made a
   a recycled car.   b refrigerator.
2 Emily's design uses
   a electricity.   b the sun's energy.
3 In the second story, people were worried that Tommy
   a had had an accident.   b had run away.
4 Tommy's mother says that she was going to
   a sell the dogs.   b lock the garden gate.
5 The weather forecast tells us that heavy rain
   a fell yesterday.   b is expected today.
6 Drivers are told to
   a phone for more   b stay at home.
       information.

C Use one of the words from the box to complete each sentence.

invented	shed	energy	recycled	puppy	flooding

1 Three days of heavy rain caused .... in the village of Hartington yesterday.
2 Clara loved her dog when it was a cute little .... but was not so happy when it grew!
3 The plane was .... by Wilbur and Orville Wright in 1903.
4 I've built a .... in the back garden to keep my tools in.
5 20% of this new car is made from .... materials.
6 Turn the lights off. We're trying to save ....

DEVELOPING CONVERSATIONS Responding to news and comments

A Five of the responses to the sentences below are not correct. Correct them.

1 A: Kate's just had a baby!
  B: Really? That's terrible!
  ....

2 A: It's great to hear some good news for a change.
  B: Absolutely!
  ....

3 A: Hey! They're testing a new drug to treat cancer and the results are very good.
  B: Really? That's great news!
  ....

4 A: They're going to pull down those old buildings by the river and create a park there.
  B: Definitely.
  ....

5 A: They should do something about the rubbish outside.
  B: Really? That's awful!
  ....

6 A: I've passed my exams! We should celebrate!
  B: Great idea!
  ....

7 A: We should take boys' old clothes to the children's home.
  B: Really? That's interesting.
  ....

8 A: This article says that goats are really useful animals.
  B: Absolutely!
  ....

B Match the responses below with the gaps in conversations 1 and 2.

> No. So is it going to snow?
> Really? That's amazing!
> They should do more
> Really? That's awful!
> Maybe we should

Conversation 1
A: I heard on the radio that a 21-year-old designed a fridge in her grandad's shed.
B: ¹.....................................
A: Yes, I know. It works without electricity, using the sun. She's shared her idea with people in Africa, and helped to build more out there.
B: ²..................................... to help people in Africa.
A: Definitely.

Conversation 2
C: Did you hear the weather forecast for tomorrow?
D: ³.....................................
C: No, but there's going to be heavy rain all over this area.
D: ⁴.....................................
C: I know. There are warnings of floods, too. And we're going out for the day!
D: Yeah, well I'm not sure. ⁵..................................... stay at home, and go another day.
C: Yeah, good idea.

PRONUNCIATION Word stress

A How many syllables do the words below have? Mark the syllable which is stressed.

1 population .... 2 research .... 3 invent .... 4 experiment .... 5 pollution .... 6 energy ....

B Write the words from the box in the correct stress list.

| study | research | population | extinct | energy | experiment | explore | shortage |
| solution | investigate | natural | pollution | participant | invent | resources | protect |

2 syllables, stress on first syllable	2 syllables, stress on second syllable	3 syllables, stress on first syllable	3 syllables, stress on second syllable	4 syllables, stress on second syllable	4 syllables, stress on third syllable

C ⬥ 9.2 Listen and practise saying the words.

VOCABULARY Animals

A Write the animals from the box below in the correct column. Some animals belong in more than one category.

dog	cat	rabbit	sheep	hen	lion
cow	shark	dolphin	whale	pigeon	horse
parrot	tiger	eagle	panther		

pets	farm animals	marine animals	birds	wild cats

B Complete the article with words from the box.

dogs	less	bones	ground	workers
success	excited	school		

HERO RATS

Bart Weetjens trains giant rats in Tanzania to find unexploded land mines and bombs in the [1]................. . Weetjens says that rats are better at doing the job than [2]................. because they have a very keen sense of smell, and they don't get as nervous or [3]................. as dogs. Also, they weigh much [4]................. , so they are less likely to cause the mines to explode and be killed.

Weetjens has already had some [5]................. in Africa with his team of rats. They cleared the area round a [6]................. in Mozambique, and made it safe for the children to return to the classroom. At the beginning of the year, they also cleared 5000 m² of land at Pfukwe, after [7]................. bringing electricity to the area had found mines there. During the clearance, the rats discovered 32 unexploded mines, and found the [8]................. of people and animals that had died in the minefield over the years.

Glossary

mine: a type of bomb that is placed in the ground and explodes when someone touches it
bomb: an object made of materials that explode and cause great damage

READING

A Read the texts. In the table, tick which environmental problems each idea helps to solve.

	magnetic fridge	methane farming	green machine	floating wind turbines
air pollution				
water shortage				
energy resources				

Cool *green* solutions for our **warm** planet

A Magnetic Fridge
Refrigerators and air conditioners eat up more electricity in the home than any other machine. Now there is a new cooling method that works using a system of magnets to make metals cool down. Camfridge, the UK company that is designing this new system, says that its fridges and air conditioners will reduce the use of electrical power by up to 40%.

B Methane Farming
The world's largest biogas factory in Penkun, Germany, makes fuel from animal waste. It produces 84,000 tonnes of the gas methane every year. This natural gas is then used as a fuel which produces enough heat for the 50,000 people who live in the town.

Glossary

biogas: gas that comes from dead plants or animals, or animal waste
fuel: any substance like coal, or gas, that can be burnt to produce heat or energy

B Which idea(s)

1 reduce the amount of electricity used? ....
2 produce electricity? ....
3 saves water? ....
4 use natural sources of power? ....
5 performs two tasks? ....

C Match the words (1–5) with the definitions (a–e).

1	magnet	a	a country's national electricity network
2	emission		
3	offshore	b	in the sea
4	float	c	sit on top of water
5	grid	d	a piece of metal which pulls other metals towards it
		e	when gases are released into the air

C Green Machine

Washing machines also require a lot of energy, as well as huge amounts of water. Now, a new company called Xeros has developed the world's first 'almost waterless' washing machine. Small magnetic metal balls attract dirt from clothes, and leave them dry. The machine uses 90% less water and 40% less electricity than normal washing and drying machines. If all households in the world change to this machine, annual CO_2 emissions will fall by 28 million tonnes.

D Floating Wind Turbines

At present, most offshore wind turbines stand on a base that is fixed to the sea floor. This means that they can only be placed in shallow water, close to land. However, the strongest winds are often further out at sea, where the water is deep. Norway has solved this problem by developing the world's first floating wind turbine. Hywind floats on the water like a boat, and is anchored ten kilometres off the Norwegian coast. It will begin feeding power into the national electricity grid this month.

GRAMMAR Past perfect simple

A Underline the actions in the sentences below. Then decide which action happened first and which happened second.

1 The biologist checked the results of the experiment and called his boss.
2 The chemistry student realised she had followed the wrong instructions.
3 Ayodele had already finished his physics exam when the teacher told them there were 30 minutes left.
4 Dr Mukabe looked at the bones and knew she had discovered a dinosaur.
5 Night had fallen by the time they got home from their trip to the Science Museum.

B Complete the sentences below with the past perfect of the verb in brackets.

1 She decided to leave after she .... the experiment. (finish)
2 When they found the cat, it .... by a car. (be hit)
3 Before he met her, he .... in love. (never be)
4 I suddenly realised I .... to tell Sarah about the party. (forget)
5 They soon learnt that the experiment .... successful. (not be)
6 When police got to the bank, the thieves .... (already leave)
7 The scientist realised that he .... to time his experiment. (forget)
8 Archaeologists studied the skeleton and realised they .... a dinosaur. (discover)

C Put the verbs in brackets into the past simple or the past perfect simple to complete the article.

200 million year-old skeleton looks like the Loch Ness monster

A young couple have found the remains of a Loch Ness-style creature that [1] .... (live) in the English Channel 200 million years ago. Scientists say that the skeleton, which is 70% complete, belongs to a 12-foot-long plesiosaur. This creature [2] .... (exist) during the Jurassic period of 150 to 200 million years ago, and looked like the Loch Ness monster with its long neck and tail.

Tracey Marler and Chris Moore, who [3] .... (discover) the remains on a beach last week, said that many of the bones were in the correct position when they found them, so they could see what the dinosaur [4] .... (look) like when it was alive. It was also possible to see how it [5] .... (die), said Mr Moore, an expert in fossils. There were teeth marks on some bones from another animal. So it seemed that another creature [6] .... (eat) the plesiosaur.

Scientists are still examining the remains, and it is hoped that the skeleton will go on public display at the Lyme Regis Museum.

09

GRAMMAR Reporting speech 1

A Match the reported sentences (1–3) with their function (a–c).

1 Emily said that she hopes to continue inventing, and making changes for a better world. ....
2 Tommy told his mother that the puppies had kept him warm all night. ....
3 His mother, Anna, said that she's delighted he's safe. ....

a to report a present feeling or opinion
b to report possible actions in the future
c to report a past action or event

B Complete the following sentences with *said*, *asked* or *told*.

1 The researcher .... I should write my answers in pen.
2 Participants were .... that they were part of a study of the effects of smells.
3 The Science Museum guide .... us that the Medical Science section was closed.
4 I .... if I could take photos, but was .... not to.
5 The teacher .... he had taken part in an interesting experiment.

Language note

Remember how to use *say* and *tell*. There is not much difference in the meaning but *tell* is used when we want to instruct or inform a person or group of people. There is a difference in form. *I said something ...* or *I said something to Ann ...* *I told John something ...* or *I told the children to do something ...*

C Report the sentences below with *said*, *asked* or *told*.

1 Doctor to patient: 'Take two aspirin and go to bed.'
   The doctor ....
2 Student to teacher: 'Could I open the window, please?'
   The student ....
3 Researcher to patient: 'Would you like to take part in an experiment?'
   The researcher ....
4 Me: 'I don't understand.'
   I ....
5 Professor to research assistant: 'Press that button when you hear a beep.'
   The professor ....

DEVELOPING WRITING
An email – expressing an opinion

A Anagele is a Kenyan student at a college in Brighton. Below is an email he wrote yesterday to his friend at home. Read the email and match the headings below (1–5) to each paragraph (a–e).

1 The weather ....   4 Opening ....
2 Closing ....   5 The town ....
3 His flatmate ....

B We use the words in the box below to connect our ideas. Use them to complete the email.

but	one thing	although	secondly	however	another

From: Anagele K
To: kitunzi@gmail.afr
Subject: First impressions of Brighton

a) Hi, Kitunzi!

How are things? I've been in Brighton for two weeks now, and I want to tell you how I'm getting on.

b) The town's really nice. ¹................... I like about it is that it's a holiday town, so there are lots of tourists. This makes it lively. ²................... , there are some great bars and restaurants to go to in the evenings, ³................... they're rather expensive. We usually eat at home, and then just go out for a drink.

c) My flatmate is an Italian guy, called Fabio. He's crazy, but great fun. When we go out, he talks to everyone, so we've already met lots of people. ⁴................... thing I like is my college. The teachers are really enthusiastic, and I'm enjoying the course – except for the homework!

d) The English weather is not so good! Grey skies every day! I haven't seen the sun since I got here! ⁵................... the buildings are comfortable and very warm inside, ⁶................... the dark atmosphere outside sometimes makes me miserable. I really miss the African sun. In general, though, I like it here.

e) Write and tell me how you're getting on.

Bye for now,

Anagele

56 OUTCOMES

Language note

Although and *but* connect opposite ideas, such as a good point and a bad point. Look at how they are used in a sentence.
Although I like living in Italy, I don't like the heat in the summer.
I like living in Italy, but I don't like the heat in the summer.

C Connect the sentences in the pairs below. Use *although*, *but* or *another thing*.

1 I like most animals. I don't like rats.

   ....

2 I know that more homes are needed in the city centre. There should be parks.

   ....

3 Paris is a beautiful city, with wide streets. I like the cafés on street corners with tables outside.

   ....

4 It's a good thing that governments are talking about climate change. They should do more.

   ....

5 I like living by the sea. It gets cold in the winter.

   ....

6 I like sweets. They're not healthy.

   ....

D Write an email to a friend in another country. Describe your town, and say what the weather is like there. Think of two things you like, and something that you don't like. Use the words from exercises B and C to connect your ideas.

Vocabulary Builder Quiz 9 (*OVB* pp34–37)

Try the *OVB* quiz for Unit 9. Write your answers in your notebook. Then check them and record your score.

A Complete the sentences with the correct form of a verb in the box.

investigate	conduct	participate	witness	protect

1 Margot .... a nasty accident outside her home last night.
2 We should all work harder to .... the environment.
3 The teacher invited students to .... in an experiment.
4 Scientists are .... experiments to see how people react to the drug.
5 Police are .... the disappearance of a ten-year-old boy.

B Choose the correct word.

1 The experiment *requires* / *refuses* two people.
2 Scientists have *suspected* / *detected* signs of life on Mars.
3 There is not enough *effect* / *evidence* to arrest the woman for the crime.
4 Police believe that the bomb was part of a *terrorist* / *soldier* attack.
5 Weather forecasts *predict* / *record* what the weather will be like the next day.

C Match the sentence halves.

1 We don't know for certain what the long-term
2 The WWF are campaigning to save
3 I got an electric
4 Taking echinacea can boost
5 Scientists were surprised by the

a your health.
b effects of climate change will be.
c findings of the experiment.
d the blue-fin tuna fish from extinction.
e shock from touching the machine with wet hands.

D Complete the sentences with the correct preposition.

1 Anil was witness .... the birth of his twin boys.
2 Magda insisted .... staying for the experiment.
3 Many teenagers dislike people .... authority.
4 I would like you to act .... chairman at the next meeting.
5 They were not prepared .... the amazing results of the experiment.

E Complete the sentences with the correct form of the word in CAPITALS.

1 Xavier was amazed by the .... shown by some of his students. CREATIVE
2 Ananya talked for an hour about .... problems. ENVIRONMENT
3 Berit gave a wonderful .... at the conference yesterday. SPEAK
4 The .... of students in the class agreed with the idea. MAJOR
5 Electricity was one of the greatest .... discoveries ever. SCIENCE

Score ___/25

Wait a couple of weeks and try the quiz again.
Compare your scores.

10 EDUCATION

VOCABULARY School and university

A Complete the conversations with the words in the boxes.

1
PE	primary	secondary	subject

A: Is your daughter still at .... school?
B: No she's 15 now, so she goes to .... school.
A: And what's her favourite .... ?
B: Well, she's very good at sports so she loves ....

2
pass	retake	fail	exams

A: I'm really worried about my .... I haven't done any work.
B: What will you do if you don't .... them?
A: If I .... I'll probably .... them next year.

3
year out	part time	leave	place

A: Are you going to university when you .... school?
B: Yes, if I get a .... But I don't want to go immediately, so I'll take a .... first.
A: Are you going to get a job?
B: Yes, but I want to do other things as well, so I'll work ....

4
finals	degree	Master's	graduate

A: When are you going to .... from university?
B: Well, I'm taking my .... in the summer, so it won't be long.
A: And what are you going to do after that?
B: If I get a good .... I'll stay at university and do a ....

Language note

In most British, North American and Australian universities, a Bachelor's degree comes first. The course is called an undergraduate course. This can be followed by postgraduate degrees – a Master's degree and then a PhD. A PhD can be in any subject, not just philosophy.

B Write these abbreviations next to the right degree.

MA	BA	MSc	PhD	BSc

	Degree	Abbreviation
1	Bachelor of Arts	....
2	Bachelor of Science	....
3	Master of Arts	....
4	Master of Science	....
5	Doctor of Philosophy	....

C Complete this table.

subject	person
biology	*biologist*
chemistry	
	economist
	geographer
	historian
	mathematician
philosophy	
	physicist
science	
sociology	

Learner tip

You can record new vocabulary in different ways. You can use tables like the one in exercise C above. You can also use diagrams to help you remember a group of words.

go to → *kindergarten* → *primary school* → *secondary school* → *university*

take a degree / an MSc in → *Biology* → *get / have a degree / an MSc in Biology*

DEVELOPING CONVERSATIONS *No?*

A **Match the speaker's first sentence (1–6) with the next sentence (a–f).**
1 I can't see the point of IT classes. ....
2 I'm not going to my PE class today. ....
3 I don't want to take a year out before university. ....
4 I don't really like history. ....
5 I don't know why people study Latin. ....
6 I'm not going to continue with chemistry next year. ....

No?

a No. I've never understood it and my teacher says I can drop it.
b No. I've hurt my leg and I can't run.
c No. Everyone knows how to use computers these days.
d No. It's a dead language. Nobody speaks it.
e No. I'm interested in the future, not the past.
f No. I want to go there as soon as possible.

LISTENING

A 🎵 **10.1 Listen to the conversation between two students. What are they discussing? Tick the correct answer.**
a The subjects they've enjoyed over the past year.
b The subjects they are going to choose to study next year.
c Their favourite subjects.

B **In the conversation you heard six sentences from the Developing conversations activity. Listen again and tick (✓) the sentences you heard.**

C **What subjects do the two students choose?**
1 The boy decides not to study ....
2 The girl decides to study ....
3 She decides not to study ....

GRAMMAR First conditionals

A **Complete these sentences with the phrases in the box below.**

> you'll find it easy to get a job.
> we'll go home early.
> if they're not quick.
> you won't pass your exams.
> if you promise to give it back.
> if you send him an email.

1 If you don't work harder, ...
2 They'll miss the train home ....
3 If you study law, ...
4 He'll reply to you ....
5 If the teacher doesn't arrive, ...
6 I'll lend you the book ....

B **Choose the correct words in these sentences.**
1 If you *are / will be* late tomorrow, you *are / will be* in trouble.
2 He *goes / will go* to the party if he *finishes / will finish* his homework.
3 If I *don't see / won't see* you tomorrow, I *call / will call* you.
4 They *don't / won't* help us if we *don't / won't* ask them.
5 If she *doesn't / won't* come to school tomorrow, we *email / will email* her.
6 You *don't / won't* pass your exams if you *don't / won't* revise.
7 If you *miss / will miss* tomorrow's lecture you *can't / won't be able to* do the assignment.
8 I *can't / won't be able to* get up in the morning if I *don't / won't* go to bed now.
9 If he *will play / plays* football tomorrow, he*'ll come / comes* home late.
10 The coach *leaves / will leave* at nine tomorrow if everyone *arrives / will arrive* on time.

Language note

In conditional sentences, use a comma when the sentence begins with *if*.
If I see you tomorrow, I'll give you the book.
Do not use a comma when *if* starts the second half of the sentence.
I'll give you the book if I see you tomorrow.

VOCABULARY Computers, the Internet and school subjects

A Use the clues to complete this crossword.

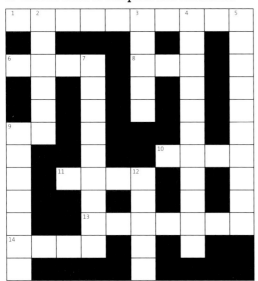

ACROSS →

1 Computer software to help you make presentations (10)
6 A diary or journal kept on the Internet (4)
8 The opposite of switch on: switch ... (3)
9 Abbreviation for Physical Education (2)
10 When you phone someone you make a ... (4)
11 To damage (4)
13 The study of the past (7)
14 To make something that is exactly like another thing (4)

DOWN ↓

2 When you are on the Internet, you are ... (6)
3 Abbreviation of photograph (5)
4 and 5 IT stands for ... (11, 10)
7 The study of the world. (9)
9 The science of movement, light, heat, etc
12 You can listen to this on MP3 files. (5)

B Match the sentence halves.

1 He said he'd left his essay at home but it was
2 Her essay was exactly the same as an article on the Internet,
3 If you miss a class you will have to
4 She was late because she was
5 The teacher liked her essay because it was full of
6 She never has any money

a chatting with her friends in the café.
b a lie because I know he hadn't done it.
c quotes from famous poets.
d because she can't organise her finances.
e copy another student's notes.
f so I think it was plagiarism.

C Fill the gaps with the correct form of the verbs in the box.

| upload | password | increase | search | mix | download | organise | cheat |

1 My teacher asked me to find some more information so I spent hours .... the Internet.
2 I really want to see the photos of last night's party. Can you .... them to your Facebook page?
3 I think he .... in the exam because I saw him looking at his neighbour's essay.
4 They are trying to .... a football match against another school this weekend.
5 The number of students at this university has .... enormously over the past few years.
6 The school is trying to .... different learning styles.
7 I'm trying to log in but I've forgotten my ....
8 I wanted to .... the reference material last night but the site was very slow.

D Match the words to make collocations.

1 chat   a messaging
2 message   b file
3 distance   c controls
4 web   d board
5 user   e site
6 instant   f name
7 MP3   g learning
8 parental   h room

READING

A Read the website of Banville School. Which kind of student do you think it is best for?

a A student who is excellent at sport but not very good at other school subjects.
b A student who wants to have a nice time at school but not work very hard.
c An intelligent student who wants to go to university and is good at music and sport.

Welcome to
Banville School

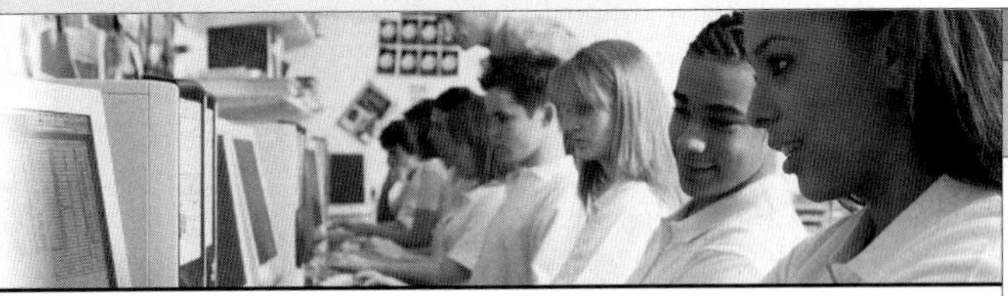

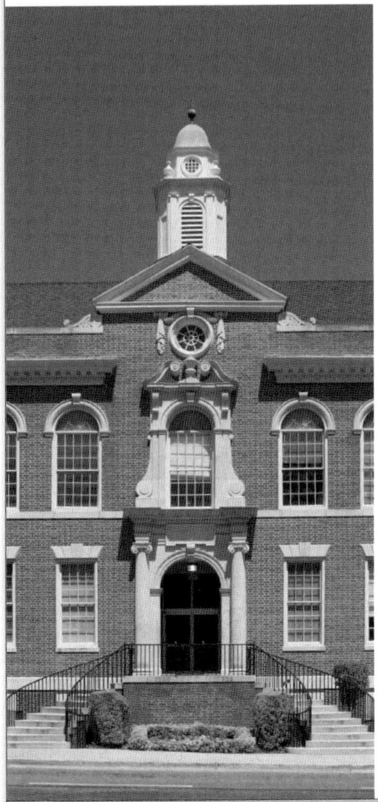

Banville School in Tapstow, North London, is a day school for boys and girls aged 11 to 18. Banville aims to provide a **stimulating and challenging environment** with **high academic standards**.

The school opened in 1786 and has been on the same site for over 200 years. But despite its long history, the school has **excellent modern facilities.** These include a new gym, a fully-equipped computer room and Internet access in every classroom. Banville is also proud to be a part of **a thriving, multicultural community** in this part of North London and students regularly take part in community projects.

Our teachers work hard to ensure that all pupils achieve their best and our exam results are **consistently above average**. Last year 87% of our students went on to continue their studies at university.

There is an **outstanding musical tradition** at the school and our students perform in more than ten school concerts every year. Banville students also excel at sport, particularly football, tennis and netball. The school has its own sports ground next to the main school buildings.

Banville is 12 miles from central London, close to the M25. The school has excellent public transport connections: Tapstow railway station is a five-minute walk away and several buses stop outside the school.

B Look at the phrases in bold. Match them to these explanations.

1 Always better than normal.
....
2 An atmosphere that makes students think and try to do their best. ....
3 A very impressive record of playing instruments and giving concerts. ....
4 A successful area containing people from many different countries. ....
5 Very good new buildings and equipment.
....
6 An expectation that students will do well in subjects such as science, languages and literature.
....

C Read the webpage again. Decide whether the statements are true (T) or false (F).

1 Banville School educates children of all ages. ....
2 The school aims to be relaxed and friendly. ....
3 The school has been in the same place for over 200 years. ....
4 Banville is building a new computer room. ....
5 It is a part of the local community. ....
6 Exam results are not particularly good. ....
7 Most students go to university after leaving Banville. ....
8 There are lots of opportunities for musicians. ....
9 The school does not have its own sports facilities. ....
10 The school is close to central London. ....

VOCABULARY Students and teachers

Fill the gaps in the text with the words in the box.

attention	relationship	subjects	approach
textbooks	standards	tests	assignment

This school takes a traditional ¹.................. to learning. Students normally study seven ².................. , including English, mathematics and one science. They will be asked to do an ³.................. every week and there are ⁴.................. at the end of every month to monitor progress. The student–teacher ⁵.................. is friendly but formal. Discipline is strict and students are expected to pay ⁶.................. in class. Students are also expected to buy their own ⁷.................. . The school takes pride in high ⁸.................. .

PRONUNCIATION Sound and spelling

🔊 **10.2 Listen to the underlined sounds. Which is the odd one out in each group?**

1 <u>ch</u>ange   <u>ch</u>eap   appro<u>ach</u>   <u>ch</u>emistry
2 <u>ch</u>eck   atten<u>ti</u>on   op<u>ti</u>onal   <u>sh</u>are
3 relation<u>sh</u>ip tradi<u>ti</u>onal ma<u>ch</u>ine   tea<u>ch</u>er

Learner's tip

When you record vocabulary, underline sounds which are spelled in unusual ways. Next to them, make a note to remind yourself how to pronounce them.

DEVELOPING WRITING A report – giving advice

A Use the information to fill the gaps in the report below.

Report Card

Name	Ahmed Al-Rashid
Course	Economics Year 2
Effort	Good
Exam mark	62%
Course work	Excellent
Contributions in class	Poor
Suggestions	Speak more in class

You have made good progress in ¹.................. 2 of your Economics course. Although your exam mark of ².................. was a little disappointing, you have worked hard and your ³.................. has been excellent. However, your ⁴.................. in class have been poor. If you speak ⁵.................. you will do much better next year.

B Use the information to complete the report for Anna Gadja. Use the model above and change the information as appropriate.

Report Card

Name	Anna Gadja
Course	History Year 2
Effort	Average
Exam mark	59%
Course work	Poor
Contributions in class	Good
Suggestions	Work harder

You have made some progress ....
....
....
....
....
....
....

GRAMMAR *Had to / could*

A Rewrite these sentences using *have to, didn't have to, could* or *couldn't*.

1 She wasn't able to finish her assignment.

....

2 It was necessary for him to stay up all night to revise.

....

3 She was able to do any sport she liked at school.

....

4 It wasn't necessary for them to do their homework.

....

5 It was impossible for me to find the book in the library.

....

6 It was necessary for us to complain about the teacher.

....

7 Was it necessary for you to stay late after class?

....

8 Were you able to understand the last question in the exam?

....

9 It was possible for him to go home early because he had finished his work.

....

10 Was it necessary for them to buy their textbooks?

....

B Find and correct five mistakes in this text.

The parents' evening at the school was a complete disaster. We have to start late because lots of the parents were stuck in a traffic jam and didn't can get to the school on time. Then there weren't enough chairs in the school hall, so lots of people must stand. Finally, the microphone didn't work, so the audience can't hear anything. Still, at least we hadn't to listen to the headmaster's speech. He's always so boring!

Vocabulary Builder Quiz 10 (*OVB* pp38–41)

Try the *OVB* quiz for Unit 10. Write your answers in your notebook. Then check them and record your score.

A Fill the gaps with the words in the box.

between	to	out	to	for	from

1 He included several quotes .... the textbook in his assignment.
2 The teacher pointed .... all the mistakes I made in the test.
3 She promised .... keep the secret.
4 The school takes a traditional approach .... discipline.
5 There is a very good relationship .... students and teachers.
6 They searched .... the information on the Internet.

B Complete the sentences with the correct form of the word in CAPITALS.

1 Please reply to this message ....   IMMEDIATE
2 You don't have to study RE next year. It's ....   OPTION
3 He's disappointed because he .... two exams last term.   FAILURE
4 They're going to .... about their teacher because they don't like her.   COMPLAINT
5 Please do not .... the students while they are revising.   DISTURBANCE
6 He gave a brilliant .... on Shakespeare.   LECTURER

C Decide whether the statements are true (T) or false (F).

1 A *deadline* is a date by which you must finish something. ....
2 A *tutor* is a student in their second year of university. ....
3 An *assignment* is someone whose job is to repair cars and machines. ....
4 An *extract* is part of a piece of writing. ....
5 *Finals* are exams at the end of a university course. ....
6 If you are *desperate* you want something very much. ....
7 Your *finances* are the amount of money that you have. ....

D Choose the correct word.

1 What's the *advantage / attention* of doing it this way?
2 The teachers asked us to write an *extract / essay* for homework.
3 She didn't check because she *assumed / mentioned* he was telling the truth.
4 He failed the exam so he has to *retake / pretend* it again next year.
5 I didn't say hello because I didn't *support / recognise* him.
6 He didn't take the test because he *set / skipped* school that day.

Score ___/25

Wait a couple of weeks and try the quiz again.
Compare your scores.

LISTENING

A 🔊 **11.1 You are going to listen to four people talking about the type of holiday accommodation they prefer. Listen and match each speaker with the accommodation they talk about.**

| hotel | tent | boat | rented house |

Speaker 1: ....
Speaker 2: ....
Speaker 3: ....
Speaker 4: ....

B Listen again and complete the sentences.
1 Speaker 1 says his type of holiday is not expensive because he and his friends .... the cost.
2 He likes having the .... to go where he wants.
3 Speaker 2 wants to .... on holiday.
4 She wants to go somewhere where there are .... for the children to do.
5 Speaker 3 doesn't like the .... of hotel breakfasts.
6 He says it's important to .... in advance, because the place is popular.
7 Speaker 4 prefers ....
8 She likes it because you don't have to pay a .... if you change your mind.

C Make collocations with words from box A and box B. Note that two words from box B are used twice.

A		B	
room	cooking	facilities	activities
be fully	Internet	deposit	fee
cancellation	organised	access	booking
make a	parking	service	
pay a	babysitting	booked	

D Complete the collocations in the sentences.
1 We chose that hotel because it had organised .... for children, which allowed us parents some freedom during the day.
2 Our room had cooking ...., so we saved money by not having to eat in restaurants all the time.
3 When we got to the hotel, we discovered it no longer had Internet ...., so Darren had to search for an Internet café to read his emails each day.
4 The receptionist told us that the hotel was fully ...., but kindly suggested we try another hotel down the road.
5 We were fortunate to find a hotel with a babysitting ...., so we could celebrate our anniversary with a romantic dinner for two.
6 The hotel looked lovely, but we changed our minds when we learnt they had no parking ...., and expected us to pay a .... of €100!
7 I'd like to make a .... for a family room for 14–21 June, please.
8 I'm sorry to hear about your accident, Sir, but I'm afraid you'll have to pay a cancellation .... of €60.
9 We decided to have a sandwich in our room and get some work done, so I called room ...., but they took an hour to send up our order!

DEVELOPING CONVERSATIONS
Giving bad news

A Answer the following questions with *I'm afraid so* or *I'm afraid not*.
1 Do you have a babysitting service?
....
2 Is it necessary to book in advance?
....
3 Can we order meals in our room?
....
4 Is there a cancellation fee?
....
5 Do you allow dogs?
....
6 Do we have to pay for the mirror we broke?
....
7 Are we too late for breakfast?
....
8 Is the lift working?
....

B Answer the following questions. Begin with *I'm afraid*, and use the words in brackets to help you.

1 Do you take Visa?
   I'm afraid ....
   (not accept credit cards / but / can pay by cheque).

2 Do you have any rooms available from the 12th to the 15th of this month?
   I'm afraid ....
   (fully booked / until / end of month)

3 Where can I park my car?
   I'm afraid ....
   have to park / car park / down the road)

4 Is this the only room you have available?
   I'm afraid ....
   (wedding party / tomorrow evening / all guests / stay in hotel)

5 Do you have a pool?
   I'm afraid ....
   (yes / closed for repairs)

6 Can I book theatre tickets through the hotel?
   I'm afraid ....
   (not have / enough staff)

DEVELOPING WRITING
An online booking form

Booking Enquiry to: Applecote Guest House

arrival	2 Sept 2010	rooms	1
nights	8	type	family
adults	2	board	B&B
children	2		
age of children	16, 9		

Your details
name Jorg Oskarsson
email josk@kambia.com
phone 0046 784 331225

Booking information
Special celebrations:
Son's 16th birthday

Children under 12
pay £10 per night.

Pets not allowed

A Read the hotel online booking form and answer the questions.

1 Who is making the booking enquiry? ....
2 Where do they want to go? ....
3 How many people are going? ....
4 When do they want to go? ....
5 How long do they want to stay? ....
6 Are they having a celebration? If so, for which occasion?
   ....
7 Will they get any discount? If so, what for?
   ....
8 Can they take their dog? ....

B Match the words (1–8) with their definitions (a–h).

1	guest house	a	how many nights you want to stay
2	nights	b	kind of accommodation: bed and breakfast, or bed and two meals, etc.
3	rooms	c	we do not accept animals in the hotel
4	type	d	how many rooms you want to book
5	board	e	special services offered when you book
6	your details	f	kind of room you want: single, double or family room
7	booking information	g	small hotel with usually no more than 10 rooms
8	pets not allowed	h	the customer's personal information

C You want to stay at the Willowmere Guest House with your family for the first two weeks of July. Complete the form below.

Booking Enquiry to: Willowmere Guest House

arrival		rooms	
nights		type	
adults		board	B&B
children			
number of children under 10			

Your details
name ....
email ....
phone ....

Booking information
Special celebrations: ....
Children under 10 pay £10 per night.
Dogs are allowed in some rooms – please request at time of booking.

Glossary

B&B: Bed and Breakfast – no other meals are available.

VOCABULARY Hotel problems

A Complete the story with words from the box.

main road	book in advance	missed	available
room service	wake-up call	filthy	bill
low	air conditioning	insects	fixed
boiling	overcharged	noisy	toiletries

Man: Hello. Have you got any rooms
¹..? We'd like one for
two nights.
Receptionist: Well, Sir, I'm afraid we're very busy, but wait
one moment. I'll just check ... You really
should ².. at this time
of year, you know.
Man: I know, but we decided to come at the last
minute.
Receptionist: Well, I'm afraid the only room we've got is
on the ground floor at the back.
Man: Never mind, we'll take it. Thanks!
Woman: This room's ³..! And
look! There are ⁴.. all
over the wall! Ugh!
Man: Yes! And it's ⁵.. in here!
I don't think the
⁶.. is working! And I'm
too tall for this shower! It's
⁷.. to the wall. And the
water pressure is too
⁸... There's hardly any
water coming out!
Woman: Well, there aren't any
⁹.. to wash yourself
with, anyway. I'll call ¹⁰..
and ask them for some soap.
Man: I didn't know the room was next to the
¹¹..! There's a lot of
traffic, and it's so ¹²..!
We won't be able to sleep!

... Next morning...

Man: Look, I asked for a ¹³.. at
6 o'clock. I've ¹⁴.. my train now!
Receptionist: I'm sorry, Sir. The receptionist on duty didn't get the
message.

... A little later...

Woman: You know, that seemed very expensive after all the
problems we had.
Man: I know ... Just one second. Let me check the
¹⁵.. again. Yes, look! They've
¹⁶.. us by €70!
Woman: I wouldn't go to that hotel again if you paid me!

GRAMMAR Second conditionals

A Put the words into the correct order to make sentences.
1 you first were, a I'd book I if room.
....
2 would you if happened do what it to you?
....
3 better would be it went home you if.
....
4 he listen him might you if called to you.
....
5 you think do better would it if left we be?
....

**B Make questions. Use the second conditional, and make any
other changes necessary.**
1 What / you do if / no hot water / your hotel bathroom?
....
2 If / I ask / you / marry me / what / you say?
....
3 you complain / if / it happen / to you?
....
4 If / I order / breakfast in my room / how much / it cost?
....
5 you think / I'm crazy / if / I buy / that hotel?
....
6 you know / what to do / if / you / on your own?
....

Learner tip

Remember to use the second conditional only for imaginary
situations, or situations that cannot be changed. Although
we use the past tense for this conditional, we are talking
about the present or the future.

C Give advice for the following situations. Begin with *If I were you …*

1 The hotel breakfast was awful this morning!
If I were you, ...
(complain / chef)

2 There are no clean towels in my room!
....
(ask / maid)

3 I've never been to London before, and I want to book a hotel there.
....
(search / Internet)

4 The waiter in the hotel restaurant was really rude and unfriendly.
....
(complain / head waiter)

5 Our room is filthy, and there are no clean sheets on the bed!
....
(tell / manager)

6 I've checked my bill and they've charged me twice!
....
(ask / refund)

LISTENING

A 🔊 **11.2 You are going to listen to three conversations with a hotel receptionist, about a guest's problem. Match the problem with the correct conversation.**

1 a door that won't open ....
2 the need to buy a present ....
3 faulty air conditioning ....

B Listen again and answer the questions.

1 In which conversation does the receptionist give the guest some advice? ....
2 In which conversation does the receptionist give the guest some instructions? ....
3 Which problem is not solved? ....

C Complete the sentences.

1 In conversation 1, the receptionist tells Mr Wiseman to .... the air conditioning.
2 Mr Wiseman says he can't .... the switch.
3 He couldn't see it because he'd ....
4 In conversation 2, the problem is urgent because Mr Arnold is .... at a charity dinner.
5 In conversation 3, the man is celebrating his ....
6 The receptionist suggests he buys his wife ....

D Complete the advice in the following conversations.

1 A: I don't know what to get my wife for her birthday.
B: If I were you, ... (get / perfume)

2 A: My husband's stuck in the bathroom!
B: If I were you, ... (call / hotel manager)

3 A: The air conditioning isn't working in my room.
B: If I were you, ... (change room)

4 A: There's no hot water in my room!
B: If I were you, ... (ask room service / call a plumber)

5 A: I'm late for an important meeting in the conference room!
B: If I were you, ... (ask / receptionist / call and explain / problem)

6 A: I don't know where to eat tonight. I'm bored with the hotel dining room.
B: If I were you .... (ask / receptionist / recommend a restaurant)

E Put the conversation between the man and his wife in the correct order.

W: OK, I'll phone reception for help. I won't be a minute … It's all right, Henri. They'll send someone up in a minute. Be patient. ....
M: Aaagh! … It's no good! It won't move! ....
W: What? OK! I'm coming. Give me two seconds … Right! You pull, I'll push. ....
M: Just a minute. I'm nearly ready … Oh wait, Cherise! I can't open the door! ....
W: Right. One, two, three … go! ....
M: Wait. Just one second … OK, ready! ....
W: Hurry up, Henri! We're going to be late! ....

READING

A Read the passage below. Decide where it comes from.

a   a travel brochure, advertising holidays in Greece

b   a newspaper

c   a blog on the Internet

B Choose the best ending for each sentence.

1   The writer says he didn't travel much as a child because he lived
   a   in the mountains.
   b   in Greece.
   c   by the sea.

2   The writer remembers his childhood holidays as being
   a   adventurous.
   b   good fun.
   c   boring.

3   One reason the family stayed at the same place every year was that
   a   it was on the beach.
   b   the owners didn't mind guests.
   c   dogs were allowed.

4   As a boy, the writer used to find the bouzouki
   a   pleasant.
   b   annoying.
   c   uninteresting.

5   Today the writer
   a   realises the value of such experiences.
   b   appreciates music.
   c   wishes he was still a boy.

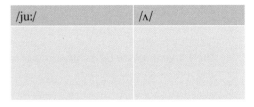

Learner tip

Sometimes in reading tasks like the one in exercise B, more than one option seems possible. Read the text carefully and choose the *best* answer.

PRONUNCIATION

A Match the underlined vowel sounds to the correct column in the table.

usually	beautiful	uninteresting
summer	suntan	useful
cute	used to	done
umbrella		

/juː/	/ʌ/

B 🔊 11.3 Listen and check. Practise saying the words in exercise A.

C 🔊 11.4 Listen and practise speaking.

1   Practise saying the telephone numbers.
   0030 2510 36754
   24210 89567
   6979 010259

2   Practise spelling these names.
   Mr Kendall. That's K – E – N – D –A – L – L.
   Mrs Tsiakos. That's T – S – I – A – K – O – S.
   Miss Pandhi. That's P – A – N – D – H – I.

D Listen again and check.

Memories of summer

I live in Volos, one of the most beautiful parts of mainland Greece. It lies on the East coast, at the foot of Pelion Mountain. I was brought up here, and as a boy, I remember spending long summers swimming and diving off rocks with my friends. We didn't need to travel far to have a holiday, as the sea was on our doorstep. Our favourite place was a beach on the far side of Pelion, where we used to rent rooms every year.

There were three families that went together, although other friends would come and visit for the day. The owners of the rooms didn't mind, and they also allowed us to take our dog, Achilles. Not many places in Greece accept dogs, so this was another reason we went there often. We kids used to spend all day on the beach, and most of the time in the water. There was a great rock that rose out of the water, and we all used to dive off it.

Evenings were spent barbecuing steaks and sausages, then playing hide-and-seek on the beach in the dark, while my father and his friend played their bouzoukis, and everyone else gathered round to sing. Sometimes others would bring their instruments and play, and one evening I remember a 16-year-old boy asked if he could join in with his violin! I used to think my parents were boring, doing that every night, but now I realise how magical it was, and I actually miss those summer evenings filled with music.

GRAMMAR *used to*

A The sentences a–d are taken from the Reading text.

1 Which three sentences talk about past habits? ....
....

2 Which sentence talks about a change of opinion? ....

a Our favourite place was a beach on the far side of Pelion, where we used to rent rooms every year.
b There was a great rock that rose out of the water, and we all used to dive off it.
c I used to think my parents were boring, doing that every night, but now I realise how magical it was ...
d We kids used to spend all day on the beach ...

B Rewrite the sentences below with *used to*.

1 When I was young, I walked to school every day.
....

2 When I was a kid, I never went on holiday with my parents, so now family holidays are special to me.
....
....

3 We went to North Wales every summer, until I went to university.
....

4 My dad went fishing with his friend every morning.
....

5 We stayed in the same place every year, so we made lots of friends there.
....

6 I swam in the sea every day of the holidays.
....

C Find five mistakes and correct them.

1 I didn't never used to like singing round camp fires, but I do now.
2 I used to travel abroad with my parents as a boy, so now I enjoy exploring Britain.
3 We use to like going to the outdoor swimming pool.
4 When I was at school, we usually go on skiing trips every February.
5 I didn't use to play much sport, but I'm in a football team now.
6 Last weekend, I used to have to get up early for a hockey tournament.
7 We usually visit my cousins in the summer holidays.
8 Rob used going to summer camp every August.

Learner tip

When you use *used to* in a sentence, it is easy to make mistakes. Always check what you have written!

Vocabulary Builder Quiz 11 (*OVB* pp42–45)

Try the *OVB* quiz for Unit 11. Write your answers in your notebook. Then check them and record your score.

A Make nouns ending in *-ment* or *-ing* from the verbs in brackets.

1 Malik goes .... (climb) every weekend.
2 The hotel offers organised .... (entertain) every Tuesday and Thursday.
3 They made an .... (arrange) to meet outside the restaurant.
4 The hotel has a .... (babysit) service.
5 .... (park) facilities are at the back of the cinema.
6 Passing your driving test first time is quite an .... (achieve).

B Match the sentence halves.

1 The hotel's in a convenient ....
2 The hotel staff gave them a lovely bunch ....
3 Our expected time of ....
4 When we booked, we paid a ....
5 Please fill in your credit card ....
6 I'd like to welcome you on ....
7 Make sure you check the use-by ....

a of flowers on their anniversary.
b details on this form.
c deposit of €150.
d behalf of all the staff of the Kent Hotel.
e location, near the town centre.
f date on that bottle of milk.
g arrival is 10.30.

C Decide whether the statements are true (T) or false (F).

1 A *site* is a place that is nice to look at. ....
2 If you pay the *standard rate*, you pay the normal amount. ....
3 We say it's a *relief* to be home when we're sad to be there. ....
4 A *digit* is an area of very dry land. ....
5 We say something is a *challenge* when it is difficult. ....
6 The London to Paris *shuttle* doesn't run regularly. ....

D Complete the sentences with one of the words in the box.

available	fully	activities	of	call	with

1 You can choose from a wide range of leisure ....
2 I'm afraid we're .... booked that weekend, Madam.
3 I'll send someone up to deal .... the problem, Sir.
4 We have a double room and a family room ...., but no singles.
5 There's a wide variety .... things to do in the town.
6 Can I have a wake-up .... at five in the morning, please?

Score ____ /25

Wait a couple of weeks and try the quiz again.
Compare your scores.

VOCABULARY Using phones

A Choose the correct words to complete the sentences.

1 I'm sorry, he's not here at the moment. Can he call you *through / back* later?
2 Can you put me *through / off* to the sales department please?
3 The receptionist put me *up / on* hold for over ten minutes.
4 I couldn't ask him about his plans because we got cut *up / off* in the middle of our conversation.
5 He was really angry with me and hung *back / up* before I could explain.
6 She's out of the office today. You could *shout / call* her on her mobile.
7 I keep calling them but I can't get through. The line's *busy / full*.
8 I don't want to phone him. He talks for hours. It's easier to send a *text / type* message.

B Choose the correct word to fill the gaps.

coverage	text	signal	busy	line

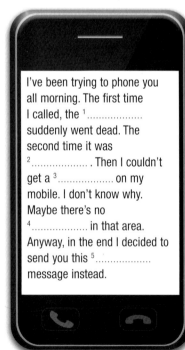

I've been trying to phone you all morning. The first time I called, the [1] .... suddenly went dead. The second time it was [2] .... Then I couldn't get a [3] .... on my mobile. I don't know why. Maybe there's no [4] .... in that area. Anyway, in the end I decided to send you this [5] .... message instead.

Language note

- -

Mobile phone (or *mobile*) is used in British English. In American English, people say *cellphone*.

DEVELOPING CONVERSATIONS
Asking for people and explaining where they are

A Fill the gaps in the phone conversation with these phrases.

Could you tell him	Could I speak to	Who's
is working from home	Can I take	My name's

Receptionist: Hello, the Ashley Corporation.
Caller: [1] .... Mr Khalil please?
Receptionist: [2] .... speaking, please?
Caller: It's Tina Morrison.
Receptionist: Hold the line, please. No, I'm sorry, Mr Khalil [3] .... today. [4] .... a message?
Caller: Yes, please. [5] .... that I called? [6] .... Tina Morrison.

B Write replies to the questions by putting the sentences (a–c) into the right order.

1 Hello. Is that Simon?
  a Simon's not up yet. ....
  b No, I'm sorry, it's Raymond. ....
  c Is it urgent? ....
2 Hi. Is Christine there?
  a Can I take a message? ....
  b She's just gone to the shops. ....
  c No, I'm afraid she isn't. ....
3 Hi, Boris?
  a Can I help you? ....
  b Boris is away today. ....
  c No, it's Dima actually. ....
4 Hello. Could I speak to Ms Seidel, please?
  a Can I take a message? ....
  b No. Don't worry. I'll call back tomorrow. ....
  c I'm afraid she's not in the office today. ....

C Match the sentence halves.

1 I'm afraid he's been off   a a meeting at the moment.
2 I'm sorry but she's in   b available right now.
3 I'm afraid that he's just   c of the door.
  walked out   d home today.
4 I'm sorry but he's working at   e away from her desk.
5 I'm afraid that he's on   f sick all week.
6 Unfortunately she's   g line's engaged at the
7 I'm sorry, he's not   moment.
8 Can she call you back? Her   h holiday this week.

LISTENING

A 🔊 **12.1 Listen to the phone conversation and <u>underline</u> the five mistakes in this message.**

> ═══◆═══ MESSAGE ═══◆═══
>
> *Tina Morrison called about your meeting next Tuesday. She's going to be away on holiday that day, so can you change the meeting to Thursday? Two o'clock at her office. If there are any problems, please call her mobile on 08857 678548.*

AN IMPORTANT MESSAGE? OK... YEP... I'M TAKING IT DOWN RIGHT NOW...

SPORTS

RECEPTION

B **Listen again and rewrite the message correctly.**

> ═══◆═══ MESSAGE ═══◆═══
>
> ....
> ....
> ....
> ....

GRAMMAR *Just, already, yet* and *still*

A **Complete these sentences with *just, already , yet* or *still*.**

1 A: What was that noise?
   B: I think someone has .... dropped a plate.
2 A: Can I see your most recent essay?
   B: I'm sorry I haven't finished it ....
3 A: Can you write to Mr Hudson to apologise for the mistake?
   B: There's no need. I've .... emailed him.
4 A: Have you managed to get Samira on the phone?
   B: No, I haven't but I'm .... trying.

B **Use the words in brackets to write answers to these questions, using *just, already, yet* or *still*.**

1 A: What is this terrible mess?
   B: I'm sorry..
      (I / spill my coffee)
2 A: Can you phone Mr Thorsen please?
   B: There's no need...
      (I / call him)
3 A: Is Anita in the office today?
   B: I don't know...
      (I / not see her)
4 A: Has the delivery arrived?
   B: No...
      (We / wait for it)
5 A: Have you told them we're going to be late?
   B: No...
      (I / not speak to them)
6 A: Where's Roger?
   B: He was here a second ago. I think ....
      ....
      (he / go out for a moment)
7 A: Has she found her mobile phone?
   B: No...
      (She / look for it)
8 A: Will you send them an invoice for those goods we sent them?
   B: I don't have to...
      (They / pay us)

Language note

Just, still and *already* normally go between the auxiliary and main verbs. *Yet* normally comes at the end of the sentence.

READING

A Quickly read the article. Tick (✓) the best summary.

a Mobile phone companies are now making big profits from poor people in Africa and Asia.

b The mobile phone is helping poor people to earn money and improve their living conditions.

c Schools are facing serious problems because teenagers are wasting too much time on their mobile phones.

d The spread of the mobile phone is worrying governments in many countries.

How Mobile Phones are Changing the World

1 When mobile phones first appeared in the early 1990s, they were status symbols for wealthy businesspeople. Phones were big and heavy, and the signal was usually poor, so people often shouted when they used them. Over the next ten years, technology improved and prices fell considerably. In many rich countries the mobile phone became the teenager's favourite toy. In just 20 years, mobiles have changed the way people do business and socialise in rich countries. But mobile technology is having a dramatic impact on life in the developing world too.

2 In Africa, arrival of inexpensive mobile phones in areas where there are no landline telephones has already helped many people to start small businesses. Before mobile phones, starting a business often meant renting a shop or an office, which was expensive. If customers called when the owner was out, business was lost. Now business owners can write their mobile number on an advertisement, put it on a noticeboard and wait for customers to call them. As a result, thousands of people can find a market for their goods or services.

3 In India, fishermen now use their mobiles to find the best market for their fish before they return to shore. A few quick calls on their mobile phones can tell them which ports to visit to find the best price for their fish and avoid unnecessary waste.

4 Farmers, too, are using mobile phones. Around the world, new mobile services provide local weather forecasts to help them plan their work. They can also have advice on farming methods and up-to-date information about prices for their crops sent to their mobile.

5 As mobile phones make business easier, they improve living conditions for hundreds of thousands of people around the world. And as they spread, becoming cheaper and more popular, it seems likely that they will change the world in ways that we can't imagine yet.

B Match the words and phrases (1–8) to their definitions (a–h).

1 status symbol   a   fruit and vegetables produced by a farm
2 socialise   b   big effect
3 dramatic impact   c   poorer countries which are growing economically
4 developing world   d   something which shows you are rich and successful
5 market   e   something that cannot be used.
6 crops   f   the way something is done
7 method   g   meet friends and acquaintances
8 waste   h   a place where things are bought and sold

C Read paragraph 1 again and answer these questions.

1 When did mobile phones first appear?
....
2 Why did people often shout when they used them?
....
3 What happened to the price of mobiles over the next ten years?
....
4 Whose favourite toy did they become?
....
5 What have mobile phones changed in rich countries?
....
6 Where else are mobile phones having an impact now?
....

D Read paragraph 2. Decide whether the statements are true (T) or false (F).

1 Mobile phones are very expensive in Africa at the moment. ....
2 Mobile phones have helped many Africans start businesses. ....
3 It has always been cheap to rent shops and offices in Africa. ....
4 Business owners often leave their mobile phone numbers on noticeboards. ....
5 At the moment, mobile phones are only being used to sell services and not goods. ....
6 There are places in Africa where there are no landline telephones. ....

E Read paragraphs 3 to 5 and complete these sentences.

1 Fishermen in India use their mobiles to find ....
2 This helps them to avoid ....
3 There are now mobile phone services for farmers which provide ....
4 This helps farmers to ....
5 They can also get advice on ....
6 In the future mobiles will change the world in ways ....

VOCABULARY Forming negatives

A Make negative adjectives using the words in the box. Write them in the correct column.

wise	fortunate	practical	fair
happy	polite	expected	common
comfortable	natural	patient	possible
pleasant			

un-	im-

B Choose negative adjectives from the boxes which have the same meaning as the underlined words and phrases.

1 He's been miserable since he lost all his money.
....
2 She's a nasty person. ....
3 He was very unlucky to fall over and break his leg.
....
4 They were very rude to the waiter in the restaurant.
....
5 The decision was unjust. ....
6 That type of bird is very rare in this area. ....
7 He couldn't sleep because the bed was hard and lumpy. ....
8 The result was not predicted. ....
9 It was not intelligent to speak to him like that.
....
10 My father is not good at DIY or fixing things.
....

PRONUNCIATION Same or different?

A 🔊 12.2 Listen to the underlined vowel sounds in these pairs of words. Decide whether they are the same (S), or different (D).

1 p<u>o</u>lite   p<u>o</u>ssible
2 p<u>o</u>ssible   c<u>o</u>mmon
3 c<u>o</u>mmon   c<u>o</u>mfortable
4 <u>o</u>btain   <u>o</u>pinion
5 h<u>o</u>le   h<u>o</u>ld
6 <u>o</u>peration   rem<u>o</u>te

DEVELOPING WRITING Text and email – abbreviations

A Look at the text message and find abbreviations for these words and phrases.

1	are	....	8	meeting	....
2	as soon as possible	....	9	possible	....
3	documents	....	10	see	....
4	evening	....	11	text	....
5	for	....	12	to	....
6	later	....	13	you	....
7	message	....	14	your	....

From: Brian

Hi Steve. Thanks 4 yr msg. R u coming 2 the meet this eve? If so, can u bring the docs we discussed? Please let me know by txt msg if this is poss asap. C u l8r. Brian

Language note

You don't have to use abbreviations in text messages and there are no rules about how to write them. The abbreviations in this activity are quite common but are not always used.

B Read Steve's email reply. Rewrite the text message as an email without abbreviations.

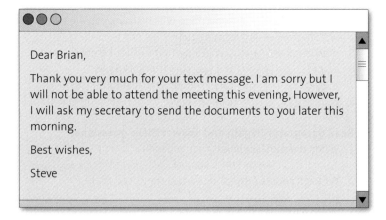

Dear Brian,

Thank you very much for your text message. I am sorry but I will not be able to attend the meeting this evening, However, I will ask my secretary to send the documents to you later this morning.

Best wishes,

Steve

From	Brian Dufriss
Subject	
Date	
To	Steve Zizek

LISTENING

A 🔊 12.3 Listen to the recorded message and answer these questions.

1 What kind of organisation has the caller phoned?
....
2 How many options are there? ....
3 What can you do if you press 1? ....
4 Which number do you press for technical support?
....
5 Which option does the caller choose? ....
6 How long is the wait time? ....

B Listen again and match the sentence halves.

1 For information about opening ....
2 Your call is ....
3 A member of our dedicated customer services team ....
4 Please note that calls may be recorded ....
5 Unfortunately we are currently experiencing a ....
6 You may find it more convenient ....

a a high volume of calls.
b will be available to speak to you shortly
c a new account, press two.
d to call back later.
e for training purposes.
f important to us.

GRAMMAR Reporting speech 2

A Choose the correct verb tense in these sentences reporting speech.

1 I'm helping my friend with her homework.
You said you *helped / were helping* your friend with her homework.

2 I haven't seen the new James Bond movie.
You said you *weren't seeing / hadn't seen* the new James Bond movie.

3 I phoned you twice on Friday.
You said you *have phoned / had phoned* twice on Friday.

4 We're going to the theatre this evening.
You said you *have been going / were going* to the theatre this evening.

5 We've seen them twice this month.
You said you *had seen / have seen* them twice this month.

6 We didn't hear from them yesterday.
You said you *haven't heard / hadn't heard* from them yesterday.

7 I spoke to him last night.
You said you *have spoken / had spoken* to him last night.

8 She hasn't called me for ages.
You said she *didn't call / hadn't called* you for ages.

B Put these sentences into reported speech.

1 Anna posted the letter on Tuesday.
She said Anna ....

2 I'm sending you the books today.
You said you ....

3 We haven't been to the office all day.
You said you ....

4 I didn't bring my notes with me.
You said you ....

5 They haven't delivered the letters yet.
They told us they ....

6 I'm going to the post office right now.
You said you ....

7 I lost my mobile phone.
You said you ....

8 I'm giving you two weeks to reply.
You said you ....

9 He has had my letter on his desk since Wednesday.
She said he ....

10 I can't remember my mobile phone number.
You said you ....

Language note

When you are writing sentences in reported speech, remember to check the personal pronouns. They will sometimes (but not always!) have to change.

Vocabulary Builder Quiz 12 (*OVB* pp46–49)

Try the *OVB* quiz for Unit 12. Write your answers in your notebook. Then check them and record your score.

A Match the sentence halves.

1 I called the help   ....
2 He went to the American   ....
3 They gave us a ride   ....
4 There are several kinds of poisonous   ....
5 We sent it by   ....
6 They're going to send a written   ....

a to the station.
b contract next week.
c Embassy to collect his visa.
d desk when I discovered the problem.
e registered post because it was important.
f snakes in this area.

B Complete the sentences with the correct form of the word in CAPITALS.

1 There's no .... for my mobile in this area.   COVER
2 He .... the robber immediately.   IDENTIFICATION
3 They've .... a new computer system.   INTRODUCTION
4 He went into hospital for an .... yesterday.   OPERATE
5 He made a good impression ....   INITIAL
6 I didn't .... you to arrive today.   EXPECTATION

C Decide whether the statements are true (T) or false (F).

1 A *refund* is an amount of money you get back when you return something.   ....
2 A *fine* is a gap or space in something.   ....
3 If you are *improper*, you show respect for other people.   ....
4 A *leaflet* is a piece of paper which gives information about something.   ....
5 A *signal* is a smal l animal with eight legs.   ....
6 If something is *urgent*, it is very important and you need to do it immediately.   ....
7 If you *misuse* something, you use it efficiently.   ....
8 If you are *fair*, you behave well.   ....

D Choose the word that does not form a collocation with the key word.

1 household — chores / bills / fares
2 automated — telephone system / irrational fear / production process
3 postal — landlord / address / delivery
4 remote — control / town / rush
5 unlimited — access / species / downloads

Score ___/25

Wait a couple of weeks and try the quiz again.
Compare your scores.

VOCABULARY Films

A Each group of words (1–6) describes a kind of film. Write down the kind of film in the box.

```
1          C
2          I
3          N
4          E
     5     M
6          A
```

1 special effects, costumes, space
2 the past, costumes, family, society
3 car chases and explosions, special effects
4 complicated plot, scary, violent
5 funny, laughter, happy ending
6 violent, special effects, kung fu

B Choose the most suitable word or phrase.
1 A scary, violent film is called *an action / a horror* movie.
2 A science-fiction film usually has a lot of *violence / special effects*.
3 A historical drama is a film that is set in the *past / future*.
4 Romantic comedies are often quite *predictable / scary*. You know what's going to happen in the end.
5 Jackie Chan stars in lots of *war /martial arts* movies set in Hong Kong.
6 Musicals usually have *scary / romantic* plots.

C Answer the quiz. If you don't know the answer, guess!

LISTENING

A You are going to hear two people talking about three films. Match the title to the kind of film you think it will be.
1 *Run and Hide*   a drama
2 *The Mansford Saga* b comedy
3 *Mr Pickles*   c thriller

B 🔊 **13.1 Listen and check your answers.**

C Listen again. Match the films to the names below.
   A *The Mansford Saga*   B *Run and Hide*   C *Mr Pickles*

1 Thierry Dumand   ....
2 Jeffrey Hinds   ....
3 Antonio Torres   ....
4 Catherine Pickard ....
5 Andreas Dumas   ....
6 Zena Williams   ....

D Decide whether the statements are true (T) or false (F).
1 Abha is searching the Internet to find out what's on at the cinema.   ....
2 Antonio Torres is the star of *Run and Hide*.   ....
3 Brad has already seen *Run and Hide*.   ....
4 Abha wants to see *The Mansford Saga*.   ....
5 They decide to go and see the Thierry Dumand film.   ....
6 *The Partygoer* is on at the Palace Cinema.   ....

Film Quiz

1 The first proper cinema showing only films opened in ...
A Paris in 1897   **B** New Orleans in 1902
C Los Angeles in 1895

2 The best-paid actor in 2008 was ...
A Johnny Depp   **B** Will Smith
C Heath Ledger

3 A historical drama is sometimes called a ...
A costume drama   **B** effects drama   **C** hat drama

4 The movie capital of India is called ...
A Hollywood   **B** Bollywood   **C** Dollywood

5 The most successful movie in the world until now is ...
A Avatar
B Harry Potter and the Philosopher's Stone
C Casablanca

6 The first films with sound were called ...
A singing movies   **B** talking movies
C laughing movies

7 The most famous prizes for film actors are called ...
A Homers   **B** Oscars   **C** Basils

8 The biggest film industry outside the USA is based in ...
A Egypt   **B** Brazil   **C** India

DEVELOPING CONVERSATIONS

Supposed to

A Match the following statements (1–6) with the subjects (a–f).

1 I'd love to hear Keiko Matsui play. She's supposed to be magical.   ....
2 I've never been, but it's supposed to be a beautiful place.   ....
3 They're supposed to have an excellent selection of wines.   ....
4 I haven't read it, but the plot is supposed to be quite complicated.   ....
5 I haven't seen it, but Daniel Day Lewis is supposed to be superb in it.   ....
6 There's an exhibition of his work at the Tate Gallery at the moment. It's supposed to be impressive.   ....

a New Zealand
b film
c a painter
d a musician
e a restaurant
f a book

B Complete the mini-dialogues with a suitable phrase from the box.

why don't you	what are you doing	amazing	are supposed to
do you fancy	really talented	would you like	is supposed to

1 A: Jen, [1] .... this afternoon?
      Have you got any plans?
    B: I'm thinking of going to see a film. [2] ....
      to come?
    A: I don't know. What's on?
    B: The new Johnny Depp film, at the Hippodrome. It [3] ....
      .... be really good.
    A: OK. I like Johnny Depp. What time does it start?

2 C: Have you got any plans for tomorrow, Tom?
    D: Not really. Why?
    C: I'm thinking of going to the new Magdalena Abakanowicz exhibition. Would you like to come?
    D: Isn't she the sculptor who designed the *Agora* figures in Grant Park?
    C: That's the one. I think she's [4] ....
    D: They're supposed to be [5] .... !
      Nine feet high, or something like that. OK, I'll come.

3 E: Are you doing anything this evening, Despina?
    F: Actually, I'm thinking of going to the Kool Kats concert.
      [6] .... come with me?
    E: Kool Kats? They're that teenage band, aren't they? They [7] .... be very good.
    F: So, [8] .... it?
    E: OK, then.

GRAMMAR *-ed / -ing* adjectives

A Choose the correct adjective in each sentence.

1 The film was all right, but I got a bit *bored / boring* at the beginning.
2 It had an *interested / interesting* plot, but the acting was rather poor.
3 I'm quite *exciting / excited* about going to see the Michael Jackson film. It's supposed to be really good.
4 I was *shocking / shocked* by the amount of violence in that film.
5 I'd read the book and really enjoyed it, but the film was *disappointing / disappointed*.
6 I find that actress so *annoying / annoyed* ! She's the same in every role.
7 We've had a *tired / tiring* day shopping in town, so let's watch a DVD at home tonight.
8 I was *confused / confusing* by the ending. Why did he leave like that?

B Rewrite the sentences with the correct adjective form of the verb in *italics*.

1 Can you stop that? It's starting to *annoy* me.
    Can you stop that? It's becoming ....
2 Jeffrey Hinds' performance really *surprised* me.
    I was .... by Jeffrey Hinds' performance.
3 Ian's behaviour *worries* me. He's been acting really strange lately.
    I'm .... about Ian's strange behaviour lately.
4 That fight scene *disgusted* me. It was too violent.
    I found that fight scene .... It was too violent.
5 Too much talking in a film *bores* me. I want action and suspense!
    I find films with a lot of talking and not much action ....
6 The dialogue *amazed* me. It was so clever!
    It was .... how clever the dialogue was.

VOCABULARY Music, art and books

A Fill the gaps with a word from the box.

albums	composer	voice	rehearse	instruments

I go to a music college in northern Italy, and I play three
[1]..................... I started playing the piano when I was five,
and the guitar at eight. For the last four years, I've been
learning the violin at college, and I'm now in the college
orchestra. We [2].................... every Wednesday and Friday. My
favourite [3].................... is Ennio Morricone, and I've got
nearly all his [4].................... The words to some of the songs
he has written for singers are very moving, but I haven't
got a good [5]...................., so I only sing them in the bath!

sculptures	auction	paintings
portrait photographer	landscape	exhibition

In my job as a [6]......................................, I meet lots of
interesting people. I was lucky enough to photograph the
Hungarian sculptor, Laszlo, last year. His bronze
[7]...................................... of political figures are superb. I met
him at an [8]...................................... of his work in Madrid,
and was impressed by the range of styles. My favourite
modern artist, however, is the [9]......................................
painter, Vitali Komarov. His [10]...................................... are
full of the rich countryside colours he sees around him.
I recently bought one of his paintings, *Branch*, at an
[11]....................................... It hangs in my study at home.

biographies	novel	letter	authors	published

One of my favourite [12].................... is Isabel Allende. She
writes passionately about relationships and events, both in
her native Chile and other South American countries. Her
well-known [13]...................., *The House of the Spirits*, is an
amazing book to read, and six months ago, I read *Paula*.
[14].................... in 1995, it is a moving memoir of Allende's
early life, written in the form of a [15].................... to her
daughter, as Paula lay dying. Although the book tells the
story of a tragic period in her life, Allende's honesty and
courage never fails. [16].................... of her life and work talk
about her courage and love of life, and I think this is clear
in all of her books.

Language note

A *biography* is a book written by one person about
another person's life.
An *autobiography* is a book in which the writer tells the
story of his / her own life and work.
A person's *memoirs* are often a series of stories
about events in their life and people they have met.

GRAMMAR Present perfect continuous

A Complete the sentences with *for* or *since*.

1 I've been playing the piano .... five years.
2 He's been working on that project .... two months
now, and he still hasn't finished!
3 You've been working on the computer .... six this
morning. Have a break!
4 We've been going to Latin American dance classes ....
2004, and we're quite good at the tango now.
5 I've been reading this book .... three weeks now.
6 We've been waiting here .... hours!

Learner tip

Use the present perfect continuous when you are interested
in the action and how long it has been going on.
Use the present perfect simple to talk about the result of
that action until now, i.e. how much / how many.
e.g. *I've been writing emails all morning*: action and how
long
I've written ten so far: result of that action and how many?

B Choose the correct form.

1 She's *been acting / acted* for ten years, and has *been starring /
starred* in six films.
2 He's *directed / been directing* several films, including *Love
Me Forever*, and for the last six months he has *worked / been
working* on a film in Africa.
3 She *started / has started* painting in 1980, and *held / has held*
exhibitions in several countries since then.
4 Mandy *is playing / has been playing* the drums since she was
eight and *is having / has had* her own drum set for three years.
5 Laura's *known / knowing* Ian for two years, and they *are going /
have been going* out together for six months.
6 The book has *been becoming / become* very popular, and has
been *published / being published* in 27 languages.

**C Complete the text with the present perfect continuous or the
present perfect simple of the verbs in brackets.**

Nobuya Sugawa is one of Japan's leading saxophonists. He
[1].................... (play) the saxophone since he was a young boy,
and [2].................... (gain) admirers all over the world.

Sugawa studied at the Tokyo University of Fine Arts and Music. He
performs in around 100 concerts a year and [3].................... (record)
more than 20 CDs, including Takashi Yoshimatsu's Saxophone
Concerto Cyber-bird with the BBC Philharmonic, and Made In
Japan. He [4].................... (work) with most of Japan's major orchestras
and several leading international orchestras.

For the last few months, Sugawa [5].................... (tour) Europe, giving
masterclasses and concerts. He will be appearing at the Royal College,
London in November, and then at the Conservatory in Madrid.

READING

A Read the movie blog below. Decide which film is

1 a fantasy   ....
2 a drama   ....
3 a romantic comedy   ....

B Which film(s)

1 is frightening?   ....
2 is amusing?   ....
3 have a complicated plot?   ....
4 is about human kindness?   ....
5 contain some violence?   ....
6 is surprising?   ....

C Make a list of adjectives that end with *-ing* from the reviews below. Add the verb form.

adjective	verb
moving	*move*

My favourite film!

A Amélie
star rating: ★★★★★

Kylie from Australia wrote:

I've seen a number of good movies in the last few years, but none as moving as this simple French story about the life of an ordinary girl. There are few special effects, and no exciting car chases, but the audience is taken on a magical bike ride with the heroine through the streets of Paris. Amélie is a funny, imaginative young woman, who tries to bring a little happiness to the people around her. As she does this, she falls in love. The director has captured the beauty of the simple things in life in this wonderful story, and shows us the extraordinary side of ordinary people's characters. Audrey Tautou is excellent as Amélie. I saw this film in the cinema when it first came out, and have watched it five times on DVD since then.

B Pan's Labyrinth
star rating: ★★★★★

Dino from Brazil wrote:

I had heard a lot about this film before I saw it, so I was worried that I would find it disappointing. However, it was amazing! Critics have been calling it *Alice in Wonderland* for adults, and I think this is true. The story is set in post-Civil War Spain, during a time of violence and hatred. A young girl called Ofelia, played by Ivana Baquero, escapes from a cruel reality into a fantasy world. *Pan's Labyrinth* is the best film that director Guillermo del Toro has ever made. He moves the action easily between Ofelia's imaginary and real worlds. The violence in Ofelia's real life is shocking, but necessary, for it shows her desperate need for escape and makes her dream world seem even more magical. The scenery inside the labyrinth is fantastic, the monsters are scary, the acting is superb, and all this is accompanied by a wonderful musical score.

C Slumdog Millionaire
star rating: ★★★★☆

Margarhita from Spain wrote:

Slumdog Millionaire is a film that both shocked and surprised me. Set on the violent streets of Mumbai, it tells the story of Jamal, a young boy who gets the chance to play the TV game show *Who Wants To Be A Millionaire*. He does well, but the show's host say's he has been cheating. Jamal gets arrested, and begins to tell the police officer the story of his life on the streets. Simon Beaufoy's screenplay is a clever adaptation of the novel *Q&A* by Vikas Swarup, and Danny Boyle's creative direction provides surprising twists and turns. The picture of life on the streets is not a pleasant one, and the way the children are treated is upsetting. It is a powerful story, and the emotional ending made me cry, along with others in the cinema.

Glossary

labyrinth: a place with many paths, so that it is difficult to understand where you are
get arrested: to be taken to the police station by the police, because they think you've done something wrong

VOCABULARY Compound nouns

A **Make a list of compound nouns from the following words.**

A	film	screen
	music	pop
	police	special

B	star	writer
	effects	business
	industry	officer

B **Match one of the compounds from exercise A with each of the pictures below.**

1 ....

2 ....

3 ....

4 ....

C **Complete the sentences with one of the compounds from exercise A.**

1 The .... in the film *2012* are really amazing!
2 There is a lot of competition in the ...., and it's hard for singers to become successful.
3 The .... asked Jane if she had stolen the money.
4 The .... generates huge amounts of money every year, but some films also cost a great deal of money to produce.
5 Michael Jackson was the most famous .... of the 20th century.
6 A .... must work really hard to create clever, realistic dialogues.

PRONUNCIATION -ed

A **Place the following past participles in the correct column.**

~~excited~~	~~bored~~	tired	disappointed
interested	starred	amazed	treated
played	surprised	directed	recorded

/ɪd/	/d/
excited	*bored*

B 🔊 **13.2 Listen and check.**

C **Practise saying the words.**

Language note

Where a verb ends in *-d, -de, -t* or *-te*, we pronounce the *-ed* ending of the past participle /ɪd/.

DEVELOPING WRITING
Blog entry – a book review

A **Carla reads a lot of online book reviews. The books blog of a local newspaper has asked readers to choose their favourite book of this year. Read Carla's entry below, and complete it with the correct adjective form of the verbs in brackets (1–3).**

B **Match the headings (1–3) with the paragraphs in Carla's entry (a–c).**
1 opinion of the book   ....
2 name of my chosen book   ....
3 description of the plot   ....

C **The underlined phrases in the text can be used to express your opinion about a book or a film. The phrase *beautiful prose* can become *wonderful screenplay / script* for a film.**
Write a similar blog entry for your own favourite book or film. Try to use some of the underlined phrases and descriptive adjectives to help you.

Language note

When we talk about the written language in a novel, we use the word *prose*. When we talk about the words that are spoken in a film, we use *script*.

posted by Carla, 06 Dec:

MY BOOKSHELF

a I have chosen *The Secret Scripture* by Sebastian Barry as my favourite book of the year. I found it very ¹ .... (move) and read it in one day.

b The heroine, Roseanne, is nearly 100 years old, and has been living in a mental hospital for 60 years. Her psychiatrist, Dr Grene, is ² .... (interest) in her, and wants to learn about how she came to be there. The story is told through the journals of these two characters. Through Roseanne's memories, the writer allows us to gradually see pieces of the truth, and her story is a ³ .... (surprise) one.

c The story develops in a clever way and Sebastian Barry's beautiful prose touches the reader's heart. Definitely worth reading!

Glossary

prose: written language using normal sentences; not poetry

Vocabulary Builder Quiz 13 (*OVB pp 50–53*)

Try the *OVB* quiz for Unit 13. Write your answers in your notebook. Then check them and record your score.

A Complete the sentences with the correct preposition.
1 She works .... the film industry.
2 He won an award .... his role in the film.
3 The censorship .... all his books and films has been relaxed.
4 There was tension .... the director and the actors this morning.
5 He is in trouble .... the neighbours for playing his drums late at night.

B Complete the sentences with the correct form of the word in CAPITALS.
1 Mozart is one of my favourite .... COMPOSE
2 Her music is loved by people from different .... backgrounds. SOCIETY
3 The plot was complicated, and the ending was .... PREDICT
4 There was a loud .... and the lights went out. EXPLODE
5 We're trying to reduce his .... to video games. ADDICT
6 James Cameron is the .... of the movie *Avatar*. DIRECT
7 Many Hollywood actors are very .... WEALTH
8 He's the .... of the local school orchestra. CONDUCT

C Choose the correct word.
1 They're busy *rehearsing / publishing* a new play at the Royal Court theatre.
2 I thought the ending was a bit *weird / light*, and didn't fully understand it.
3 She wrote a *novel / biography* of her mother's life.
4 The gallery hopes to *generate / experience* public interest in graphic art.
5 The film is about a *current / corrupt* police officer who sells drugs.
6 The National Youth Orchestra gave an amazing *concert / programme* last night.

D Match the sentence halves.
1 He never raises his
2 The paintings will be put up
3 The band are busy recording
4 It's a TV drama that deals
5 An exhibition of his work is opening
6 I fell asleep halfway

a for auction next month.
b with teenagers' problems.
c through the film.
d at the gallery on Saturday.
e voice when he's angry.
f their new album.

Score ___/25

Wait a couple of weeks and try the quiz again.
Compare your scores.

14 THINGS

GRAMMAR Relative clauses

A Complete these sentences by joining them to a phrase in the box using *which, who* or *where.*

helps you to get dry	horse racing takes place
cleans carpets	you can watch the latest movies
hold water	prepares food in a restaurant
you can keep fit	make things from wood

1 A gym is a place ....
2 A chef is a person ....
3 A vacuum cleaner is a thing ....
4 Carpenters are people ....
5 A cinema is a building ....
6 A towel is a piece of cloth ....
7 A racecourse is an area ....
8 Buckets are containers ....

Language note

In relative clauses you will sometimes see *that* used instead of *who* or *which*. For example:
He's the man that drives the bus. = He's the man who drives the bus.
It's a machine that drills holes. = It's a machine which drills holes.

B Choose the right word in these sentences.
1 She's the woman *which / who* sold me her car.
2 It's a place *where / which* you can go to be alone.
3 They're the people *who / when* saw the robbery.
4 It's the time of day *who / when* people relax after work.
5 Here comes the man *when / who* knows all the answers.
6 This is the room *which / where* we keep the records.
7 We're the people *which / who* are paying for the party.
8 This is the day *who / when* we remember the great successes of the past.

C Complete the conversation with *who* or *which.*
A: What's the name of that restaurant [1] .... does Moqueca?
B: I don't remember. And what's Moqueca!?
A: It's a famous Brazilian dish [2] .... is made of fish.
B: Oh, now I remember. And all the people [3] .... work there are Brazilians, right?
A: Yes, that's the place.
B: It's the Carnicero.
A But a Carnicero is a person [4] .... prepares different cuts of meat! A butcher, in English. That's a funny name for a fish restaurant.
B: It's not a fish restaurant. It's a place [5] .... serves everything.

VOCABULARY Things in the house

A Read the clues 1–10, and write the rooms or things in the house in the grid.

```
 1        L
 2        I
 3        V
 4        I
 5        N
 6       G
 7        R
 8        O
 9        O
10        M
```

1   You wipe surfaces with this.
2   A container for rubbish.
3   This keeps you warm in bed.
4   You need a hammer to bang this into a piece of wood.
5   You fry food in this.
6   This is a place where you keep your car.
7   You use a needle to repair clothes with this.
8   You need this to see into dark corners.
9   This removes the creases from clothes, when it's hot.
10 This tool bangs nails into wood.

B Fill the gaps in these words and match them to the pictures.
1   mop and b _ _ _ _ t.   3 dustpan and b _ _ _ h.
2   n _ _ _ _ e and thread.   4 h _ _ _ _ r and nails.

a
b
c
d

DEVELOPING CONVERSATIONS

A Complete these conversations with the phrases in the box.

> Yes, there are some in the fridge.
> Can I make a drink?
> Have you got a needle and thread?
> There's a first aid kit in the kitchen cupboard.
> Have you got today's paper?
> Where do you keep the plasters?
> Yes, the coffee is on the shelf.
> Have you got any snacks?
> There's a sewing box on the shelf.
> There's one on the bathroom wall.
> Can I borrow a hairdryer?
> It's on the table by the TV.

1 A: I'd like to wash my hair. ....
   B: ....
2 A: I've just cut my finger. ....
   B: ....
3 A: I'm feeling hungry. ....
   B: ....
4 A: A button has come off my shirt. ....
   B: ....
5 A: I'm thirsty. ....
   B: ....
6 A: I'd like to check the sports news. ....
   B: ....

B Fill the gaps in these sentences with the prepositions in the box.

on	under	in	in	next	in	at	on

1 You'll find a mop in the cupboard .... to the kitchen door.
2 There's a needle and thread .... the drawer.
3 There's a torch on the table .... the side of the bed.
4 You'll find some towels .... the shelf in the bathroom.
5 There's a rubbish bin .... the desk in the study.
6 You'll find a vacuum cleaner .... the corner of the garage.
7 There's a notebook .... the table.
8 There's a clean shirt .... the wardrobe.

LISTENING

A 🔊 14.1 Two cleaners are starting their day's work at a hotel. Listen to their conversation. Put a tick next to the four things that they have to do.

> ### TO DO
> Clean carpets in lobby   Wipe mirrors
> Tidy reception area   Sweep front steps
> Clean marble floor in   Polish glasses in bar
>   dining room   Put up picture

B Listen again and make a list of the things they need to do each job.
1 ....
2 ....
3 ....
4 ....

C Where can they find the things that they need? Match these places to the things you have listed above.
1 in the drawer in the staff room
   ....
2 in the cupboard behind the reception area
   ....
3 in the cellar
   ....
4 under the stairs
   ....

D At the end of the conversation one of the cleaners can't find the right word. What is it? ....

14

VOCABULARY Containers

A Choose the word that does **not** collocate with the container.

1 a can of — cola / beer / shampoo
2 a packet of — biscuits / bread / sweets
3 a jar of — fish / honey / jam
4 a carton of — milk / orange juice / butter
5 a bar of — soap / cheese / chocolate
6 a box of — sausages / cereal / tissues
7 a pot of — yoghurt / crisps / tea
8 a tin of — eggs / baked beans / tomatoes

B Match the words (1–6) to the clues (a–f).

1 metal ....
2 glass ....
3 plastic ....
4 cardboard ....
5 cloth ....
6 paper ....

a this material is often made from wool or cotton
b you can make many things from this material including bags and bottles and sheets.
c a material which you can see through
d this is made from layers of paper stuck together
e iron and aluminium are examples of this material
f this is made from wood or rags

"I felt an incredible sense of freedom"

READING

A Quickly read the article. Which of these sentences is the best summary?

a The article is about a man who destroyed his home and family life because he couldn't stop buying things.
b It's about a man destroyed everything he owned as a work of performance art.
c It tells the story of a man who lost everything that he owned because of bad luck.
d It's about a man who was always breaking things, including some very valuable objects.

THE MAN WHO DESTROYED EVERYTHING

In February 2001, the artist Michael Landy destroyed everything he owned. He rented an empty shop on London's busiest shopping street, Oxford Street. He took all his possessions there and with the help of ten assistants, started to make a list of everything – his car, his books, his works of art, his photographs, his clothes, his passport, his driving licence, his toothbrush – absolutely everything! When they had written all 7,227 items onto huge cards Landy and his assistants started the serious business. One by one, they placed Michael Landy's things onto a conveyer belt which took them to a machine that destroyed them.

Why did Landy do this? For him, it was a work of performance art, which he called *Break Down,* and he even invited the public to come along and watch. During the two weeks that it took to destroy all his possessions, 45,000 people visited the shop in Oxford Street. Landy believed that *Break Down* could make people think again about the consumer society that they live in and reflect on their shopping habits and possessions.

At the end of the process, Michael Landy was left with nothing except his cat. So how did he feel?

'I felt an incredible sense of freedom,' he said, 'the possibility that I could do anything.'

Since then, Michael Landy has become one of the most respected artists in the UK but he certainly took an unusual route to career success!

Glossary

conveyer belt: a moving strip which carries things from one place to another
performance art: a live work of art in which the artist plays a part
consumer society: a society in which shopping is very important

84 OUTCOMES

B **Read the article again and answer the following questions.**

1 Where did the event happen?

....

2 How many assistants did Michael Landy have?

....

3 How many things did he own?

....

4 What was the event called?

....

5 What did he want people to think about?

....

6 What one thing did he have at the end?

....

7 How did he feel at the end of the event?

....

8 What has happened to Michael Landy since 2001?

....

C **Decide whether the statements are true (T) or false (F).**

1 Oxford Street is London's busiest shopping street.
....

2 Michael Landy didn't own a car. ....

3 His things were destroyed by a conveyer belt. ....

4 Michael Landy didn't want publicity. ....

5 The event lasted two weeks. ....

6 He saved his works of art. ....

D **Fill the gaps in the conversation with these sentences.**

> We all have too many possessions these days.
> I think he made a good point.
> You're always going shopping.
> It was so wasteful!
> But he could have given them to charity.
> Why do you think that?

A: I think Landy's *Break Down* was a stupid idea.

B: 1...

A: He didn't need to destroy his things.

2...

B: I disagree.

3...

A: What point was he trying to make?

B: I think he was trying to say something about the consumer society.

4...

A: 5...

It would have been more useful. And I don't think I have too many possessions!

B: Yes you do!

6...

GRAMMAR *must, mustn't, don't have to*

A **Match the sentences with the same definitions.**

1 There is a law that tells you to do this. ....

2 There is no law that tells you to do this. ....

3 There is a law that tells you not to do this. ....

a You mustn't do this.

b You don't have to do this.

c You must do this.

B **Complete this hotel information sheet with *You must*, *You mustn't* or *You don't have to*.**

Information for Guests

1 .... return the keys to reception when you leave.

2 .... smoke in the children's play area.

3 Check out time is 11.00 am. ....
leave your room before then on your last day.

4 .... use your mobile phones in the quiet room.

5 The coffee is free. .... pay for it.

6 If you want to check out late, ...
tell reception the day before.

7 Towels are available at the swimming pool.
.... bring your own.

8 You can use the sauna any time ....
book in advance.

9 The swimming pool is very shallow.
.... dive into it.

10 .... wear your swimming costume in the dining room.

GRAMMAR Verbs with two objects

A Choose the correct word.
1 She bought the shirt *for / to* me.
2 He sent the parcel *for / to* them.
3 They brought the books *for / to* our house.
4 He cooked roast beef *for / to* her.
5 Can you lend your bike *for / to* me for the afternoon?
6 Will you give that plate *for / to* him?
7 Will you read the letter *for / to* us?
8 Can you pour some orange juice *for / to* her?

B Change the order of the two objects in these sentences.
1 He gave the books to me.
  He gave ....
2 I bought you a cup of coffee.
  I bought ....
3 He poured a glass of milk for me.
  He poured ....
4 I sent you a postcard.
  I sent ....
5 She made a sandwich for me.
  She made ....
6 He read them the report.
  He read ....
7 The lent their car to us.
  They lent ....
8 We cooked dinner for them.
  We cooked ....

PRONUNCIATION
/g/ and /k/, /b/ and /p/

A 14.2 Say these pairs of words. Then listen and tick (✓) the word you hear.

1	glass	class	6	good	could
2	gave	cave	7	ban	pan
3	bin	pin	8	bad	pad
4	bear	pair	9	goal	coal
5	gold	cold	10	boring	pouring

LISTENING

A 14.3 Listen to the conversation. Decide whether the statements are true (T) or false (F).
1 Rachel has just returned from Scotland. ....
2 She brought back a present which is a bit like a handbag. ....
3 You wear it over your shoulder. ....
4 In Scotland the men wear them. ....
5 It has four tassels on the front. ....
6 It's called a kilt. ....

WRITING

A Read this paragraph about haggis, a famous Scottish dish. In which order do you read these things? Number them 1 to 4.
The writer's opinion of haggis ....
The writer's recommendation ....
A definition of haggis ....
The writer's first experience of haggis ....

B Write a description of one of these things. Use the notes to help you organise your writing.
- Your favourite place
- Your favourite food
- A movie you've seen recently
- Your favourite piece of music
- Your favourite book.

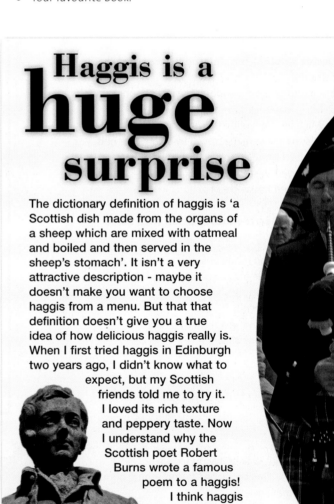

Haggis is a huge surprise

The dictionary definition of haggis is 'a Scottish dish made from the organs of a sheep which are mixed with oatmeal and boiled and then served in the sheep's stomach'. It isn't a very attractive description - maybe it doesn't make you want to choose haggis from a menu. But that that definition doesn't give you a true idea of how delicious haggis really is. When I first tried haggis in Edinburgh two years ago, I didn't know what to expect, but my Scottish friends told me to try it. I loved its rich texture and peppery taste. Now I understand why the Scottish poet Robert Burns wrote a famous poem to a haggis! I think haggis is probably my favourite food of all time, although I don't think I could eat it every week. Don't take my word for it, though. You really have to try haggis for yourself!

The guide books say that ...
The dictionary definition of X is ...
The newspaper reviews say that ...
Most people think that ...

But that does not give you a true idea of how *amazing* / *delicious* / *special*, *etc.* X really is.

When I first *saw* / *heard* / *tried etc* X, I thought ...
(Describe your first experience of X.)

I think that X is ... (Give your opinion of X.)

But don't take my word for it, you really have to *see* / *try* / *taste*, *etc.* X for yourself.

Vocabulary Builder Quiz 14 (*OVB* pp54–57)

Try the *OVB* quiz for Unit 14. Write your answers in your notebook. Then check them and record your score.

A Fill the gaps with the words in the box.

> forecast warming rid going turned break

1 We got .... of all our rubbish last weekend.
2 They were always arguing so they decided to .... up.
3 Have you seen the weather .... for next week?
4 Roma and Leo have been .... out with each other for ages.
5 He had a party because he .... 21 last week.
6 Our summers are much hotter now because of global ....

B Decide whether the statements are true (T) or false (F).

1 A *vegetarian* is someone who doesn't eat meat.   ....
2 A *sticker* is a small piece of material that you put over a cut on your skin.   ....
3 You use *a plaster* for boiling water.   ....
4 A *mortgage* is an amount of money you borrow to buy a house.   ....
5 A *refugee* is someone who has left their country to escape from danger.   ....
6 A *tap* is a connection between different parts of a website.   ....
7 An *expert* is an amount of money that you spend.   ....

C Complete the sentences with the correct form of the word in CAPITALS.

1 We made a big .... in spending last year.   REDUCE
2 I made a mistake because I was very ....   CONFUSING
3 She's a very .... person.   ATTRACT
4 It was very hard to .... of all their rubbish.   DISPOSAL
5 She's much more .... than her boss.   EFFICIENCY
6 We need to increase the amount of .... that we do.   RECYCLE

D Choose the word that does not collocate with the key word.

1 *rubbish* / *waste paper* / *clue*   bin
2 *petrol* / *kitchen* / *desk*   drawer
3 *curtain* / *sink* / *towel*   rail
4 *gold* / *coal* / *soap*   mine
5 *football* / *neighbour* / *management* team
6 *tennis* / *racing* / *basketball*   court

Score ___ /25

Wait a couple of weeks and try the quiz again.
Compare your scores.

15 THE ECONOMY AND MONEY

VOCABULARY The economy and quality of life

A **Find the words and phrases from the list below hidden in the box. The missing words read up ↑ , down ↓ , to the left ← or to the right →.**

C	O	T	D	E	R	U	K	A	E	W	N	P	U
X	Y	O	O	A	O	N	I	D	Q	W	X	Y	L
W	C	L	C	B	T	E	S	C	E	T	N	T	E
T	N	L	X	T	I	M	E	O	F	F	P	I	V
A	E	U	I	Y	N	P	K	S	A	L	A	R	Y
S	R	E	N	A	W	L	Z	T	M	H	J	U	T
Z	R	F	I	Q	O	V	O	I	C	E	C	R
Q	U	A	L	I	T	Y	O	F	L	I	F	E	O
S	C	M	A	K	L	M	B	L	Y	A	R	S	P
T	R	I	T	E	U	E	M	I	R	C	H	B	S
Y	P	L	I	C	I	N	Z	V	Q	D	U	O	N
P	W	C	O	I	W	T	P	I	Y	F	G	J	A
U	L	O	N	S	T	R	O	N	G	G	O	W	R
Q	I	M	A	V	E	R	A	G	E	R	S	A	T

1	average	6	family	11	strong
2	climate	7	inflation	12	time off
3	cost of living	8	job security	13	transport
4	crime	9	quality of life	14	unemployment
5	currency	10	salary	15	weak

B **Choose the correct word or phrase to complete the sentences.**
1 One of the biggest problems at the moment is *unemployment / inflation.* Many skilled people are out of work.
2 The *pace of life / cost of living* is quite fast in this city, and a lot of people suffer from stress.
3 While the economy is doing badly, most people are interested in having *job security / a high salary.*
4 More and more people are moving out of the city to find a better *average salary / quality of life.*
5 People are becoming more and more worried about *climate change / crime* as temperatures rise and there is less rain than in the past.
6 Our currency is *weak / strong* at the moment, so it's not a good time to travel abroad.
7 The rate of *inflation / crime* is rising at the moment, and the cost of living is high.
8 Although Gina has a good *currency / salary,* she doesn't have much job security.

LISTENING

You're going to listen to Carlos and Yelena speaking. Carlos is a native Argentinian, and Yelena is from the Czech Republic.

A 🔊 **15.1 Listen and answer the questions.**
1 Does Yelena like living in Argentina?
....
2 Is the economy doing well?
....
3 Why does she want to leave?
....
....

B **Listen again and complete the sentences with one word.**
1 According to Carlos, the cost of living in Prague is .... than it is in Argentina.
2 Yelena says that unemployment is .... in Prague than it is in Argentina.
3 According to Yelena, houses are .... in the Czech Republic.
4 Carlos says that eating out is less .... in Argentina.
5 Yelena says that salaries are .... in the Czech Republic.
6 Yelena thinks it is important for Miguel and her to decide where they will both feel .... to live.

C **Tick (✓) the arguments Yelena gives to support her decision to move to Prague.**
1 It is important for Miguel to understand her culture and language.
2 Prague is a better place to bring up children.
3 They will find a better paid job easily.
4 Cars are cheaper in the Czech Republic.
5 She doesn't have a good quality of life in Argentina.
6 They need to live in both countries to decide where to raise a family.

GRAMMAR Time phrases and tense

A **Match the sentence halves.**

1 House prices are currently ....
2 Unemployment has fallen ....
3 According to the government, the economy will ....
4 The cost of living has gone up over ....
5 Rents used to be a lot cheaper ....
6 The government is going to announce ....
7 According to newspaper reports, inflation is falling ....
8 The pace of life used to be much ....

a improve over the next few months.
b the last two years.
c slower when I was a child.
d at the moment.
e rising and many people can't afford to buy their own home.
f since this time last year.
g when I was a student.
h the new budget in two weeks' time.

B **Put the words in the sentences into the correct order.**

1 used to / on education / the government / spend more
....
2 a new shopping centre / yesterday / they opened / on the ring road
....
3 she's going to / next week / in advertising / a new job / start
....
4 three jobs / he's had / in the last two years
....
5 improving / at the moment / the economy is
....
6 in the last five years / three loans / she's had / from the bank
....

C **The tense is wrong in the sentences below. Correct the mistakes.**

1 Unemployment used to rise over the last few months.
....
2 The average salary has been higher when I was at school.
....
3 Inflation will fall since last year. ....
4 The price of petrol has risen again in the next few weeks.
....
5 The cost of living used to fall at the moment, and prices are lower. ....
6 I think the economy has improved next year.
....

DEVELOPING CONVERSATIONS
Comparing prices

A **Below are lists of average prices for certain items in two countries, Celtonia and Faroland. Compare the prices and complete the sentences about them. Use phrases such as *more / less expensive than, cheaper than, much cheaper than*, etc.**

	Celtonia	Faroland
three-bedroom house	€200,000	€300,000
four-door saloon car	€20,000	€25,000
petrol	€1 per litre	€1.20 per litre
computer (PC)	€750	€1000
iPod	€200	€200

1 Houses are ....
to buy in Celtonia than in Faroland.
2 In Celtonia petrol is .... in Faroland.
3 Cars are ....
in Faroland than they are in Celtonia.
4 Computers are .... in Celtonia.
5 An iPod, however, costs ....
in Celtonia as in Faroland.
6 Generally, the cost of living in Celtonia seems to be
.... it is in Faroland.

B **Complete the replies to the following statements with an example from the lists in exercise A.**

A: Clothes are cheaper in Faroland than in Celtonia.
B: I know. You can buy Designer jeans for €60, whereas they cost €70 in Celtonia.

1 A: Houses are much cheaper in Celtonia.
B: I know. You can buy a three-bedroomed house for €200,000 there, whereas
....
2 A: Cars are more expensive in Faroland.
B: I know. A four-door saloon costs €25,000 in Faroland, whereas
....
3 A: However, petrol is only slightly more expensive in Faroland.
B: I know. It costs €1.20 there,
....
4 A: If you want a new computer, you should go to Celtonia. They're much cheaper there.
B: I know. They cost only €750 in Celtonia,
....

15

READING

A Read the newspaper article about Professor Muhammad Yunus and complete the sentences.

1 Professor Yunus used to work as

....

2 In 1983, he formed

....

3 In 2006, Professor Yunus was awarded

....

B Decide whether the statements are true (T) or false (F).

1 Professor Yunus was a university student in 1974. ....
2 Professor Yunus was upset by the famine in Bangladesh. ....
3 The woman's story showed him how traders took advantage of the poor. ....
4 Professor Yunus helped the woman and other workers by offering them a loan. ....
5 He did not expect them to pay back the money. ....
6 Everyone paid back the money they had borrowed. ....
7 In 1983, Professor Yunus started a bank to help poor people. ....
8 The bank is not very successful. ....

C Complete the sentences with a word or phrase from the box.

loan	micro-credit	borrowed
lend	interest	pay back

1 People usually pay a lot of .... on a business loan, and it often takes them a long time to pay back the money.
2 Riko, can you .... me £50? I haven't got enough money to pay the bill.
3 Several banks are setting up .... systems for small businesses to help the economy improve.
4 Hi, Camille! Look, I'm sorry for the delay. I'll .... the money I owe you at the end of the week, OK?
5 I'm fed up! Ming .... £100 from me three months ago, and he still hasn't paid it back!
6 Right, David! Here's £1,000 towards your car. Remember it's a .... , so I expect to be paid back!

Nobel Prize Winner receives Medal of Freedom

Professor Muhammad Yunus has many reasons to be proud. He was awarded the Nobel Peace Prize in 2006, and has just been presented with the Medal of Freedom by United States President, Barack Obama.

When famine hit Bangladesh in 1974, Professor Yunus was teaching Economics at Chittagong University. He was deeply shocked by the number of people dying in the streets, and wanted to do something to help.

He mixed with villagers, learning about their lives and their problems. One woman made bamboo stools. She was skilled and hardworking, but did not have the money to buy the bamboo. She was forced to borrow from a trader who then paid a low price for the stools, which he would then sell for a good profit. The woman's profit was just a penny a day! Professor Yunus discovered that this was true for many villagers. Together with one of his students, he made a list of 42 people who worked like this woman. He decided to lend them the total amount they needed to become independent in their work – about £1 per person – and told them it was a loan, but without interest. The Professor then persuaded a bank to provide such loans, with him as guarantor. The bank was not enthusiastic, but the system worked, and all the loans were paid back.

Professor Yunus realised that a new bank was needed; a bank that was owned by the people. In October 1983, the Grameen (Village) Bank was formed. Over the next few years, it made small loans to some of the poorest people in Bangladesh, so that they could become self-employed and escape poverty. It was a huge success. Since then, the bank has grown so much that it now has almost 8 million members, and 96% of them are women. Grameen's system of micro-credit is one of the most successful banking systems in the world, with 98% of all loans paid back in full.

Professor Yunus has given the people of Bangladesh hope and a sense of pride.

> **Glossary**
>
> **famine:** period when large numbers of people have little or no food and they die
>
> **stool:** a seat with legs but no support for the back
>
> **guarantor:** person who promises to make sure a loan is paid back

VOCABULARY Money verbs

A Choose the best word in *italics* to complete the sentences.

Ming Woo had no money, and he [1] *left / owed* €5,000 to the bank. He [2] *borrowed / lent* €5 from his brother and bought a lottery ticket. Fortunately, he [3] *won / saved* €10,000! Ming paid the money to the bank, and [4] *left / gave* his brother €1,000. Then he bought a second-hand car for €3,000. That [5] *left / saved* him with €1,000. He decided to [6] *lend / save* it, and put it in the bank. Ming Wu is more careful with his money now. He is worried that he might [7] *drop / lose* his job. He saves €100 every month. But he still [8] *plays / spends* the lottery every week!

B Complete the sentences with the most suitable word(s) from the box.

loan	credit card	attention	bill
interest	to do it	paid	back

1 Sinead didn't have much cash, so she paid for the meal by ....
2 Ameet spent too much money last month and couldn't afford to pay the electricity ....
3 Can I borrow €50? I promise I'll pay you .... !
4 Our TV needed repairing and we paid the technician €65 ....
5 The sales manager talked for an hour at the meeting, but few people paid much ....
6 Oh, no! I've spent all my wages and I'll have to wait another two weeks until I get .... !
7 I don't want to ask the bank for a loan, as I'll have to pay a lot of ....
8 Danil wanted to buy a new car, so he took out a ....

LISTENING

A 🎵 15.2 Listen to two people talking, and answer the questions.

1 What is Isabel doing?
2 Does she say it is easy or difficult?
3 Does Primo like the idea?

B Listen again. Choose the most suitable answer.

1 Isabel is
  a writing out a cheque. c paying bills through the Internet.
  b writing an email.
2 How does Primo feel about what she is doing?
  a Surprised.   b Uninterested.   c Enthusiastic.
3 Isabel says this system
  a saves you money.   c is complicated.
  b is good for the environment.
4 Primo worries about
  a security.   b expense.   c wasting time.
5 Isabel agrees that
  a it's expensive.   c it is difficult.
  b there are some risks.
6 When he goes to pay bills in Scotland, Primo sometimes finds it difficult to
  a work out the money.   c remember his ID number.
  b understand the cashier's accent.
7 Isabel says her way
  a wastes money.   b is slower.   c saves time.
8 Finally, Primo
  a thinks it's a good idea.   c doesn't like the idea.
  b is uncertain.

PRONUNCIATION

A Say the words. Choose the word in each group that does not belong.

/aɪ/	price	online	bill	buy	twice
/əʊ/	loan	grow	owe	owl	own
/aʊ/	amount	through	pound	round	sound
/eɪ/	save	paid	said	sales	wage

B 🎵 15.3 Listen to the sentences, and practise saying them. Stress the words in bold.

1 **Buy** a house when the **price** is **right**, and pay your bills on**line**.
2 Take out a **loan** to buy your **own home**, then **owe** the bank money until you **grow old**.
3 Twenty-five **pounds** for a meal may not **sound** much but is a large **amount** for a pizza.
4 I got **paid** a good **wage** for my job in **sales**, and was able to **save** for a holiday in **Wales**.

GRAMMAR
Present tenses in future time clauses

A Six of these sentences contain mistakes. Find and correct them.

1 I'll pay back the money I owe you as soon as I'll be able to.
2 Call me after you'll transfer the money. OK?
3 I lend you the money until you get paid.
4 I'm going to talk to the manager as soon as he arrives at the bank.
5 When I find a job, I open a savings account.
6 I'm going to invest in Dave's company after I retire.
7 As soon as I'll get confirmation of payment, I'll let you know.
8 When I'll have enough money, I'll buy a new car.

B Choose the correct word in *italics* to complete the sentences.

1 I'll leave home *when / until* I finish college.
2 Oliver is going to pay me back *before / as soon as* he comes home.
3 Don't buy a flat *after / until* you're sure where you're going to live.
4 I'm going to see what different banks offer *before / after* I take out a mortgage.
5 You'll be able to pay bills online *until / after* you register.
6 Don't forget to pay the bill *as soon as / until* it arrives.

C Complete the sentences with the correct form of the verb in brackets.

1 We .... (cancel) your credit card as soon as we get home.
2 Don't buy that laptop until you .... (have) enough money to pay for it.
3 Inflation .... (not fall) until the government takes action.
4 When the economy .... (recover) unemployment will fall.
5 I .... (not invest) any money until the price of shares .... (fall).
6 As soon as I .... (win) the lottery, I .... (take) you to Hawaii.
7 Before you .... (take out) a bank loan, always .... (check) how much interest you will have to pay.
8 After I .... (finish) university, I .... (come) to work for you.

VOCABULARY Dealing with banks

A Complete the sentences with one of the verbs in the box.

change	make	charge	transfer	pay	cancel	open	take out

1 Farouq and Heba want to buy their first house, and so they are going to .... a mortgage.
2 I'm afraid my credit card has been stolen, so I need to .... it.
3 Yes, my husband and I would like to .... a joint account, please.
4 The banks are planning to .... us £2.40 every time we take cash from a cash machine!
5 Yes, I'd like to .... a complaint. You've overcharged me for this meal.
6 I want to .... some money into my account, please.
7 Could you .... €1,000 from my account to Ms Yoko Wong in Tokyo, please? Just a moment and I'll give you her account number.
8 Just a moment, Vikram! I haven't got any euros! I need to .... some money.

B Look at the situations and write what you will do.
e.g. You are travelling to the USA, but you haven't got any dollars.
I will change some money.
1 You want to send some money to your brother, who lives in Prague.
....
2 Your parents have sent you some money for your birthday. You take it to the bank. ....
3 Someone asks you to translate an article. You want to be paid for this.
....
4 You want to buy a flat, but need to borrow some money from the bank.
....
5 You've just started your first job and want to put your money in a bank.
....
6 You think someone has stolen your credit card details.
....

Language note
- -
Some verbs can go with more than one noun to form collocations.
e.g. *take out ~ a loan; ~ a mortgage; ~ some money*
When you see a verb + noun collocation, use your dictionary to see if the verb can form other collocations, and make a list.

DEVELOPING WRITING
Email – giving information and advice

Sanjida is going to be a foreign exchange student at Edinburgh University. She has written to the university asking about the cost of living for students there. Below is the reply from the International Office.

A **Read the reply, and fill the gaps with one of the following words and phrases.**

cost	spend	pay	expenses	cost of living	charges

● ● ○

From	info@internat.office.ed.uk
To	Sanjida Beiz
Subject	re: cost of living in Edinburgh

Dear Sanjida,

1) You asked about the ¹.................... in Edinburgh. Edinburgh is quite an expensive city, so as a student here, you'll need to budget carefully.

2) You will ².................... £170 per week to stay in a university hall of residence. This includes the ³.................... of electricity, hot water, Internet access and your breakfast. The university canteen ⁴.................... students £13 a week for lunches. Then you will need to think about social ⁵...................., such as a cinema tickets, haircuts, clothes, drinks and so on. So, you can expect to ⁶.................... at least £210–220 per week.

3) We look forward to welcoming you here. Don't hesitate to write again if you have any more questions.

Best wishes,

Gavin Stewart

B **What do the following amounts refer to?**
£170:..
£13:...
£210–220:...

C **Place the paragraph headings in the correct order.**
a) information and advice ....
b) closing statement and offer of extra help ....
c) reason for writing ....

D **Paco is a foreign exchange student who is coming to study in your city. He is going to stay in your house. He has written an email asking you for information about the social life. Read the notes you have made below. Then write Paco an email with some information. Use paragraphs like the model above.**

college student centre - films, parties, discount prices at bar
local cinema / theatre - student prices
art gallery - free
sports facilities - some are expensive
eating out - expensive!

Vocabulary Builder Quiz 15 (*OVB* pp58–61)

Try the *OVB* quiz for Unit 15. Write your answers in your notebook. Then check them and record your score.

A **Decide whether the statements are true (T) or false (F).**
1 If you *divide* something, you share it between two or more people. ....
2 *Goods* are things that are bought and sold. ....
3 A *bill* is a card with numbers or pictures on it. ....
4 An *election* is when people in a country vote to choose a new government. ....
5 The *minimum* is the largest amount possible. ....

B **Correct the error in the collocations.**
1 It's an old motorbike so it doesn't worth much.
2 Our insurance police covers fire and flooding.
3 It cost us €10,000 to repair the harm to the house.
4 In times of recession, people want more job safety.
5 She decided to buy shame in the company.

C **Choose the correct word.**
1 My father took out a *will / loan* to build his factory.
2 The President's *population / popularity* has decreased.
3 I *suspect / support* the thieves had help from one of the staff.
4 Our *salary / currency* is strong now, so it's a good time to go abroad.
5 He left all his money to a children's *charity / company*.

D **Match the sentence halves.**
1 The second-hand car was in ....
2 It will take the economy a long time to recover ....
3 Luciano took out a ....
4 The government has promised to invest ....
5 The bank charges an interest ....

a rate of 8%.
b more money in schools.
c immaculate condition.
d loan to pay for his car.
e from the recession.

E **Complete the phrasal verbs.**
1 Prices have gone .... again, and it's becoming difficult to afford the basics.
2 I'm cold! Can you turn .... the air conditioning?
3 You're driving too fast! Please slow ....
4 Samir was too shy to ask Marianna ....
5 She turned old dresses .... skirts to save money.

Score ___/25

Wait a couple of weeks and try the quiz again. Compare your scores

16 DATES AND HISTORY

VOCABULARY Describing parties

A **Fill the gaps in these sentences with the words in the box.**

office	leaving	launch	house-warming
surprise	reception	dinner	end-of-term

1 To celebrate a marriage, there is often a wedding ....
2 When a new book or product is introduced there is sometimes a .... party.
3 If you don't know a party is going to happen, it's a .... party
4 An .... party happens just before school or university holidays.
5 People who work together sometimes have an .... party.
6 A .... party happens when someone moves to a new job.
7 When people move to a new house or flat they sometimes have a .... party.
8 If you invite people round to your house to eat in the evening, it's a .... party.

B **Match the sentence halves.**

1 There wasn't much food, just a few bowls ....
2 I couldn't hear anyone because the background ....
3 The party was held in a converted ....
4 The DJ played such bad music that he cleared ....
5 They met each other at a birthday ....
6 They had a terrible argument and ruined ....

a party last year.
b of olives and nuts.
c the dance floor in five minutes.
d the whole evening.
e warehouse near the river.
f music was much too loud.

C **Choose the word or phrase in italics which does not complete the answer.**

1 A: So where did you go last night?
   B: I was at a *leaving / launch / host / dinner* party.
2 A: What were the other guests like?
   B: They were all very *easy to talk to / comfortable and convenient / warm and friendly / cold and distant*.
3 A: Did you like the venue?
   B: Oh, yes. It was *impressive / amazing / backward / elegant*.
4 A: What kind of food did they have?
   B: It was mostly *spicy / grilled / general / cold*.
5 A: What was the wedding like?
   B: Well, it was very *modern / traditional / formal / full*.
6 A: Where did they hold the event?
   B: It was on the *past / ground / top / dance* floor.

DEVELOPING CONVERSATIONS Linked questions

Fill the gaps in the conversation with these questions.

Was anyone I know there?	And what was the venue like?
Did you have a good time?	Was there anything to eat?
Or did you hang out with your friends?	What time did you leave?
Is he the person you went to school with?	What's he like?

A: How was the party last night? [1]...
B: Yes, it was pretty good actually.
A: [2]...Did you stay really late?
B: No. It was probably about midnight.
A: [3]...Was it a nightclub?
B: Yes, it was that new place in the middle of town, near the river. Do you know it?
A: I know the one you mean, but I've never been inside. So what about the food? [4]...
B: Not really. Most of it had gone by the time I arrived.
A: Oh, that's a shame. So did you meet any new people?
   [5]...
B: With friends mostly.
A: Who was there? [6]...
B: Yes, Peter was there. Do you remember him?
A: Have I met him? [7]...
B: That's him, yes. Anyway, he introduced me to a friend of his, who was rather nice.
A: Really? [8]...
   Are you going to see him again?
B: Well, it's a long story ...

LISTENING

A ✆ 16.1 Listen to the conversation. Tick (✓) the best description.
a Two people discussing a party the night before.
b Someone complaining to a friend about her neighbour's noisy party.
c Two people planning a surprise party for a friend.
d Someone talking about a party with a professional party planner.

B Listen to the conversation again and correct the mistakes in these notes.

Kind of party	18th birthday
Atmosphere	Fun and noisy
Venue	Nightclub in shopping mall
Food	Hot buffet
Music	Live band
End time	1.00–2.00 am

C Fill the gaps in these questions with the phrases in the box. Then listen again to check.

| would you like | what kind of | what time can you think |
| sort of venue | have you got | are you going to |

1 .... party is it going to be?
2 What .... do you want?
3 .... any suggestions?
4 .... of anywhere else?
5 And .... serve any food?
6 What kind of music .... ?
7 .... would you like the party to finish?

PRONUNCIATION

A ✆ 16.2 Listen to these three extracts from the listening activity. Mark where the intonation rises or falls at the ends of the sentences.

1 A: With lots of people? ↗
   B: Oh, yes, at least a hundred.

2 A: How about a cold buffet?
   B: Yeah, a cold buffet's good.

3 A: Shall we say three to four in the morning?
   B: Yeah, that's great.

B ✆ 16.3 Will these sentences will have rising or falling intonation? Mark them with rising or falling arrows, then listen and check.

1 Where did you go last night?
2 Did you see what she was wearing?
3 Why were you so rude to him?
4 Have you been here before?
5 How many people here do you know?
6 Are you going to eat something?
7 Who's that man in the sunglasses near the bar?
8 Do you have the time?

Language note

Rising intonation means that the pitch increases and is often used in *Yes / No* questions. Falling intonation means that it decreases and is often used in *wh-?* questions. Intonation is often marked with an arrow pointing up ⟶ or down ⟶.

VOCABULARY

A **Read the clues 1–8 and write the answers in the grid.**

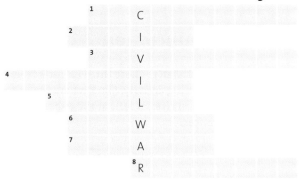

1 C
2 I
3 V
4
5 L
6 W
7 A
8 R

1 When a foreign power invades and then controls a country, there is an ...
2 In the nineteenth century, the British ... included India, Canada and Australia.
3 France had one in 1789; Russia had one in 1917.
4 When someone is killed by the government for a crime it is an ...
5 Waterloo, Stalingrad and the Somme were all famous ...
6 When someone becomes a king, he is ...
7 A king or a queen is a ...
8 A country like France or the USA which does not have a king or a queen.

B **Choose the right words in these sentences.**
1 India gained *independence / conversion* from the UK in 1947.
2 The French Emperor Napoleon was *gained / defeated* at the Battle of Waterloo.
3 Kenya was a British *quarter / colony* for many years.
4 The city of New York was *declared / founded* by the Dutch in 1614.
5 There were big political changes in the first *decade / decimal* of the 21st century.
6 British women gained the *vote / voice* for the first time in 1918.

C **Fill the gaps in the sentences with the words in the box.**

Kingdom	royal	Union	Civil	ruled	parliament

1 The North and South of the USA fought each other in the American .... War.
2 Buckingham Palace is the most famous of Britain's .... palaces.
3 Queen Victoria .... the British Empire for 64 years.
4 In a democracy, new laws are discussed in ....
5 UK stands for United ....
6 The UK has been a member of the European .... since 1973.

READING

A **This is an extract from a history of a state in the USA. Quickly read the text. Tick (✓) the state that it describes.**
a California
b Florida
c Hawaii
d Texas

THE LONG HISTORY OF THE NEWEST STATE

Glossary

settlers: people who move to live in a new area of the world
missionaries: people who try to persuade others to become Christians
territory: in the USA, an area controlled by the government that is not a state
naval base: a place where navy (fighting) ships are kept

B Read the extract again and complete this timeline.

500   *The first settlers arrived.* ....

1778 ....

1779 ....

1805 ....

1820 ....

1893 ....

1898 ....

1941 ....

1959 ....

1961 ....

This American state is famous for its beautiful beaches and volcanoes and, of course, was also the childhood home of US President Barack Obama who was born here in 1961. But the newest state in the union (it became the 50th state in 1959) has a long and fascinating history.

The first settlers arrived on the islands around AD 500 but little is known about them until 1778, when the British explorer Captain James Cook stayed here on his way to Australia. At first the people of the islands were generous to him and may have thought he was a representative of their god. But when he returned a year later, Cook argued with the local rulers and was killed.

At the end of the 18th century, the rulers of the islands were continually fighting each other for power, but in 1805 Kamehameha I became the islands' first king and established a monarchy which ruled successfully for many years.

The fate of Cook did not discourage other Westerners. In 1820 the first Christian missionaries arrived and before long European and American sailors and traders were a familiar sight in the streets of the islands' main ports such as Honolulu. However, as Western influence grew during the 19th century, the monarchy became weaker. In 1893 a group of American businessmen seized power in a revolution. Five years later, the islands were made a territory of the USA.

Under American rule, the economy continued to grow during the 20th century and Pearl Harbor became one the USA's most important naval bases. It was here that the Japanese launched their surprise attack in December 1941 which brought the USA into the Second World War.

GRAMMAR
Prepositions and nouns / -ing forms

A Correct the mistakes in these sentences.

1 After to win the election, the President introduced a series of reforms.
2 Everything depends on be honest about the situation.
3 We are all opposed raising taxes.
4 This problem was caused of cutting costs.
5 He was banned from to leave the country.
6 We are not involved in import products from the USA.
7 Before enter parliament, he was a successful businessman.
8 These decisions led in the current crisis.

B Choose the right prepositions in this text.

The current problems in the country date [1] *from / to* the late 1980s. That was when the President was involved [2] *by / in* a major scandal. He was accused [3] *to / of* receiving bribes from big businesses. There was an election and the majority of the population voted [4] *for / of* the opposition party but the President ignored the result. The crisis led [5] *to / in* a civil war which lasted for seven years and resulted [6] *in / for* the deaths of more than 5,000 people.

C Put the verbs in brackets into the correct form.

1 The country has problems .... (date) from the 1980s.
2 There was a major scandal .... (involve) the President.
3 It was said that he had .... (receive) bribes from big business.
4 With the majority of the population .... (vote) for the opposition, the President faced defeat.
5 By .... (ignore) the results of the election, he hoped to stay in power.
6 The crisis led to a civil war .... (last) more than seven years.
7 The war lead to thousands of people .... (become) refugees.
8 The discovery of oil resulted in lots of oil companies .... (buy) land.
9 The settlers depended on .... (farm) to live.
10 The President was accused of .... (take) millions out of the country.

Language note

Most prepositions have many different functions, so it is often difficult to find their exact equivalent in another language. It is best to learn them as part of a sentence or a phrase.

DEVELOPING WRITING

A Read the text and put these events into the right order.

The Normans sailed across the English Channel. ....
William was crowned king. ....
King Harold was killed. ....
The Normans established a camp. ....
The Normans and the English fought a battle. ....
William marched to London. ....

B Look at the text again.

1 Why is the date 1066 important?
....
2 What is the connection between William and modern Britain?
....
3 Underline these words in the text: *First, Next, Meanwhile, After*
4 Which word means 'at the same time as'? ....

C Write a paragraph about an important event in the history of your country.

• Write a sentence to introduce the subject
• Include at least three steps in the story. Link them together with expressions such as *First, Next, Meanwhile* and *After*.
• Finish with a concluding sentence.

LISTENING

A 🔊 16.4 Listen to a tour guide talking about the Bayeux Tapestry. Decide whether the statements are true (T) or false (F).

1 The Bayeux Tapestry shows the events leading to the Norman invasion of England. ....
2 The Normans walked to England. ....
3 The tapestry shows the Battle of Hastings. ....
4 The tapestry doesn't show the death of King Harold. ....
5 The tapestry was made in 1070. ....
6 Queen Matilda was King Harold's wife. ....
7 The tapestry was definitely made by King William's brother. ....
8 There is a copy of the tapestry in Reading, England. ....

The Norman Conquest

In the UK, every schoolchild knows the date 1066. That was the year of the Norman invasion of England, which changed British history forever. William, Duke of Normandy, left France with his army in September of that year.

First, the Normans crossed the English Channel, landing at Pevensey Bay on the south coast of England. Next, William established a camp near the town of Hastings. Meanwhile, the new English king, Harold Godwinson, was marching towards Hastings with his army.

The two armies met on 14 October and fought a fierce battle in which Harold was killed. After the battle, William marched north to London where he was crowned king on Christmas Day.

William the Conqueror became the first in a long line of British kings and queens which includes the current monarch, Elizabeth II.

GRAMMAR Verb patterns

A In each pair, match the sentence halves.

1 I forgot   telling her to go home early.
   I remember   to post the letter.

2 He spent two weeks   doing nothing.
   She decided   to review all the work.

3 They hated   to play tennis.
   They persuaded us   going to the theatre.

4 I'd like   watching TV this evening.
   I don't feel like   to help my parents with their business.

5 She enjoyed   to help with her assignment.
   She asked me   taking her brother to school.

6 Her new boss offered   to help her sort out the accounts.
   The new job stopped   her spending so much time at home.

B Use the prompts to write answers to the questions.

1 A: Do you always drive to work?
   B: Yes. *I / hate / take the bus.*
   ....

2 A: Do you still smoke?
   B: *No. I / stop / smoke / last year*
   ....

3 A: What are you doing for your holiday next year?
   B: *I'd like / go / Hawaii*
   ....

4 A: Do you want to come to the cinema this evening?
   B: No, thanks. *I / feel like / watch TV at home*
   ....

5 A: Why doesn't your phone work any more?
   B: *Because / I forget / pay my bill*
   ....

6 A: What was the last thing you remember before the accident?
   B: *I remember / see / my brother's face*
   ....

7 A: What did you do between school and university?
   B: *I / spend a year / work for my father's business*
   ....

8 A: Have you had a meeting with your boss yet?
   B: Yes. *I manage / speak to her yesterday*
   ....

Learner tip

Now that you have come to the end of the Workbook, look through it again and make a list of any language points that you are uncertain about. Ask your teacher to help you with them.

Vocabulary Builder Quiz 16 (*OVB* pp62–65)

Try the *OVB* quiz for Unit 16. Write your answers in your notebook. Then check them and record your score.

A Fill the gaps with the words in the box.

| side   dates   ruined   connection   settled   accused |

1 Our family .... in the USA 100 years ago.
2 The company was .... of corruption.
3 There is a close .... between the two events.
4 Our musical talent comes from my mother's .... of the family.
5 The castle .... from the thirteenth century.
6 Bad weather .... the holiday.

B Complete the sentences with the correct form of the word in CAPITALS.

1 The whole family is very .... and friendly.   WARMTH
2 The country has been .... since 1971.   INDEPENDENCE
3 The agreement was a very .... event in our history.   SIGNIFICANCE
4 The government is .... to any kind of compromise.   OPPOSITION
5 We .... our euros into dollars at the airport.   CONVERSION
6 She made a very good first .... at the interview.   IMPRESSED

C Decide whether the statements are true (T) or false (F).

1 A *buffet* is a fight between two armies.   ....
2 If you *convert* something you change it into something else.   ....
3 A *battle* is a period of ten years.   ....
4 A *citizen* is someone who performs operations on patients.   ....
5 Something that is *remarkable* is very unusual.   ....
6 A *tragedy* is a very sad event.   ....
7 If you *lease* a building to someone, you allow them to use it in return for money.   ....

D Choose the word that does not collocate with the key word.

1 background   *colony / noise / music*
2 ex-   *husband / decade / girlfriend*
3 moving   *film / empire / experience*
4 oil   *rule / company / exports*
5 nomadic   *bowl / tribe / society*
6 gorgeous   *dress / agriculture / cake*

Score ___ / 25

Wait a couple of weeks and try the quiz again. Compare your scores.

AUDIOSCRIPT

UNIT 01

🌀 1.1

1 Babur Wahidi

I was born in Afghanistan but grew up in the city of Bradford. There were a lot of people from different countries living in the area, so the primary school I attended was a multicultural school. There were children from India, Turkey and Afghanistan in my class. The teachers were really good. They were caring, open minded and patient. I liked the school and had a good time there.

I think I was sometimes treated differently at secondary school because I was Afghan ... Nothing terrible, but I was called bad names by some of the students. This changed when they realised I could play football. I played in the school football team, and the situation improved.

2 Joe Allbright

My childhood was spent on a farm in Shropshire. I really remember two things about growing up there. The first was the feeling of freedom. For example, being able to run across the fields. I had jobs to do, like feeding the chickens, and helping with the harvest, but I could also ride my bike all over the place, or go for a ride on my horse. In that way, I was very lucky. [Pause] The other thing ... the second thing I remember was *not* positive. I often felt lonely because there were no other children living nearby to play with. I didn't have the company of brothers or sisters either. That was difficult during school holidays.

3 Carrie Hutton

My dad was in the army. And because Dad was in the army, we lived in a lot of different parts of the world, and I changed schools a lot. I made new friends, and then left them after only a year, sometimes even six months. We stayed in Cairo for three years when I was a teenager, and I had some really good friends there. It was hard to say goodbye. At first, I was angry with my father, and didn't try to make friends at my new school in Dubai. But in the end, I did. I made new friends. I guess the good thing about moving around was that I learnt several languages, and I also learned how to make friends easily. Now, starting a new job or moving to a new town doesn't worry me at all. In fact, I can't imagine staying in one place for too long!

🌀 1.2

Yeah, well my two kids are quite different from each other. People don't believe them when they say they're brother and sister! Jill's the oldest, at 16, and she's tall and slim, with blonde hair, whereas Paul, at 14, is rather short, and overweight. He really likes his food, and doesn't like sport. I get angry with him for spending so much time in front of his computer! Jill's the sporty one in the family, and plays volleyball and tennis. She's friendly and outgoing, and is always out at the weekends, either playing in a match, or shopping with friends. I hope Paul will start going out more soon, but he says he doesn't want to. He's very shy. Still, at least they both like swimming,

and go twice a week. Neither of them likes reading much, but they both enjoy going to the cinema, and sometimes do that together.

🌀 1.3

1

Ralph and I both like playing sport, but neither of us likes watching it on TV!

2

All of my friends are Linkin Park fans.

3

None of us is very patient.

🌀 1.4

1 Both of us
2 All of them
3 Neither of them
4 None of us
5 Many of you

UNIT 02

🌀 2.1

L = Larry; M = Maria; K = Keith

L: For most of us, shopping is a leisure time activity. However, this is not true for everyone. On the show this morning are two guests who have a medical problem called compulsive shopping disorder. This means they can't *stop* shopping. In fact some experts think that 10% of British people are compulsive shoppers. Yes, an amazing 10%! Maria Lomax, you've had this problem for over ten years. How did it start?

M: Well, Larry, I didn't know it was a problem until I realised I couldn't stop buying things. I wasn't happy unless I was shopping. Then I started having money problems, and this caused arguments with my husband. He finally made me go to see a doctor.

L: Really! That's awful. And how bad did the problem get?

M: Well, to give you an example, when I went into a shop and found a top I liked, I used to buy it. But not one top. I'd buy one in every colour. I have 50 bags of clothes in my wardrobe. That's 50 bags of clothes that I've never worn. I also have 135 pairs of shoes.

L: 135 pairs of shoes!! Really? Amazing. OK, can I now turn to you, Keith. Can you tell us about your problem. Do you buy too many clothes?

K: Clothes, no ... But I *do* have 104 pairs of trainers. Most of them I've never worn.

L: You're joking! Do you do a lot of sport then?

K: No. I go running twice a week, but I just like trainers. But the problem started with books and CDs. I bought lots of CDs – hundreds of them. And I also bought books. I have thousands of books that I have never read. My wife started complaining about all the CDs and books. I stopped buying them. But then I turned my attention to trainers. That caused more problems between my wife and me. She told me that I had to stop. I had to stop buying things or she would leave me.

L: And did she leave you?

K: No, I'm happy to say she didn't leave me.

L: That's good. Compulsive shopping disorder is generally a woman's condition, though, isn't it? Maria?

M: I don't know, to be honest.

K: A lot of people think that but studies show that although there *are* more women compulsive shoppers, the number of men with the problem is increasing.

L: And do you think women and men buy different things? I mean, do women buy more clothes?

K: Yes, I think there is a difference between men and women. I think women tend to buy clothes and shoes, while men buy CDs, tools, electrical goods.

L: Well, that is very interesting. I'd like to thank both of my guests for coming on the show and talking to us about a growing problem. *[fade out]*

2.2

food and drink
toiletries and cosmetics
electrical goods
market research
special offer
good value
Far East

Unit 03

3.1

S = Socrates, C = Claire, W = Waiter
Part 1

S: Have you been here before?

C No, I haven't.

S: Well, I think you'll like it. It's the best Greek restaurant I've ever been to outside Greece.

C: I've never eaten Greek food before

S: So prepare to enjoy yourself! You're going to love it! Shall I order several dishes for us? Then you can try some different things.

C: Oh ... er ... OK.

S: Waiter!

W: Are you ready to order, Sir?

S: Yes. Could we have the...um...souvlaki and spetsofai, please?

W: Certainly. Any salads with that?

S: I think we'll have tzatziki and... a Greek salad, please.

W: Would you like anything to drink?

S: Shall we have some wine, Claire?

C: That would be lovely. Red, please.

S: A bottle of the house red, please.

W: Thank you, Sir.

3.2
Part 2

C: Mm, this souvlaki is delicious, Socrates. What meat is it, exactly?

S: It's pork, actually ... You haven't tried the spetsofai yet. That's the spicy sausage with peppers.

C: It's too spicy for me, I'm afraid. I don't like hot food.

S: Oh, sorry! I didn't know.

C: No problem. You like it, anyway. Er ... what's this?

S: Tzatziki. Yoghurt and cucumber salad.

C: Let's see ... Ugh! No! ... They've put too much garlic in! Could I have some water, please?

S: They haven't put enough in for me. I love garlic!

C: Well, I don't like garlic much, actually. The Greek salad and the souvlaki are lovely, though.

S: Well, I'm glad you enjoyed some of the food.

W: Would you like to see the dessert menu, Sir?

S: Claire, would you like something?

C: Oh no, thanks! I couldn't eat another thing! Could I have a coffee, please?

S: OK. Could we have two filter coffees, please?... Oh, and could you bring us the bill, too?

W: Certainly, Sir.

3.3
1 would
2 shall
3 enough
4 juice

3.4
1
would
count
could
book
2
shall
champagne
chant
pancake
3
enough
rough
cough
hungry
4
juice
root
boil
fruit

UNIT 04

🔊 4.1
I = Interviewer, M = Megan
Part 1

I: I'd like to welcome Megan Bradshaw to the studio this morning. Megan, thanks for coming in.

M: Good morning David, and thank you for inviting me.

I: Megan, you're a firefighter. Now there aren't many women firefighters, are there?

M: Well, the answer to your question is yes and no. Most firefighters *are* men but that is changing. There are now over 200 women firefighters in London.

I: Over 200! I'm surprised! And how long have you been a firefighter?

M: About four years now. I joined the fire service as soon as I left school.

I: Really!? So, what does the job involve? What do you have to do?

M: Well, most people think that firefighters only put out fires! Obviously we have to put out fires, but only one in five calls is actually for help at a fire.

I: Really? Only one in five? So if only one in five calls is about fires, what do you do most of the time?

M: We rescue a lot of people and animals. So, for example, we go out to road and train accidents. And because these are accidents we do a lot of first aid, and look after any injured people.

I: I see. And what do you do if you aren't fighting fires or at the scene of an accident. Do you just sit around drinking coffee?

M: No … not at all! It's a very hard job so you have to be very fit. We do a lot of fitness training – we train every day. We also check the fire engine and our equipment.

I: I see. And what other work do you do?

M: Education is a big part of the job.

I: Education?

M: Yes, fighting fire is also about education. We go out a lot. To schools and to businesses. We give a lot of talks about safety – it's important that people know about fires and how to stop them. So, there isn't much time for coffee!

🔊 4.2
Part 2

I: … You seem to be busy all the time! So, do you enjoy the job?

M: Yeah, I enjoy rescuing someone from a fire or a car accident. It feels great when you help someone. I also like giving talks in schools, and talking to the children. I work in a team of six people and that relationship with my team mates is also important to me. The variety of work is good as well.

I: And are there any things you don't like about your work?

M: Yes, some. The job is hard, physically and emotionally. The most difficult part of the job is when someone dies in a fire or a car accident. That is hard, very hard. If that happens, we are all upset for days. Yes, that is still the most difficult part of the job.

I: Yes, that must be terrible.

M: Yes, yes it is. Oh, and I really don't like writing reports. We have to write a lot of them … on fires and accidents. No, I don't like that but it's part of the job.

I: Well, Megan, thank you very much for coming in this morning. It's been very interesting finding out about the work you do …

🔊 4.3
I = Interviewer; Y = Yoko; V = Viktor

I: It is the biggest change in the work environment for over 100 years. 'Teleworking', using computers, email and the phone so that you don't need to be in an office. You can work from anywhere but most teleworkers work from home. And it's growing fast! My guests on the programme this morning are both teleworkers. Yoko and Viktor, welcome.

Y/V: Thank you.

I: So Viktor, why did you decide to work from home?

V: I was working an eight-hour day and spending four hours travelling. One evening I was sitting on the train when I said to myself, 'Enough! I want to work to live not live to work!' So I left the company and went freelance. That was two years ago, and since then I've spent more time with my wife and our two children. I'm not so tired, as I don't spend so much time travelling. I've also joined a gym, so it was a great decision.

I: Yoko, did you make the decision for the same reason?

Y: Not exactly. I'm a single parent, and I was working in an office until 5.30 every day. My kids were coming home from school alone, to an empty house. François is nine and Georges is seven. I wanted someone to be there but babysitters were expensive. Then while I was talking to a friend about it one day her husband came in, and he told me about teleworking. He gave me the addresses of a couple of websites, and I did some research. Then I talked it over with my boss, and we agreed to change some of my work duties, so that I could stay with the company, but work from home. I've been much happier since I made the change, as I'm also there for my boys if they get ill.

🔊 4.4
1 I was working an eight-hour day.
2 My kids were coming home from school alone.

4.5

1

was

was

was

I was working

I was working

I was working an eight-hour day.

2

were

were

were

My kids were coming

My kids were coming

My kids were coming home from school alone.

4.6

1

We were discussing marketing plans when the lights went out.

2

Sam was writing his report when his boss called.

Unit 05

5.1

D = Dave, H = Heidi, B = Beret

D: Right, then, girls! Have you decided what you're going to do to get fit? How about you, Heidi?

H: Yeah, I have, actually. I really like water sports, but want to try something different, so I'm going to have a go at underwater rugby!

D: Oh, Heidi you're joking! Isn't that for men? A bit violent for you!

H: No, it isn't. Dave, why do you think 'girls' can't do anything?!
'Girls can't play football, you know. It's not a sport for girls. Heidi, do you think it's good for 'girls' to play basketball?' Wake up, Dave! 'Girls' can play golf, 'girls' can swim, 'girls' can climb mountains, girls can ...

D: OK, OK, I'm sorry!

H: Anyway, back to underwater rugby ... Not many people play it, so most teams are mixed – men and WOMEN.

B: Well, I've never heard of it. Rugby in water? I just can't imagine it.

H: Yeah, well ... You wear a mask and snorkel and flippers, and you use a ball ... a ball filled with salt water.

B: And what do they do for the, err, the you know, the goal?

H: Oh, they use a heavy metal bin. A bin is placed at either end of the pool, and that's the goal.

D: Aren't you afraid of getting hurt?

H: Oh, Dave! Stop it!

D: Stop what?

H: Stop the *'aren't you afraid of getting hurt?'* Anyway, no I am not afraid of getting hurt. You play the game under *water*. So you can't really hurt yourself. I'm having my first lesson tomorrow evening.

D: Have you got all the gear?

H: Not yet. I'm going to go to the sports shop later.

B: Sounds fun.

H: Yeah. And how about you, Beret? Are you going to do anything?

B: I'm not sure yet. I might play volleyball, or tennis. I enjoyed those sports at school.

D: Why don't you come with me and try something new? I'm going to play sepak takraw!

H/B: What?

D: Sepak takraw. It's really popular in Asia. It's rather like volleyball, only you can't hit the ball with your hands or arms. You use your legs and feet.

H: You use your legs and feet! That sounds impossible!

D: Yeah, it's pretty hard to do, and you've got to be quite fit.

H: Come with me instead, Beret! We'll have some fun.

B: To be honest, Heidi, I'm not a very good swimmer. I don't like going underwater. So, I might try sepak ... whatsit, especially if it's like volleyball.

D: Well, we're meeting at the gym on Wednesday, at 7pm.

B: OK, I've decided. I'm going to try sepak takraw.

5.2

1

largest

cyclist

fastest

2

challenging

marathon

badminton

3

ski

beat

easy

team

4

win

instruct

business

5

play

break

race

UNIT 06

🔊 6.1

L = Landlady, T = Tenant

L: Right, I'll show you your room. It's not very big but it's clean and bright. You've got a little TV and you've got a nice view out of the window here.

T: Oh yeh, that's nice.

L: And you share the bathroom with the gentleman who lives in the next room.

T: That's fine for me.

L: Now, there are a few house rules that you have to follow.

T: OK.

L: This is a non-smoking house, so I'm afraid you can't smoke in any of the rooms.

T: That's OK, I don't smoke anyway.

L: That's good. And you can cook your food downstairs in the kitchen, but not after eight o'clock in the evening because that's when I cook my dinner.

T: That's no problem. Anything else?

L: No, not really. Do you have any questions?

T: Yes. It's a bit cold in here. Is the heating off?

L: Yes, don't worry about that. It comes on at six in the morning and goes off at nine when everyone goes to work. Then it comes on again at six o'clock at night. The heating bills are included in the rent. Is that OK with you?

T: Yes, that's fine.

L: Good. Well, I'm sure you'll be very comfortable here.

T: So how much do I have to pay in advance?

L: The first two months rent please.

T: Two months? Oh, OK.

UNIT 07

🔊 7.1

Conversation 1

W = woman; M = man

W: Hello, there! Are you OK?

M: No, not really. I've got a terrible headache, and a sore throat. It hurts when I swallow.

W: Oh, you poor thing! Have you taken anything for it?

M: Well, I took an aspirin, but it still hurts.

W: Maybe you should go to see a doctor.

M: Mm, I don't like going to the doctor's.

W: Well, you ought to go if your headache's still bad. And why don't you take some throat sweets? Here, I've got some in my bag ... Go on, try them.

M: Thanks. Mmm, yeah, that's nice.

Conversation 2

M = man; W = woman

M: Hey! Are you OK?

W: Aah! Oh dear! I feel really dizzy!

M: Here, why don't you sit down for a minute? Shall I get you a glass of water?

W: What...? Oh, yes, please. Thanks.

M: Here you are. Is that better?

W: Mm, yes, a little, thanks. I don't know what happened. I just suddenly felt very weak, and couldn't stand up.

M: Perhaps you ought to see the nurse. Have you eaten anything today?

W: Well, I had a piece of toast on the way to the office.

M: And it's now five in the afternoon! You should eat something!

🔊 7.2

I = Interviewer, A = Dr Aziz

Part 1

I: I'm delighted to welcome to the programme today Dr Emil Aziz, who specialises in Down's Syndrome research.

A: Thank you for inviting me.

I: Thank you for coming. Now, Dr Aziz, I've read that one in every 1,000 babies born in the UK will have Down's Syndrome or DS.

A: Yes, yes, that's correct. About one in every thousand.

I: And do you think that people ... well, that *most* people really understand this condition?

A: Well, Georgia, one of the problems is that people often think that Down's Syndrome is a mental illness. It is not. It is a condition that occurs before birth. It is *not* a disease, the person is not *ill*, and so does not *'suffer'* from the condition.

I: But they do have learning difficulties, don't they?

A: Well, that's not an easy question to answer. Yes, a person with Down's Syndrome will have *some* difficulty in learning. But some people will have more problems and some people will have less. *Most* people will learn to talk, read and write, and *many* go to ordinary schools and lead enjoyable, semi-independent lives.

I: That's important to know. And how about physical problems? People with Down's Syndrome usually have physical disabilities, don't they?

A: Ah, another mistaken belief! They *do* have certain physical characteristics that make them look different. For example, their faces may look different. So, people often think this means they are also stupid.

I: Really?

A: And people sometimes think they can't do things like walk and play games. But the public need to realise that people with DS just *look* different. They are *people*, however, like you and me. Most of them are very healthy, active and strong

I: Yes, that's important to know. And ... talking of being healthy, active and strong, can you tell us about these football clubs here in London?

A: Yes, there are three football teams in London: the Fulham Badgers, QPR Tiger Cubs and Charlton Upbeats. They are all doing very well, and the players are enthusiastic and hardworking. I've been told that they're the only teams whose players are never late for training!

I: That's fantastic! So, doesn't anyone with DS ever have a physical disability?

A: Yes, sometimes, but this is often caused by another problem, not by DS itself. Thanks to research, and the wonderful work done by many charities and support groups throughout the UK, children with Down's Syndrome can get the right care and education to lead active lives, and an increasing number are able to then work in the community.

🔊 7.3
Part 2

I: Can you give us an example, Dr Aziz, of someone who has done just that?

A: Certainly! The story of Ruth Cromer is well-known to anyone involved with DS. She attended school, succeeded in learning to read and write, did not listen to teachers who told her she couldn't do things, and taught herself to type. She became an actress, and has been on TV several times. She also writes articles and gives speeches about the condition.

I: Amazing! Dr Aziz, that was extremely interesting. Thank you for coming to talk to us, and making us more aware that people with Down's Syndrome are *people*, first and foremost.

A: Thank *you* for inviting me, Georgia.

🔊 7.4
central
musical
industrial
physical

unbelievable
enjoyable
reliable
curable

🔊 7.5
1
The flat is really central.
2
Most kids are pretty musical.
3
That part of town is really industrial.
4
Rugby's a very physical game.
5
That's unbelievable!
6
The course was enjoyable.
7
The cars they make are very reliable.
8
A lot of diseases are curable.

UNIT 08

🔊 8.1
1 crossroads
2 roundabout
3 underground
4 playground
5 traffic lights
6 sports ground
7 town hall
8 police station
9 traffic warden
10 sports programme
11 town centre
12 police woman

🔊 8.2
Go out of the railway station, turn left and then take the first right by the church on the corner. Go straight down the road until you come to a crossroads with some traffic lights. Turn left, go past the monument on your right and then you'll come to a roundabout. Go right at the roundabout and you'll find it at the bottom of the road, just to the left of the bridge.

🔊 8.3
A = woman, B = man

A: Excuse me?

B: Yes.

A: How do I get to the town hall? I'm afraid I'm lost.

B: The town hall. Let me think. OK. Go out of the park, turn left and walk past the playground. After a few minutes you'll come to a roundabout. Let me think. Yes, at the roundabout go straight on until you come to a bridge over the river at the bottom of the road. Stay on this side of the river and turn right. Go straight on for a while and then I think you'll see the town hall on the next corner.

A: Thank you very much.

🔊 8.4
G = Greg; A = Anna
Part 1

A: So how was your road trip on the famous Route 66 then?

G: Anna, it was absolutely fantastic. I loved it. I loved every minute of it.

A: Tell me more. Where did you start?

G: Well, we hired a car and started in Chicago. Then we drove over to Los Angeles on the west coast.

A: Wow! How many miles did you drive?

G: In total ... in total it was 2,448 miles.

A: 2,448? Really!?

G: Yep!

A: And how long did that take you?

G: 16 days.

A: 16 days. Wait … that's , err … that's about 150 miles a day, right? That's not very fast.

G: No, it isn't but Route 66 isn't a big motorway. It's only a normal road.

A: Oh, right.

G: And because, you can't drive fast in America, you see more.

A: You really had a good time, didn't you?

G: I did, I did, yeah. It was a fantastic holiday … a really good one.

8.5
Part 2

A: You really had a good time, didn't you?

G: I did, I did, yeah. It was a fantastic holiday … a really good one. [fade]

A: And what were the best bits?

G: That's a difficult question. We saw and did a lot on those 16 days. Hmm …. I really loved St Louis. St Louis is a pretty big city on the Mississippi River.

A: That's the biggest river in the US, isn't it?

G: Yeah, it's big, really big. We went out on a paddleboat and we saw that famous arch.

A: That famous arch!? What famous arch?

G: The Arch of St Louis – it's a famous monument. It's almost 200 metres high.

A: Wow, that is high. And what other things did you see?

G: Well, we went to this amazing place near Amarillo, in Texas. We wanted to visit this crazy monument called Cadillac Ranch.

A: Cadillac Ranch?

G: Yeah, it was built by a Texan millionaire. It's made of ten cars – they are all cadillacs. They are buried nose down in the ground.

A: Sounds crazy.

G: Yeah crazy but cool. And you can put graffiti on them. Can you imagine that? You can cover them in graffiti! … After that we went to the Grand Canyon National Park to see the canyon.

A: Oh, the Grand Canyon. I've always wanted to go there.

G: It was wonderful. It's beautiful … very beautiful. Imagine this place – it's 227 miles long and in some place it's a mile deep.

UNIT 09

9.1

… And on a happier note, a young scientist from Yorkshire has discovered a clever way to help people in the poorer countries of Africa. Emily Cummins, aged 21, has invented a fridge that works without electricity, and she did it in her Grandad's garden shed!

The fridge works using the sun's energy. Emily won £5,000 from York Merchant Adventurers for her design and took a year off from her studies to go to Africa and test out her idea. She helped make more than 50 electricity-free refrigerators during the trip, using such materials as recycled car parts, and the locals named her 'The Fridge Lady'. Emily said that she hopes to continue inventing, and making changes for a better world.

More good news now on the little boy who went missing yesterday. Four-year old Tommy Jones has been found alive and well. He went missing from his home near Burnham Woods yesterday afternoon with his two Labrador puppies. His family were worried that he had run away. However, searchers found both him and the dogs safe this morning. They were fast asleep under a tree. Tommy told his mother that the puppies had kept him warm all night. He is now resting at home. His mother, Anna, said that she's delighted he's safe, but she's going to lock the garden gate in future.

… And finally, the weather forecast. Heavy rain will spread across the south of England today. Floods are expected in some parts so if you are driving, be very careful. Telephone the Environment Agency Floodline for the latest warnings.

9.2

study   shortage
extinct   explore   invent   protect   research
energy   natural
solution   pollution   resources
experiment   investigate   participant
population

UNIT 10

10.1
A = boy; B = girl

A: So what subjects are you going to choose next year?

B: It's difficult. I can't decide. What about you?

A: Well, I know the subjects I'm *not* going to choose.

B: Really?

A: Yes! I don't really like history.

B: No?

A: No. I'm interested in the future, not the past.

B: Oh. I quite like history. In fact, I think I might take history next year. I'm interested in the past. It was more exciting than the present, anyway.

A: Why don't you do Latin as well, then?

B: Oh no! I don't know why people study Latin.

A: No?

B: No. It's a dead language. Nobody speaks it. But what about you? If you're interested in the future, what about IT?

A: IT? Are you joking? I can't see the point of IT classes.

B: No? Why?

A: Everyone knows how to use a computer these days.

B: That's not true. A lot of people can't use a computer.

A: Well, I know how to use one, so why study it?

B: Because it might help you to find a job. In fact, I think I might take IT as well as history. That's a good idea. This is great! I've made three decisions already.

🔊 **10.2**

1

change cheap approach chemistry

2

check attention optional share

3

relationship traditional machine teacher

🔊 **11.1**

Speaker 1

Well, we're 3 couples, actually. None of us has children, so there's no need to worry about them falling into the water! We rent a small yacht every summer, and when you share the cost, it's not very expensive. It's great having the freedom to go where we want, and do some great sailing.

Speaker 2

I want to relax on holiday, and not run around after the kids all the time, so a place with a babysitting service and organised activities for children is my first choice. To be honest, I'm not the outdoor type, who likes sitting in a tent. I prefer the comfort of a hotel bar and restaurant. Internet access is also useful, so that I can check my emails.

Speaker 3

We like a certain amount of comfort, but don't want the fixed timetable of hotel breakfasts. So we rent a little place near the beach every year. It's got cooking facilities, and a barbecue outside. It's quite popular, though, so we book well in advance!

Speaker 4

Hotels are nice, but to be honest, we prefer sleeping in a tent! It's actually quite comfortable! OK, you need to organise the equipment, but you don't need to make a booking or pay a deposit. You choose where you want to go, and if you change your mind, you don't pay a cancellation fee. It's a lot cheaper!

UNIT 11

🔊 **11.2**

Conversation 1

R = Receptionist, M = Mr Wiseman

R: Reception. Can I help you?

M: Hello. Mr Wiseman here ... Room 214. I'm not happy with my room. Could you give me another one?

R: I would if there was one available, Sir, but I'm afraid we're fully booked this weekend. What seems to be the problem? Perhaps we can sort it out.

M: The air conditioning's on too high. It's freezing in here.

R: No problem, Sir. Just turn it down.

M: I might be able to if I could find the switch!

R: It's on the wall by the door.

M: Well, I can't ... Oh, wait ... just a second. Yes, found it! I'd put my coat over it! Thanks very much.

Conversation 2

R = Receptionist, W = Mrs Arnold

R: Reception.

W: Oh, hello. I'm Mrs Arnold, from room 304. Could you send someone up, please? My husband's stuck in the bathroom.

R: Oh, dear! Is the door locked, Madam?

W: No, it's stuck. I've tried pushing it but it won't move.

R: Right. Wait a moment. I'll see if someone's available ... Jeff? Can you send someone up to 304? The bathroom door's stuck ... Really? Well, can't you go? ... I see. Well, as soon as you can, then ...
Mrs Arnold?

W: Yes?

R: I'm afraid my colleague's very busy right now. It'll be about ten minutes.

W: But what are we going to do? My husband's the main speaker at the charity dinner, and it starts in five minutes! Call the manager, please!

R: I'll see what I can do, Mrs Arnold.

Conversation 3

R = Receptionist, M = Mr Dominguez

R: Hello, Reception.

M: Oh, er, hello. It's Mr Dominguez here, in the executive suite. I wonder if you could help me.

R: If I can, Sir, certainly. What's the problem?

M: Oh, no problem exactly. It's our wedding anniversary, and I didn't have time to buy my wife a present. Is there anything I could order from here?

R: If I were you, I'd order a big bouquet of red roses. We have an arrangement with a local flower shop. I could phone them for you.

M: Lovely idea. Could you order them for me then and have them sent up to the room?

R: Certainly, Sir.

M: Great! Thanks a lot.

🔊 **11.3**

used to

usually

useful

beautiful

cute

umbrella

uninteresting

summer

suntan

done

🔊 **11.4**

Double 0 – 3 – 0   2 – 5 – 1 – 0   3 – 6 – 7 – 5 – 4

2 – 4 – 2 – 1 – 0   8 – 9 – 5 – 6 – 7

6 – 9 – 7 – 9   0 – 1 – 0 – 2 – 5 – 9

Mr Kendall. That's K – E – N – D – A – L – L

Mrs Tsiakos. That's T – S – I – A – K – O – S

Miss Pandhi. That's P – A – N – D – H – I

UNIT 12

🔊 12.1

R = Receptionist, T = Tina Morrison

R: Hello, the Ashley Corporation.
T: Could I speak to Mr Khalil please?
R: Who's speaking, please?
T: It's Tina Morrison.
R: Oh, I'm sorry, Mr Khalil is working at home today. Can I take a message?
T: Yes, please. Could you tell him that I called? It's Tina Morrison. It's about our meeting next Thursday. I'm sorry but I'm going to be away on business that day, so can we change the meeting to Friday? The same time, three o'clock at my office. He knows where it is. If there are any problems, tell him to call my mobile on 08897 6576548. Thanks.
R: I'll pass that message on to him.
T: Thanks, bye!

🔊 12.2

1 polite possible
2 possible common
3 common comfortable
4 obtain opinion
5 hole hold
6 operation remote

🔊 12.3

Thank you for calling Lucibello Bank. You now have four options. To check your current bank balance, press one. For information about opening a new account, press two. For technical support with our internet banking services, press three. For all other queries or to speak to an adviser, press four.

[beep]

Thank you for calling Lucibello Bank. Your call is important to us. A member of our dedicated customer services team will be available to speak to you shortly. Please note that calls may be recorded for training purposes. Unfortunately, we are currently experiencing a high volume of calls and your call is being held in a queue. Your wait time at the moment is approximately 12 minutes. You may find it more convenient to call back later. Thank you for calling Lucibello Bank. Your call is important to us.

UNIT 13

🔊 13.1

B = Brad, A = Abha

B: Have you found the website, Abha?
A: Yes, here it is. Now, let's see what's on... Films showing now ... There's that new thriller, *Run and Hide*, directed by Antonio Torres. Andreas Dumas is in it. It's supposed to be good.
B: Mm, I've heard it's nothing special. Kate went and saw it last Friday, and she said she was bored. It was too predictable, she said. She knew who the killer was long before the end.
A: OK ... Well, then how about *The Mansford Saga*? Jeffrey Hinds is in it. Mm, I like him!
B: What's it about?
A: It's a family drama, set in 1860. They're rich but they lose their money, and then have to struggle to survive. Sounds interesting. Zena Williams is in it too.
B: It sounds boring to me! Isn't there anything lighter on, like a comedy, for instance?
A: Right! Here's one. *Mr Pickles*, starring Thierry Dumand and Catherine Pickard. Wasn't he in that film we saw a couple of weeks ago?
B: *The Partygoer*, yes. He's good. Shall we go and see that, then?
A: OK. It's on at the Palace, in Walker Street.
B: That's not far. We can walk there. What time does it start?
A: The first showing is at 3, and then there's another one at 5.30.
B: Let's go to the 5.30 one. Then I'll take you to that nice Italian place afterwards. They do a great carbonara.
A: OK, Brad. Great.

🔊 13.2

excited
bored
tired
disappointed
interested
starred
amazed
treated
played
surprised
directed
recorded

UNIT 14

🔊 14.1

A: Morning! Have you got everything ready?
B: Of course not. I've only just arrived... What do we need today?
A: Well we have to clean the carpets in the lobby, so we'll need the vacuum cleaner.
B: Where's that, then?
A: Usual place. Under the stairs.
B: Right.
A: And we've got to clean the marble floor in the dining room ...
B: ... so we'll need the mop and the bucket.
A: That's in the cupboard behind the reception area. And we'll also need a cloth because we've got to wipe all the mirrors.

B: And remind me – where do we keep the cloths?

A: In the drawer in the staff room, of course.

B: Oh yeah.

A: And we also need a hammer and some nails because we have to put up a picture.

B: And where do we keep those?

A: Down in the cellar.

B: Oh yes, it's dark down there isn't it? We'll need ... we'll need ... what do you call it? A ... A ...

A: What are you talking about?

B: Well, the light doesn't work down there so we'll need a ... You know. We'll need a ... a ...

🔊 14.2

1 class
2 gave
3 bin
4 pair
5 gold
6 could
7 ban
8 pad
9 goal
10 pouring

🔊 14.3

G = Gianni; J-P = Jean-Paul

G: Hi Jean-Paul! So how was Rachel's trip to Scotland?

J-P: Oh, hi Gianni! Yeah, she had a great time. But she brought me back this really strange present.

G: Really? What's it like?

J-P: Well, it's a bit like a handbag but you wear it round your waist.

G: Round your *waist*?

J-P: Yes. It's made of leather and apparently in Scotland men wear them.

G: Oh I know what it is. Does it have three tassels on the front?

J-P: Tassels?

G: Yes, extra bits of leather that hang down.

J-P: Yes, it does.

G: It's called a sporran. It's a traditional part of Scottish dress. You wear it with a kilt.

J-P: A *sporran*? How do you know that?

Unit 15

🔊 15.1

C = Carlos; Y = Yelena

C: So, you're moving to Prague. But I thought you liked living here.

Y: I do, but if Miguel and I get married, I want him to know something about my country, and to understand the culture, the language, and so on.

C: Can't you just go for a holiday?

Y: You don't learn much from a holiday, Carlos! No, we've decided to go for two or three years, and then see where we'd prefer to live and bring up a family.

C: OK, but the cost of living's really high in Prague, isn't it?

Y: Not much higher than it is here in Argentina. Also, unemployment has fallen there in the last few years, and is lower than it is here. So, I think we'll find jobs fairly easily.

C: But the economy's doing better here now, though, and you get paid quite well, don't you?

Y: Yes, Carlos. It's not that I don't like it here. I'm happy, and have a good quality of life, but things are getting more expensive, and it's not easy to buy a house here. In the Czech Republic, house prices are generally cheaper, and so are cars.

C: Perhaps, but eating out is cheaper here, and as you told me, you can't beat the night life here!

Y: True, but I'm thinking more of the future. The salaries are higher in Prague. I could get paid more for doing the same job as I'm doing now.

C: Do you think Miguel will like it there?

Y: I have no idea! That's why I want him to try it. Don't worry, Carlos! You're not going to lose your best friend! I just think it's important for us to see where we are both happier, and we can't do that if we don't try living in both countries. Anyway, you can come and visit!

C: Yeah, I suppose you're right.

🔊 15.2

P = Primo, I = Isabel

P: What are you doing, Isabel?

I: Oh, just paying some bills.

P: What, you're paying them online? I didn't know you could do that.

I: Yes, it's easy, too. You can do it through your bank, or the service itself. I pay my phone bill to the phone company's bill payment service on its website.

P: Really? It must save you a lot of time!

I: Yes, and it's good for the environment, too. You don't use any paper! I pay my mortgage and electricity through the online banking service. I just order the bank to transfer the amount each month.

P: Is it safe, though? I mean, don't you worry about someone stealing your bank details and then taking all your money?

I: Well, there are some risks, but we change ID numbers and security codes fairly often, so they're difficult to copy. You should try it, Primo. It would be much easier for you.

P: Mm, perhaps I'll try it myself. I hate standing in the queue for hours waiting to pay the electricity bill! And then I often can't understand what the cashier says! The Scottish accent is not easy!

I: I know! This way it only takes you a few minutes, and no need to talk!

P: Sounds great!

🔊 15.3

1

<u>Buy</u> a house when the <u>price</u> is <u>right</u>, and pay your <u>bills</u> onl<u>ine</u>.

2

Take out a <u>loan</u> to buy your <u>own home</u>, then <u>owe</u> the bank money until you <u>grow old</u>.

3

Twenty-five <u>pounds</u> for a meal may not <u>sound</u> much but is a large <u>amount</u> for a pizza.

4

I got <u>paid</u> a good <u>wage</u> for my job in <u>sales</u>, and was able to <u>save</u> for a holiday in <u>Wales</u>.

UNIT 16

🔊 16.1

A: So what kind of party is it going to be? It's your birthday, isn't it?

B: Yes, it's my 21st birthday, so I want something big and noisy.

A: With lots of people? How many do you want to invite?

B: Oh, at least a hundred.

A: OK. And what sort of venue do you want? Have you seen somewhere you like?

B: Hmm. I don't know. Have you got any suggestions?

A: I know a really good new nightclub in a shopping mall just out of town.

B: Oh no. I don't think so. Can you think of anywhere else?

A: Well, there's also a really good converted warehouse near the beach. You can get at least a hundred people in there.

B: That sounds great.

A: And are you going to serve any food? How about a cold buffet?

B: Yeah, a cold buffet's good.

A: And what kind of music would you like?

B: Well, definitely not background music. I want a really good DJ and I want it to be loud.

A: No problem. And what time do you want the party to finish? It will be late, won't it?

B: No earlier than three.

A: Shall we say three to four in the morning?

B: Yeah, that's great.

🔊 16.2

1

A: With lots of people?

B: Oh yes, at least a hundred.

2

A: How about a cold buffet?

B: Yeah, a cold buffet's good.

3

A: Shall we say three to four in the morning?

B: Yeah, that's great.

🔊 16.3

1 Where did you go last night?
2 Did you see what she was wearing?
3 Why were you so rude to him?
4 Have you been here before?
5 How many people here do you know?
6 Are you going to eat something?
7 Who's that man in the sunglasses near the bar?
8 Do you have the time?

🔊 16.4

Now, this room contains the famous Bayeux Tapestry. As you can see, at this end it shows the events leading to the Norman invasion of England in 1066. As we walk round, you'll see the Normans' sea journey to England, the Battle of Hastings itself and the death of King Harold. We are not sure exactly when the tapestry was made but it dates from the 11th century. One legend says that it was made by William the Conqueror's wife, Queen Matilda. However, many historians now think that King William's brother paid for the tapestry to be made. This is the original tapestry, but there is also a copy at the Museum of Reading in England. Right, are there any questions so far?

ANSWER KEY

UNIT 01

VOCABULARY People you know

A
1 brother;
2 flatmate;
3 dad;
4 housewife;
5 cousins;
6 colleagues

B
1 impatient;
2 stupid;
3 plain;
4 unfit;
5 mean;
6 uncaring

C
1 patient;
2 fit;
3 mean;
4 clever;
5 uncaring;
6 attractive, plain, caring;

GRAMMAR Question formation

A
1 Question: When did you start learning English?
Example answer: Two years ago.
2 Question: How long have you known your best friend?
Example answer: Twelve years.
3 Question: What is your favourite food?
Example answer: Vegetable lasagne.
4 Question: Do you like Madonna?
Example answer: Yes, I do / No, not really.
5 Question: How much do you pay to go to the cinema in your country?
Example answer: Eight euros.
6 Question: Is your hair dark or fair?
Example answer: It's dark.
7 Question: Why do you like your best friend?
Example answer: Because she's honest, and we like the same things.
8 Question: How old are you? Do you still go to school? Or do you work?
Example answer: I'm 23, and I work in a bank.

B
1 Why do you like him?
2 How long have you been waiting?
3 Did you like Kerry's new boyfriend?
4 When did you meet your wife?
5 How do you make that delicious spaghetti dish?
6 Where are you from?

DEVELOPING CONVERSATIONS Responding naturally

A
1 Bangalore, in India.
2 Two weeks.
3 Yes, I've got one brother and two sisters.
4 Yes, I am. Business Studies at the university.
5 Yes, I do. I share a flat with another student.
6 No, I don't. He's really untidy and mean.

B
1 Where are you from?
Example answer: Okinawa
2 How long have you been studying English?
Example answer: Three years.
3 Do you like the language?
Example answer: It's OK.
4 Do you get on with your classmates?
Example answer: Yes, they're good fun.
5 Do you live near your language school?
Example answer: Not very near.

LISTENING

A
1 c;   2 e;   3 b;   4 a;   5 d

B
Speaker 1 D; Speaker 2 A; Speaker 3 C

C
1 d;   2 b;   3 f;   4 a;   5 e;   6 c

GRAMMAR Present simple

A

fact	regular occurrence / habit
1	3
2	4
5	6

B/C

never	hardly ever	sometimes	usually	always
0%				100%
	not very often	quite often		

D
1 I often go to the cinema at the weekend.
2 How often do you visit your grandparents?
3 They go to the local gym twice a week.
4 I meet up with my old school friends two or three times a year.
5 Do you sometimes need to speak English at work?
6 David quite often visits his sister in Toronto.
7 I sometimes hear Rachel arguing with her flatmate.
8 I hardly ever see Wendy any more.

E
1 grow
2 stay
3 seems
4 believe
5 don't eat
6 are
7 live
8 studies
9 marries
10 has

READING

A
1 c;   2 a;   3 b;   4 b

B
1 F;   2 T;   3 F;   4 F;   5 T;   6 F

C
1 keeps;
2 human;
3 paints;
4 spend;
5 plays;
6 family

GRAMMAR Similarities and contrasts
1 both;
2 whereas/but;
3 both, neither;
4 All;
5 Neither;
6 None, all;
7 whereas/but;
8 whereas/but

LISTENING

Example answers:
Similarities: They both like swimming and going to the cinema.
Differences: Jill is tall and slim, whereas Paul is short and overweight; Jill goes out a lot and does sport, but Paul stays at home and plays on his computer.

VOCABULARY Character and habits
A
1 friendly; 3 calm; 5 honest;
2 neat; 4 clever; 6 kind

B
1 f; 2 d; 3 b; 4 c; 5 a; 6 e

C
1 strict; 3 soft; 5 open;
2 wise; 4 determined; 6 patient

DEVELOPING WRITING Character reference
A
1 Two years;
2 kind, caring, calm, and a good student;
3 plays tennis, reads books, and watches films

B
1 Dear 4 In her spare time;
2 Thank you for; 5 I am sure;
3 also; 6 any more information

C
1 B; 2 F; 3 C; 4 A; 5 D; 6 E

D
Example answer:
From: Peter North
To: Mrs Mojewski
Subject: Reference for Rashid Kirijian
Dear Mrs Mojewski,
Thank you your letter, asking me about my student, Rashid Kirijian.
I have known Rashid for two years. He is clever and hardworking, friendly and polite. He is good at Polish, and wants to practise speaking the language, as he is hoping to be a translator. In his spare time, Rashid likes playing basketball and swimming. He plays in a water polo team three times a week.
I think you will find him to be good company. I hope you enjoy your time together!
Please write back to me if you need any more information or have any questions.
Yours sincerely,
Peter North

VOCABULARY BUILDER QUIZ 1
A
1 cousin; 3 generous; 5 wise
2 liberal; 4 neighbour;

B
1 healthy; 5 dirty;
2 behaviour; 6 successful;
3 messy; 7 lucky;
4 spice(s); 8 argument

C
1 happy; 3 beautiful; 5 fresh
2 enthusiastic; 4 lucky;

D
1 to; 5 in;
2 for; 6 to;
3 into; 7 with
4 on;

UNIT 02
VOCABULARY
A
mobile phone, watch, hat, camera, tie, coat, laptop

B
1 wide selection 6 thick
2 good quality 7 bright
3 good value 8 reliable
4 suit 9 last
5 smart 10 complicated

C
1 children 3 school 5 play
2 a meal 4 an effort 6 meal

LISTENING
A
1 F; 2 T; 3 F; 4 F; 5 F; 6 T

B
1 Maria's husband told her to go and see a doctor.
2 It has caused problems between Keith and his wife.

DEVELOPING CONVERSATIONS Complimenting
A
1 great/good; 6 Did they have it in any other colours;
2 love
3 did you get it; 7 good / great;
4 Cool; 8 good value;
5 much was it; 9 they have

GRAMMAR Past simple
A
1 c; 2 e; 3 b; 4 d; 5 a

B
1 bought; 4 gave;
2 sold; 5 costs;
3 went, found; 6 spent, saw

C
1 did you go; 6 did you get;
2 was; 7 bought;
3 Did you find; 8 did;
4 didn't have; 9 found;
5 got/did get; 10 didn't you buy

DEVELOPING CONVERSATIONS
Making offers and checking
A
Making offers: Would you like a; Do you want me to; Do you want to
Checking: You don't mind; Are you sure
Responding: Of course; Not at all
Accepting the offer: Thanks; Thanks a lot
1 Would you like a 6 Do you want to
2 Do you want me to 7 You don't mind
3 Are you sure 8 Not at all
4 Of course 9 Thanks a lot/Thanks
5 Thanks/Thanks a lot

GRAMMAR Comparatives

A

1 c;   2 b;   3 a;   4 c;   5 b

B

1 Have you got/Do you have a larger one?
2 Have you got/Do you have anything cheaper?
3 Have you got/Do you have one of a better quality?
4 Have you got/Do you have anything more modern?
5 Have you got/Do you have anything more comfortable?

READING

A

food and drink	clothing	toiletries and cosmetics	electrical goods
wine cheese chicken	shirt trousers skirt	toothbrush face cream lipstick	hairdryer vacuum cleaner dishwasher

B

2

C

1 b;   2 a;   3 a;   4 b

D

1 greater ability;
2 are more interested than men;
3 greater consumers;
4 more popular;
5 most noticeable;
6 younger men;
7 more interested in;
8 more active role

GRAMMAR Passives

A

1 The report found little change in food and drink shopping habits.
2 However, the report found interesting changes in the purchase of toiletries and electrical goods.
3 Cosmetics companies are now targeting men.
4 Women now buy electrical goods more often.
5 The UK is importing cheap clothing from China and the Far East.
6 Children affect many purchasing decisions.

B

2 A man was caught stealing ladies' perfume yesterday.
3 Pleasant aromas are used by shop owners to encourage customers to buy more.
4 The staff of many small shops are being fired due to the economic crisis.
5 The store was opened (by two businessmen) in 1947.
6 The shop's customers are encouraged to buy its products over the Internet.

C

1 was forced;
2 was bought;
3 has been introduced;
4 sells;
5 has been kept

DEVELOPING WRITING An email – informal writing

A

1 c
2 To thank him for her birthday present and to tell him her news.
3 She went shopping
4 Enrique is coming to stay in Milan and they are going on a camping trip.

B

1 went;
2 played;
3 thought;
4 wished;
5 gave;
6 decided;
7 bought;
8 paid

C

Hi, James!; Dear Julie; How are you?; It was great to hear from you again; I wanted to ask you something; Write soon; Take care; Best wishes

D

Example answer:
Hi, Elena!
Thanks for your email. I'm glad you like the top, and enjoyed your birthday. It sounds like you had a good night out! Can't wait to go to some of these night clubs you mention!
Well done with your shopping. I also bought a new sleeping bag last week, and some new climbing shoes. So, don't worry, I won't forget to pack them! My dad's already got me some money in euros, so I'm ready for the trip!
Are we going to the beach? If so, I'll pack my swimming things. Can you think of anything else I need to bring? Let me know. Can't wait to see you!
Take care,
Enrique

VOCABULARY BUILDER QUIZ 2

A

1 unreliable;
2 clever/wise;
3 pretty;
4 tight;
5 uncomfortable;
6 open

B

1 brand;
2 temple;
3 designs;
4 receipt;
5 fine;
6 guide;
7 quality

C

1 d;   2 f;   3 b;   4 a;   5 c;   6 e

D

1 F;   2 T;   3 T;   4 F;   5 F;   6 T

UNIT 03

VOCABULARY Restaurants

A

1 fast food;
2 Japanese;
3 seafood;
4 Mexican;
5 Italian;
6 Chinese

B

1 e;   2 a;   3 b;   4 c;   5 d

C

food	staff and service	describing the restaurant
choice disgusting good selection portions delicious dishes	friendly and polite helpful slow fast and efficient	busy view crowded terrace

D
1 choice, good selection
2 helpful, disgusting
3 busy
4 terrace, view
5 friendly and polite, portions
6 fast and efficient
7 delicious
8 dishes, crowded

DEVELOPING CONVERSATIONS
Suggestions and deciding where to go

A
1 How about that Thai place round the corner?
Well, we could go to that vegetarian restaurant in the square, instead.
2 How about the new sushi bar on Samson Street?
Well, we could go to that Greek restaurant down the road instead.
3 How about that seafood restaurant in the centre?
Well, we could go to The Cooking Pot on James Street instead.

B
1 d;   2 b;   3 e;   4 f;   5 c;   6 a

GRAMMAR Present perfect simple

A
1 d;   2 e;   3 f;   4 c;   5 a;   6 b

B
1 Have you ever eaten
2 Have you been, I've been
3 Have you ever tried
4 I've made
5 has never eaten
6 Have you read

C
1 Have you been, I came, I've never been, Have you visited, I haven't, I went
2 Have you been, I went, Was he

READING

A
A France;   C Ireland;
B Vietnam;   D Austria

B
1 A, C, D;   2 B;   3 A;   4 D;   5 B

C
1 f;   2 h;   3 e;   4 j;   5 b;   6 i;   7 d;
8 a;   9 c;   10 g

D
1 coffee, orange juice, ice cream
2 football team, restaurant, person, Mexican
3 food, ingredients, dishes, colours
4 fruit, fish, water, vegetables, bread
5 fast, spicy, health, junk, frozen
6 reasonable, discount, full, half

GRAMMAR too, not ... enough

A
1 too spicy;   4 chilled enough;
2 too hard;   5 too expensive;
3 cooked enough;   6 not big enough

B
1 haven't been;   4 I've never heard;
2 too slow;   5 wasn't hot enough;
3 Have you tried;   6 has had

C
Answers may vary. Example answers:
The kitchen is too untidy to work in.
The kitchen is too dirty to cook in.
The chef has got too much work.
There isn't enough room to work in *or* The room isn't big enough.

LISTENING

A
Greek restaurant

B
1 tzatziki, spetsofai, souvlaki;
2 wine

C
1 It's too hot / She doesn't like sausage.
2 No, she doesn't. There's too much garlic in it.
3 No, they don't. (They just have coffee.)

D
Socrates is enthusiastic. Claire likes some of it

E
1 c;   2 a;   3 d;   4 b

GRAMMAR Offers, request, permission, suggestions

A
1 c;   2 a;   3 b;   4 d;   5 a;   6 d;
7 c;   8 b

B
1 No, thank you. I don't drink (alcohol). Could you bring me a bottle of sparkling water, please?
2 Could I leave early, please?
3 (To be honest) I don't feel like Chinese / noodles. Could we go for a pizza, instead?
4 Shall I help you look for them, Sir?

VOCABULARY Describing food

A
1 d;   2 f;   3 c;   4 a;   5 e;   6 b

PRONUNCIATION

A
1 could, book;   3 rough, hungry;
2 champagne, pancake; 4 root, fruit

DEVELOPING WRITING A review – a restaurant

A
1 The Flying Fish
2 The Taj Mahal

B

1 (A) delicious. squid soft and juicy, cooked perfectly. (B) tasty and well-prepared. Vindaloo spicy and full of flavour.
2 (A) good. Staff extremely helpful. (B) not good. Staff unfriendly and service slow.
3 (A) room too dark, couldn't see food. (B) pleasant, nicely decorated.
4 (A) reasonable, good value for money. (B) very expensive, disappointing

C

Answers will vary slightly, but students should choose from the following for each section.
Name of restaurant: Answers will vary.
1 quality of food: delicious, full of flavour, well-prepared, tasteless, overcooked
2 the service: friendly and polite, fast, helpful, unfriendly and rude, slow
3 the interior design: modern, tastefully decorated, well-lit, dark, unwelcoming
4 the price: reasonable, good value for money, cheap, too expensive

VOCABULARY BUILDER QUIZ 3

A

1 e;   2 g;   3 b;   4 h;   5 a;   6 c;
7 d;   8 f

B

1 stuffing;   3 service;   5 bookings;
2 painting;   4 allergy;   6 choice

C

1 raw;   3 skins;   5 tip;
2 delicious;   4 incredible;   6 dishes

D

1 in;   3 down;   5 down
2 stall;   4 advance;

UNIT 04

VOCABULARY Jobs and experiences at work

A

1 e;   2 a;   3 b;   4 g;   5 f;   6 h;
7 d;   8 c

B

1 care assistant;   5 secretary;
2 teacher;   6 sales manager;
3 chef;   7 architect;
4 pilot;   8 builder

DEVELOPING CONVERSATIONS Questions about jobs

A

1 b;   2 c;   3 e;   4 f;   5 a;   6 g;   7 d

B

1 What do you do?
2 Do you enjoy it?
3 What are the hours like?
4 Is the money good?
5 Do you get on with the people you work with?

LISTENING

A

1 F (there are over 200 women firefighters in London);
2 F (only one in five calls is about a fire);
3 T;   4 T;   5 F;   6 T

C

The following should be ticked:
rescue people and animals; write reports on accidents; go to fires; check equipment; give first aid; make visits to schools; do fitness training

D

1 Megan enjoys rescuing people.
2 She also likes giving talks in schools talking to the children.
3 The most difficult part of the job is when someone dies.
4 Megan really doesn't like writing reports.

GRAMMAR Present continuous and present simple

A

1 do you do;   6 are you working;
2 Do you work;   7 are designing;
3 run;   8 Do you ever get;
4 do you work;   9 don't work;
5 are working;   10 share

B

1 organise;   5 are preparing;
2 experience;   6 is looking;
3 have;   7 are placing;
4 am checking;   8 is

VOCABULARY Activities at work

A

1 are installing, is causing;
2 am doing, am gaining;
3 am studying;
4 am attending, are advertising

B

1 working on;   4 learning;
2 teaching;   5 organise;
3 advising;   6 negotiate

C

1 negotiate: an evening;
2 do: an offer;
3 run: a negotiation;
4 make: some research

GRAMMAR Plans and wishes for the future

A

1 d;   2 f;   3 a;   4 b;   5 c;   6 e

B

1 I'm not going to go and live abroad.
2 I wouldn't like to work with animals.
3 I'm not thinking of becoming a firefighter.
4 I'm not planning to stay in my present job.
5 I wouldn't like to become a doctor.
6 I'm not expecting to continue studying next year.

C

1 planning to;   5 would like to;
2 am going to;   6 am planning to;
3 am planning to;   7 am hoping to;
4 am going to;   8 would like to

READING

A

1 B;   2 C;   3 A

B

1 C;   3 A;   5 C;
2 B and C;   4 B and C;   6 A

C

1 long hours;
2 my work experience;
3 job advertisement;
4 marketing department;
5 night shift

VOCABULARY Forming words

A

verb and noun		verb	
volunteer	experience	manage	negotiate
interview	offer	advertise	
research	work	apply	

B

1 manage/management;
2 advertise/advertisement;
3 apply/application;
4 negotiate/negotiation

GRAMMAR Past continuous and past simple

A

1 was working;
2 ran across the room;
3 were you doing;
4 was buying;
5 didn't notice;
6 was travelling

B

1 went;
2 bought;
3 woke;
4 was raining;
5 didn't want;
6 called;
7 was getting;
8 went;
9 was cleaning;
10 was sitting

LISTENING

1 Viktor was working an eight-hour day and spending four hours travelling. He wanted to spend more time with his family.
Yoko was working in an office until 5.30 every day. Her kids were coming home to an empty house. Babysitters were too expensive, so she wanted to be there for them.

2 Viktor made his decision while he was travelling home from work.
Yoko made her decision while she was talking to a friend about the problem, and her friend's husband told her about working from home.

DEVELOPING WRITING
A formal email, asking for information

B

Information and an application form

C

1 B; 2 C; 3 D; 4 A

D

informal email	formal email
Hi Gill	**Dear Ms Dunn**
I'm working in a pub at the moment.	At present, I am studying marine biology at Southampton University.
Can you send me the photos from your party?	Could you please send me more information?
Thanks a lot.	Thank you very much.
Can't wait to hear from you!	I look forward to hearing from you.
Lots of love	Yours sincerely
Charlie	Chad Duffy

E

Example answer: Dear Mr Norman,
I saw your advertisement for researchers on the Natural History Museum's website, and I am writing to ask for further information about the position.
At present, I am a second-year post-graduate student, studying for a PhD in Marine Biology at Southampton University. I have a special interest in endangered sea plants, and am hoping to gain some work experience in this area.
I am very interested in the post. Could you please send me an application form, and some more information about which seas you are studying and whether we will be going on study trips?
I look forward to hearing from you.
Yours sincerely,
Chad Duffy

VOCABULARY BUILDER QUIZ 4

A

1 presentation;
2 advertisement;
3 installation;
4 application;
5 contribution;
6 management;
7 negotiations;
8 development

B

1 T; 2 F; 3 T; 4 F; 5 T

C

1 forward;
2 form;
3 skills;
4 fight;
5 click;
6 make

D

1 weight;
2 pension;
3 depressing;
4 unemployed;
5 studio;
6 competitive

UNIT 05

VOCABULARY Activities, places and equipment

A

play	go	do
cards	fishing	exercise
golf	cycling	Pilates
football	swimming	gymnastics
	walking	

B

1 tennis;
2 90 minutes;
3 dance;
4 form of exercise;
5 volleyball;
6 sports equipment;
7 answers may vary: tennis, basketball, badminton, volleyball;
8 ten to fifteen;
9 answers may vary: football, rugby, hockey;
10 game

DEVELOPING CONVERSATIONS
Introducing negative comments

A

1 the acting wasn't (very) good.
2 I was disappointed that/because Chelsea didn't win.
3 I don't like romantic novels.
4 I can't stand swimming.
5 I'm useless at tennis.
6 I think golf's boring.

B

Suggested answers:
1 I must admit;
2 to be honest;
3 I have to say
4 it was too difficult.
5 I prefer dancing.
6 I don't like sport much any more.

GRAMMAR
Might, present continuous, *be going to* + verb

A

1 c;   2 e;   3 a;   4 f;   5 b;   6 d

B

1 We're meeting;
2 I'm thinking of going;
3 What are you doing; I might go;
4 I'm going to do; I might do;
5 Are you going to come; are you going to meet?
6 I'm going to watch

C

1 are meeting;
2 are you coming / are you going to come, I might go;
3 What are you doing? I'm going to go;
4 are having; are we going to do

LISTENING

A

1 underwater rugby;   3 tennis;
2 sepak takraw;   4 badminton

B

Dave: sepak takraw
Heidi: underwater rugby
Beret: sepak takraw

C

1 Heidi likes water sp0rts.
2 Dave suggests that girls can't do certain sports.
3 Because Beret is not a good swimmer.
4 Because it's played under the water.
5 legs and feet
6 Because sepak takraw is like volleyball, which Beret likes playing.

VOCABULARY Sports and games verbs

A

1 beat;   3 won;   5 supported;
2 scored;   4 timed;   6 throw

B

football pitch; tennis racket; tennis court; running track; golf course; golf clubs; swimming gear; swimming pool; dance class; sports event

C

1 football pitch   3 tennis racket   5 golf course
2 swimming gear   4 running track

D

1 d;   2 f;   3 a;   4 c;   5 b;   6 e

GRAMMAR Superlatives

A

1 most exciting;   6 hardest;
2 biggest;   7 worst;
3 easiest;   8 most popular;
4 best;   9 fittest;
5 most expensive;   10 most successful

B

1 This is the most expensive car I've ever bought.
2 This is the most exciting sport I've ever tried.
3 That's the biggest pizza I've ever seen.
4 That was the best game he's ever played.
5 She's the most successful tennis player I've ever known.
6 That was the easiest game I've ever won.

C

1 longest;   4 fastest;   6 largest;
2 largest;   5 most expensive;   7 longest
3 most challenging;

D

a 24 hours;   d 8 days;   f 594;
b 98,772 people;   e $132 million; g 31 hours
c 3,000 miles;

PRONUNCIATION

/ɪ/	/eɪ/	/æ/	/ɪst/	/iː/
win	play	challenging	largest	ski
instruct	break	marathon	cyclist	beat
business	race	badminton	fastest	easy
interesting	stadium	exam	longest	team
pretty	game			complete
				achieve

VOCABULARY Word families

A

adjective	noun	adjective	noun
tired	tiredness	homeless	homelessness
happy	happiness	weak	weakness
aware	awareness	ill	illness
conscious	consciousness	lazy	laziness
fit	fitness	mad	madness

B

1 homelessness;   3 lazy;   5 madness;
2 populated;   4 awareness;   6 weak

READING

A

The picture features a yoga breathing technique.

B

1 T;   2 F;   3 T;   4 F;   5 T;   6 T

DEVELOPING WRITING
A blog – your favourite game

A

1 chess;
2 His father taught him when he was five;
3 12 years;
4 He's going to play in a tournament

B

1 b;   2 c;   3 a

C

Answers will vary. Suggested answers: join a club;
I've been a member for ... ; it's the most exciting / enjoyable / interesting ... ; team game; you can meet people;
I play against / with; practise / train hard; do well;
take part in a match/tournament ...

Vocabulary Builder Quiz 5

A

1 beat;	3 pitch;	5 Supporters
2 club;	4 campaign;	

B

1 for;	3 from;	5 of / about
2 at;	4 to;	

C

1 awareness;	3 consciousness;	5 illness
2 invention;	4 cycling;	

D

1 b;   2 e;   3 a;   4 c;   5 d

E

1 bat;	3 racket;	5 full
2 scores;	4 an opponent;	

UNIT 06

Developing conversations
Explaining where places are

A

1 So where are you from?
2 Really? Whereabouts?
3 Where's it near?
4 So what's it like?
5 How big is it?
6 What do you like most about living there?
7 Have you always lived there?
8 And is there anything you don't like about it?

Vocabulary Cities and areas

A

1 plant;	4 system;	7 culture;
2 square;	5 coast;	8 climate
3 area;	6 bank;	

B

1 industrial;	5 beach;	8 factories;
2 historic;	6 24-hour culture;	9 murders;
3 rural;	7 bank;	10 desert
4 parks;		

Pronunciation /s/ or /z/?

1 de<u>s</u>ert /z/	6 coa<u>s</u>t /s/	11 boat<u>s</u> /s/
2 indu<u>s</u>trial /s/	7 <u>s</u>ystem /s/	12 pla<u>c</u>e /s/
3 hi<u>s</u>toric /s/	8 mu<u>s</u>eum /z/	13 <u>c</u>ircle /s/
4 factorie<u>s</u> /z/	9 fore<u>s</u>t /s/	14 dangerou<u>s</u> /s/
5 <u>s</u>quare /s/	10 bar<u>s</u> /z/	

Reading

A

1 B;   2 C;   3 A

B

1 C;   2 A;   3 C;   4 B;   5 A;   6 A

Grammar have to / don't have to / can

A

1 can;	4 don't have to;	7 don't have to;
2 doesn't have to;	5 don't have to;	8 can
3 can;	6 have to;	

C

1 have to;	4 can;	7 have to;
2 don't have to;	5 have to;	8 have to
3 can;	6 can;	

Listening

A

c

B

1, 2, 4, 5

C

1 T;	2 T;	3 F;	4 T;	5 T;	6 F;
7 T;	8 F				

Developing writing
A letter - describing where you live

A

c

B

1 C;   2 D;   3 A;   4 B

C

1 Because he has just found somewhere to live.
2 In a small room in a family house in Portsmouth.
3 It's near to the university and the beach.
4 A bed, a desk and a chair.
5 A TV.
6 Because the family has small children who go to bed early.
7 He can't invite guests to his room during the week.
8 The rent is very cheap.

D

1 F;   2 T;   3 F;   4 T;   5 F;   6 T

Vocabulary Staying with people

A

1 d;	2 b;	3 a;	4 g;	5 h;	6 c;
7 f;	8 e				

B

1 H;	2 G;	3 G;	4 G;	5 H;	6 H
7 G;	8 H				

Developing conversations Asking for permission

A

1 mind if I borrow your umbrella?
2 OK if I switch on the TV?
3 mind if I use your computer?
4 OK if I take some food from the fridge?
5 mind if I invite a friend to stay tonight?
6 borrow your phone to make a quick call?

B

1 a;   2 a;   3 b;   4 a;   5 b;   6 b

C

Suggested answers:
1 you mind if I;
2 actually, I'd rather you didn't;
3 it OK if;
4 of course;
5 help yourself / feel free;
6 help yourself / feel free

GRAMMAR Future

A
1 I won't do it again.
2 I'll pay you back.
3 I'll pick you up in the car.
4 I'll get it.
5 I'll look into it.
6 I won't be able to.
7 I'll carry them for you.
8 I'll see who it is.

B
1 P;   5 IR;
2 O;   6 IR;
3 O, IR;   7 O;
4 IR;   8 IR

C
1 'll;   4 won't;
2 'll;   5 'll;
3 'll;   6 won't;

VOCABULARY BUILDER QUIZ 6

A
1 a;   2 d;   3 f;   4 e;   5 c;   6 b

B
1 tiring;   4 spare;
2 hard;   5 free;
3 noisy;   6 rural

C
1 wall;   4 show;
2 square;   5 basin
3 takeaway;

D
1 T;   2 F;   3 F;   4 T;   5 T;   6 F

UNIT 07

VOCABULARY Illnesses and health problems

A

B
1 water;   5 aches;
2 swallow;   6 last;
3 sweating;   7 concentrate;
4 sneezing;   8 cough

GRAMMAR
Giving advice (*should, ought to, why don't you*)

A
1 should;   5 should;
2 why don't you;   6 why don't you;
3 you ought to;   7 should;
4 should;   8 you ought to

B
1 I *don't* think you should …;
2 Maybe you should *put* …;
3 … He *ought* to stop …;
4 Why *don't* you …;
5 You ought *to* stay …;
6 You *oughtn't to* / *shouldn't* eat …

DEVELOPING CONVERSATIONS
Common questions about illness

A
1 Are you OK?
2 Have you been to the doctor's about it?
3 Are you taking anything for it?
4 Have you been to the doctor's about it?
5 Are you OK?
6 Are you taking anything for it?

B
1 e;   2 d;   3 f;   4 b;   5 a;   6 c

LISTENING

A
1 He has a headache and sore throat.
2 She feels dizzy and weak (because she hasn't eaten).

B
1 You should go to the doctor; take some throat sweets.
2 You should sit down; you ought to go to see the nurse.

C
He tells her to eat something.

D
1 b;   2 a

LISTENING

A
1 b;   2 c;   3 b;   4 a

C
1, 4, 6

D
1 school;   4 an actress;
2 read and write;   5 speeches/talks
3 type;

VOCABULARY Forming words

A

	-able		-al	
inevitable	believable	physical	musical
affordable	curable	financial	emotional
comparable	acceptable	industrial	cultural
enjoyable	reliable	central	occasional

C
1 occasional;   4 financial;   7 cultural;
2 industrial;   5 affordable;   8 enjoyable
3 emotional;   6 central;

D

1 musical;	3 emotional;	5 reliable;
2 affordable;	4 financial;	6 enjoyable

PRONUNCIATION

A

unbe**lie**vable	**mu**sical	en**joy**able
in**dus**trial	re**li**able	**phy**sical

DEVELOPING WRITING A webpage – fundraising

A

1 Different Strokes
2 Her son had a stroke when he was small, and Different Strokes helped them.
3 She's going to take part in the London to Paris Cycle Ride.
4 She's hoping to raise €2,000.

B

1 e;	2 a;	3 c;	4 f;	5 d;	6 b

C

Example answer:
Target: £5,000
Raised so far: £1,140
Donate now!
My Story
In 2005, I had a car accident and suffered a bad head injury. Afterwards I discovered that I could not speak. The medical name for this is aphasia. I suffered from this for two years. During this time, I received a lot of help and support from Speakability. Their speech therapists helped me to speak again. I decided that I wanted to help other people with this problem. I'm going to walk from Edinburgh to Brighton next month to raise money to help fund training for Speakability's speech therapists.
Thank you for your support.

VOCABULARY Parts of the body

A

1 legs;	5 lips;	
2 face;	6 ear;	
3 finger;	7 stomach;	
4 hair;	8 feet	

B

1 eye hair;	4 back arm;
2 yellow hair;	5 mouth pain
3 armstand;	

GRAMMAR Imperatives

A

1 call;	5 Don't take;
2 put;	6 Let;
3 Don't leave;	7 Drink;
4 eat;	8 Don't touch

B

1 f;	2 d;	3 b;	4 d;	5 c;
6 e;	7 a;	8 c		

C

Example answers:
1 Take these painkillers three times a day.
2 Go to bed and rest.
3 Don't eat so many sweets. Eat more fruit.
4 Drink hot drinks and fruit juice.
5 Stay at home and put on this cream twice a day.

Reading

A

1 hydrotherapy;	3 nutrition
2 aromatherapy;	

B

1 rub;	5 burn;
2 radiator;	6 steam;
3 gargle;	7 symptoms;
4 remedy;	8 virus

C

1 a;	2 b,c;	3 b;	4 a,c;	5 a

VOCABULARY BUILDER QUIZ 7

A

1 anxious;	5 cultural;
2 acceptable;	6 depressed;
3 disabled;	7 generous
4 religious;	

B

1 I've got an upset stomach;
2 Take a deep breath;
3 She's made a speedy recovery from the flu;
4 He broke out in a rash after touching the cat;
5 Don't forget to brush your teeth after eating sweets

C

1 T;	2 F;	3 T;	4 F;	5 F;	6 T;	7 F

D

1 put on an;	3 wise;	5 back;
2 throat;	4 cold;	6 suffer from

UNIT 08

VOCABULARY Places in town

```
                    ¹Z O O
              ²M U S E U M
                    ³B A N K
               ⁴B R I D G E
               ⁵R A I L W A Y
          ⁶P O L I C E
⁷S P O R T S G R O U N D
⁸R O U N D A B O U T
              ⁹S U B W A Y
         ¹⁰C R O S S R O A D S
    ¹¹T R A F F I C
              ¹²M O N U M E N T
         ¹³P L A Y G R O U N D
```

B

1 sports TV
2 police day
3 town shop (you can say, 'a shop in town')
4 cross shirt
5 traffic car (you can say, 'cars in a traffic jam')
6 play person
7 bus drink
8 church person. (you can say a *church goer*.)

PRONUNCIATION Stress on compound nouns

A

'crossroads	'roundabout	'underground
'playground	'traffic lights	'sports ground
town 'hall	pol'ice station	'traffic warden
'sports programme	town 'centre	pol'ice woman

DEVELOPING CONVERSATIONS Giving directions

A

1 Excuse me. How do I get to the sports ground?
2 Excuse me. Is there a tube station near here?
3 Excuse me. Do you know where the police station is?
4 Excuse me. Do you know the way to the town hall?
5 Excuse me. Can you tell me how to get to the museum, please?
6 Excuse me. Where's the nearest bank?

B

1 c   2 d   3 g   4 b   5 h   6 f
7 a   8 e

LISTENING

A

The sports ground

B

1; 4; 5; 6; 7; 8; 9; 10

C

1 The town hall.
2 He says, 'Go straight on at the roundabout.'
3 The cinema.

READING

A

b

B

1 F;   2 T;   3 F;   4 T;   5 F;   6 F;
7 F;   8 F

GRAMMAR Articles (*a, an, the* and no article)

A

1 a;	3 a;	5 the, a;	7 a, the;
2 the;	4 a, the;	6 a, the;	8 a, the

B

1 0, the;   2 0, a;   3 0, a;   4 0, a;   5 the, a;   6 a, 0

C

1 0;   2 the;   3 0;   4 the;   5 the;   6 the

D

You can travel across the USA by 0 bus, train or plane, but for the real experience, you have to drive. There's no need to buy a car, because renting a car is easy. There are 0 car hire offices at all major airports and most companies will offer a one-way rental which means that you don't have to return the car to the same office.

LISTENING

A

1 a;   2 b;   3 b;   4 a;

B

1 river, park;   3 cadillac, monument
2 river, paddleboat;

C

1 St Louis;   3 Grand Canyon
2 Cadillac Ranch;

VOCABULARY Transport

A

car	bike	train	plane	foot
motorway	ride	station	check in	walk
park	helmet	platform	airport	umbrella
traffic jam	cycle lane	underground	flight	zebra crossing

B

1 A ride; B helmet, cycle lanes
2 B flight, check in, airport
3 B station, platform
4 traffic jam, motorway, park
5 B walk, zebra crossing, umbrella

C

1 the car;   4 the policeman;
2 crashed;   5 the website;
3 the licence;   6 an airport

GRAMMAR Quantifiers

A

a 2;   b 1;   c 3

B

1 There isn't much traffic on the road.
2 There isn't a lot of traffic on the road.
3 There isn't any traffic on the road.

C

1 There aren't many car parks in this town.
2 There's a strike today, so there's no public transport.
3 It's very polluted here because there's a lot of industry in this area.
4 I can't lend you anything because I've only got a little money on me.
5 She's in a terrible hurry because she only has a few minutes before her bus arrives.

D

many, much, any, a few, much, a lot of

DEVELOPING WRITING

A

1 Dinner on Saturday
2 Take the tube to Scott's Park and then walk
3
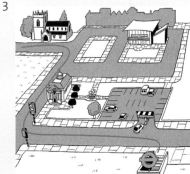
4 23 Avenue Road.
5 Ring the top bell.
6 Call Peter on 09736727887.

B

Example answer:
From: (Your name)
Subject: Lunch on Friday
Date: (Today's date)
To: Martine Kovacs
Hi Martine,
I'm pleased to hear that you can come round for lunch on Friday. It's probably best if you take the tube to Scott's Park station and then walk to my house. When you come out of the station, turn left and go down the road until you come to the traffic lights. Then, turn right, go past the town hall and take the second turning on the right. This is the High Street and I am at number 23, opposite the cinema.
If there's a problem, give me a call on (your phone number).
Look forward to seeing you at 1.00 on Friday.
Best wishes,
(Your name)

VOCABULARY BUILDER QUIZ 8

A
1 couple;   4 pray;
2 hard-working;   5 licence;
3 exit;   6 trust

B
1 e;   2 f;   3 d;   4 a;   5 b;   6 c

C
1 freely;   4 sailing;
2 global;   5 cancelled;
3 delayed;   6 chaos

D
1 F;   2 T;   3 F;   4 T;   5 T;   6 F;   7 F

UNIT 09

VOCABULARY Science and nature

A
1 exploring;   3 investigating;   5 invented;
2 studied;   4 discovered;   6 extinct

B
1 d;   2 a;   3 e;   4 b;   5 c

C
1 shortage;   3 research;   5 resources;
2 extinct;   4 pollution;   6 experiments;

LISTENING

A
Emily Cummins 2; Tommy Jones 3; weather forecast 1

B
1 b;   2 b;   3 b;   4 b;   5 a;   6 a

C
1 flooding;   3 invented;   5 recycled;
2 puppy;   4 shed;   6 energy

DEVELOPING CONVERSATIONS
Responding to news and comments

A
Suggested answers:
1 Really? That's great news / fantastic / wonderful!
2 No change
3 No change

4 Really? That's good news / great / really good.
  Yes, I know. It's really good.
5 Definitely / Absolutely.
6 No change
7 Good idea.
8 Really? That's interesting.

B
1 Really? That's amazing!
2 They should do more
3 No. So is it going to snow?
4 Really? That's awful!
5 Maybe we should

PRONUNCIATION

A
popu**la**tion – 4 syllables
research – 2 syllables
in**vent** – 2 syllables
ex**per**iment – 4 syllables
pol**lu**tion – 3 syllables
energy – 3 syllables

B

2 syllables, stress on first syllable	2 syllables, stress on second syllable	3 syllables, stress on first syllable	3 syllables, stress on second syllable	4 syllables, stress on second syllable	4 syllables, stress on third syllable
study shortage research* natural*	extinct explore invent protect research*	energy natural*	solution pollution resources	experiment investigate participant	population

* both pronunciations are acceptable

VOCABULARY Animals

A

pets	farm animals	marine animals	birds	wild cats
dog cat rabbit horse parrot	sheep hen cow rabbit horse	shark dolphin whale	eagle parrot pigeon	lion tiger panther

B
1 ground;   5 success;
2 dogs;   6 school;
3 excited;   7 workers;
4 less;   8 bones

READING

A

	magnetic fridge	methane farming	green machine	floating wind turbines
air pollution		✓		✓
water shortage			✓	
energy resources	✓	✓	✓	✓

B

1 a, c; 2 b, d; 3 c; 4 b, d; 5 c (washes and dries)

C

1 d; 2 e; 3 b; 4 c; 5 a

GRAMMAR Past perfect simple

A

1 checked, called; 4 looked at, had discovered;
2 had followed, realised; 5 had fallen, got home
3 had already finished, told;

B

1 had finished; 4 had forgotten; 7 had forgotten;
2 had been hit; 5 had not been; 8 had discovered
3 had never been; 6 had already left;

C

1 lived; 3 discovered; 5 had died;
2 existed; 4 had looked; 6 had eaten

GRAMMAR Reporting speech 1

A

1 b; 2 c; 3 a

B

1 said; 3 told; 5 said
2 told; 4 asked, told;

C

1 told his patient to take two aspirin and go to bed.
2 asked if she could open the window.
3 asked if the patient would like to take part in an experiment.
4 said I didn't understand.
5 told the research assistant to press the button when he heard a beep.

DEVELOPING WRITING

An email – expressing an opinion

A

1 d; 2 e; 3 c; 4 a; 5 b

B

1 One thing; 3 but; 5 However;
2 Secondly; 4 Another; 6 Although

C

Answers may vary slightly. Suggested answers:
1 *Although* I like most animals, I don't like rats.
2 *Although* more homes are needed in the city centre, there should be parks.
3 Paris is a beautiful city, with wide streets. *Another thing* I like are the cafés on street corners with tables outside.
4 It's a good thing that governments are talking about climate change, *but* they should do more.
5 *Although* I like living by the sea, it gets cold in the winter.
6 I like sweets but they're not healthy.

VOCABULARY BUILDER QUIZ 9

A

1 witnessed; 3 participate; 5 investigating
2 protect; 4 conducting;

B

1 requires; 3 evidence; 5 predict
2 detected; 4 terrorist;

C

1 b; 2 d; 3 e; 4 a; 5 c

D

1 to; 2 on; 3 in; 4 as; 5 for

E

1 creativity; 3 speech; 5 scientific
2 environmental; 4 majority;

UNIT 10

VOCABULARY

A

1 A: Is your daughter still at <u>primary</u> school?
   B: No she's fifteen now, so she goes to <u>secondary</u> school.
   A: And what's her favourite <u>subject</u>?
   B: Well, she's very good at sports so she loves <u>PE</u>.
2 A: I'm really worried about my <u>exams</u>. I haven't done any work.
   B: What will you do if you don't <u>pass</u> them?
   A: If I <u>fail</u> I'll probably <u>retake</u> them next year.
3 A: Are you going to university when you <u>leave</u> school?
   B: Yes, if I get a place. But I don't want to go immediately, so I'll take a <u>year out</u> first.
   A: Are you going to get a job?
   B: Yes, but I want to do other things as well, so I'll work <u>part time</u>.
4 A: When are you going to <u>graduate</u> from university?
   B: Well, I'm taking my <u>finals</u> in the summer, so it won't be long.
   A: And what are you going to do after that?
   B: If I get a good <u>degree</u> I'll stay at university and do a <u>Master's</u>.

B

1 BA; 2 BSc; 3 MA; 4 MSc; 5 PhD

C

subject	person
biology	*biologist*
chemistry	*chemist*
economics	*economist*
geography	*geographer*
history	*historian*
mathematics/maths	*mathematician*
philosophy	*philosopher*
physics	*physicist*
science	*scientist*
sociology	*sociologist*

DEVELOPING CONVERSATIONS

A

1 c; 2 b; 3 f; 4 e; 5 d; 6 a

LISTENING

A

b

B

I don't really like history.
No. I'm interested in the future, not the past.
I don't know why people study Latin.
No. It's a dead language. Nobody speaks it.
I can't see the point of IT classes.
No. Everyone knows how to use a computer these days.

C
1 history, Latin and IT
2 history and IT

GRAMMAR First conditionals

A
1 If you don't work harder, you won't pass your exams.
2 They'll miss the train home if they're not quick.
3 If you study law, you'll find it easy to get a good job.
4 He'll reply to you if you send him an email.
5 If the teacher doesn't arrive, we'll go home early.
6 I'll lend you the book if you promise to give it back.

B
1 are, will be;
2 will go, finishes;
3 don't see, will call;
4 won't, don't;
5 doesn't, will email;
6 won't, don't;
7 miss, won't be able to;
8 won't be able, don't;
9 plays, 'll come;
10 will leave, arrives

VOCABULARY

A

¹P	²O	W	E	R	³P	O	⁴I	N	⁵T
	N				H		N		E
⁶B	L	O	⁷G		⁸O	F	F		C
	I		E		T		O		H
	N		O		O		R		N
⁹P	E		G				M		O
H			R			¹⁰C	A	L	L
Y		¹¹H	A	R	¹²M		T		O
S			P		U		I		G
I			¹³H	I	S	T	O	R	Y
¹⁴C	O	P	Y		I		N		
S					C				

B
1 b; 2 f; 3 e; 4 a; 5 c; 6 d

C
1 searching;
2 upload;
3 cheated;
4 organise;
5 increased;
6 mix ;
7 password;
8 download

D
1 h; 2 d; 3 g; 4 e; 5 f; 6 a; 7 b;
8 c

READING

A
c

B
1 consistently above average
2 stimulating and challenging environment
3 outstanding musical tradition
4 thriving multinational community
5 excellent modern facilities
6 high academic standards

C
1 F; 2 F; 3 T; 4 F; 5 T; 6 F;
7 T; 8 T; 9 F; 10 F

VOCABULARY

1 approach;
2 subjects;
3 assignment;
4 tests;
5 relationship;
6 attention;
7 textbooks;
8 standards

PRONUNCIATION Sound and spelling

1 *che*mistry   2 *che*ck   3 tea*che*r

DEVELOPING WRITING A report – giving advice

A
1 Year;
2 62%;
3 course work;
4 contributions;
5 more

B
Model answer:
You have made some progress in Year 2 of your History course. Although your exam mark of 59% was disappointing, your contributions in class have been good. However, your course work has been poor. If you work harder, you will do much better next year.

GRAMMAR Had to / could

A
1 She couldn't finish her assignment.
2 He had to stay up all night to revise.
3 She could do any sport she liked at school.
4 They didn't have to do their homework.
5 I couldn't find the book in the library.
6 We had to complain about the teacher.
7 Did you have to stay late after class?
8 Could you understand the last question in the exam?
9 He could go home early because he had finished his work.
10 Did they have to buy their textbooks?

B
The parents' evening was a complete disaster. We *had to* start late because lots of the parents were stuck in a traffic jam and *couldn't* get to the school on time. Then, there weren't enough chairs in the school hall, so lots of people *had to* stand. Finally, the microphone didn't work, so the audience *couldn't* hear anything. Still, at least we *didn't have to* listen to the headmaster's speech. He's always so boring!

VOCABULARY BUILDER QUIZ 10

A
1 from;
2 out;
3 to;
4 to;
5 between;
6 for

B
1 immediately;
2 optional;
3 failed;
4 complain;
5 disturb;
6 lecture

C
1 T; 2 F; 3 F; 4 T; 5 T; 6 T; 7 T

D
1 advantage;
2 essay;
3 assumed;
4 retake;
5 recognise;
6 skipped

UNIT 11

LISTENING

A
1 boat
2 hotel
3 rented house
4 tent

B
1 share
2 freedom
3 relax
4 (organised) activities
5 fixed timetable
6 book
7 sleeping in a tent
8 cancellation fee

C
room service, be fully booked, cancellation fee, make a booking, pay a deposit, cooking facilities, Internet access, organised activities, parking facilities, babysitting service

D
1 activities;
2 facilities;
3 access;
4 booked;
5 services;
6 facilities, fee;
7 booking;
8 fee;
9 service

DEVELOPING CONVERSATIONS Giving bad news

A
1 I'm afraid not;
2 I'm afraid so;
3 I'm afraid not;
4 I'm afraid so;
5 I'm afraid not;
6 I'm afraid so;
7 I'm afraid so;
8 I'm afraid not

B
1 I'm afraid we don't accept credit cards, but you can pay by cheque.
2 I'm afraid we're fully booked until the end of the month.
3 I'm afraid you'll have to park in the car park down the road.
4 I'm afraid so. There's a wedding party tomorrow evening and all the guests are staying in the hotel.
5 I'm afraid not. It is currently closed for repairs.
6 I'm afraid not. We don't have enough staff to offer that service.

DEVELOPING WRITING
An online booking form

A
1 Jorg Oskarsson;
2 Applecote Guest House;
3 four (two adults, two children);
4 2 September 2010;
5 eight nights;
6 yes – son's 16th birthday;
7 yes – £10 per night for the one child under 12;
8 no

B
1 g;   2 a;   3 d;   4 f;   5 b;   6 h;
7 e;   8 c

VOCABULARY Hotel problems
1 available;
2 book in advance;
3 filthy;
4 insects;
5 boiling;
6 air conditioning;
7 fixed;
8 low;
9 toiletries;
10 room service;
11 main road;
12 noisy;
13 wake-up call;
14 missed;
15 bill;
16 overcharged

GRAMMAR Second conditionals

A
1 If I were you, I'd book a room first. / I'd book a room first if I were you.
2 If it happened to you, what would you do? / What would you do if it happened to you?
3 It would be better if you went home.
4 He might listen to you if you called him. / If you called him, he might listen to you.
5 Do you think it would be better if we left?

B
1 What would you do if there was no hot water in your hotel bathroom?
2 If I asked you to marry me, what would you say?
3 Would you complain if it happened to you?
4 If I ordered breakfast in my room, how much would it cost?
5 Would you think I was crazy if I bought that hotel?

C
Answers may vary. Possible answers:
1 If I were you, I'd complain to the chef.
2 If I were you, I'd ask the maid.
3 If I were you, I'd search on the Internet.
4 If I were you, I'd complain to the head waiter.
5 If I were you, I'd tell the manager.

LISTENING

A
1 2;   2 3;   3 1

B
1 3;   2 1;   3 2

C
1 turn down;
2 find;
3 put his coat over it;
4 the main speaker;
5 wedding anniversary;
6 roses

D
1 I would get her some perfume.
2 I would call the hotel manager.
3 I would change room.
4 I would ask room service to call a plumber.
5 I would ask the receptionist to call and explain that there's a problem.

E
W: Hurry up, Henri! We're going to be late!
M: Just a minute. I'm nearly ready ... Oh, wait, Cherise! I can't open the door!
W: What? OK! I'm coming. Give me two seconds ... Right! You pull, I'll push.
M: Wait. Just one second ... OK, ready!
W: Right. One, two, three ... go!
M: Aaagh! ... It's no good! It won't move!
W: OK, I'll phone reception for help. I won't be a minute ... It's all right, Henri. They'll send someone up in a minute. Be patient.

READING

A
c

B
1 c;   2 b;   3 c;   4 c;   5 a

PRONUNCIATION

A

/juː/	/ʌ/
used to	umbrella
usually	uninteresting
useful	summer
beautiful	suntan
cute	done

GRAMMAR *used to*

A

1 a, b, d; 2 c

B

1 When I was young, I used to walk to school every day.
2 When I was a kid, I never used to go on holiday with my parents, so now family holidays are special to me.
3 We used to go to North Wales every summer, until I went to university.
4 My dad used to go fishing with his friend every morning.
5 We used to stay in the same place every year, so we made lots of friends there.
6 I used to swim in the sea every day of the holidays.

C

1 I **never use** to like singing round camp fires, but I do now.
3 We use**d** to like going to the outdoor swimming pool.
4 When I was at school, we **used to** go on skiing trips every February.
6 Last weekend, I **had** to get up early for a hockey tournament.
8 Rob **used to go** to summer camp every August.

VOCABULARY BUILDER QUIZ 11

A

1 climbing; 4 babysitting;
2 entertainment; 5 Parking;
3 arrangement; 6 achievement

B

1 e; 2 a; 3 g; 4 c; 5 b; 6 d; 7 f

C

1 F; 2 T; 3 F; 4 F; 5 T; 6 F

D

1 activities; 4 available;
2 fully; 5 of;
3 with; 6 call

UNIT 12

VOCABULARY Using phones

A

1 back; 5 up;
2 through; 6 call;
3 on; 7 busy;
4 off; 8 text

B

1 line; 4 coverage;
2 busy; 5 text
3 signal;

DEVELOPING CONVERSATIONS
Asking for people and explaining where they are

A

1 Could I speak to; 4 Can I take;
2 Who's; 5 Could you tell him;
3 is working at home; 6 My name's

B

1 b, a, c; 3 c, b, a;
2 c, b, a; 4 c, a, b

C

1 f; 2 a; 3 c; 4 d; 5 h; 6 e; 7 b;
8 g

LISTENING

A

Tina Morrison called about your meeting next <u>Tuesday</u>. She's going to be away on <u>holiday</u> that day, so can you change the meeting to <u>Thursday</u>? <u>Two o'clock</u> at her office. If there are any problems, please call her mobile on <u>08857678548</u>.

B

Tina Morrison called about your meeting next Thursday. She's going to be away on business that day, so can you change the meeting to Friday? Three o'clock at her office. If there are any problems, please call her mobile on 088976576548

GRAMMAR *Just, yet, already* and *still*

A

1 just; 2 yet; 3 already; 4 still

B

1 I've just spilled my coffee.
2 I've already called him.
3 I haven't seen her yet.
4 We're still waiting for it.
5 I haven't spoken to them yet.
6 He's just gone out for a moment.
7 She's still looking for it.
8 They've already paid us.

READING

A
b

B

1 d; 2 g; 3 b; 4 c; 5 h; 6 a; 7 e;
8 f

C

1 the early 1990s;
2 because the signal wasn't always very good;
3 it fell dramatically;
4 teenagers in rich countries;
5 the way people do business and socialise
6 in the developing world

D

1 F; 2 T; 3 F; 4 T; 5 F; 6 T

E

1 the best market for their fish; 4 plan their work;
2 unnecessary work; 5 farming methods;
3 local weather forecasts; 6 that we can't imagine yet

VOCABULARY Forming negatives

A

un-		im-
fortunate	expected	practical
common	comfortable	possible
wise	natural	polite
fair	pleasant	patient
happy		

B

1 unhappy; 5 unfair; 9 unwise;
2 unpleasant; 6 uncommon; 10 impractical
3 unfortunate; 7 uncomfortable;
4 impolite; 8 unexpected;

PRONUNCIATION Same or different?

A

1 ✗; 2 ✓; 3 ✗; 4 ✓; 5 ✓; 6 ✗

DEVELOPING WRITING Text and email – abbreviations

A

1 R; 5 4; 9 poss; 12 2;
2 ASAP; 6 l8r; 10 c; 13 u;
3 docs; 7 msg; 11 txt; 14 yr
4 eve; 8 meet;

B

Answers may vary. Example answer:
From: Brian Dufriss
Subject: This evening's meeting
Date: 14 January 2010
To: Steve Zizek
Dear Steve,
Thanks for your messages. Are you coming to the meeting this evening? If so, could you please bring the documents that we discussed?
Please let me know if this is possible as soon as you can.
See you soon,
Brian

LISTENING

A

1 a bank; 4 three;
2 four; 5 four;
3 check your bank balance; 6 approximately 12 minutes

B

1 c; 2 f; 3 b; 4 e; 5 a; 6 d

GRAMMAR Reporting speech 2

A

1 were helping; 4 were going; 7 had spoken;
2 hadn't seen; 5 had seen; 8 hadn't called
3 had phoned; 6 hadn't heard

B

1 She said Anna had posted the letter on Tuesday.
2 You said you were sending me the books today.
3 You said you hadn't been to the office all day.
4 You said you hadn't brought your notes with you.
5 They told us they hadn't delivered the letters yet.
6 You said you were going to the post office right now.
7 You said you had lost your mobile phone.
8 You said you were giving me two weeks to reply.
9 He said he had had my letter on his desk since Wednesday.
10 You said you couldn't remember your mobile phone number.

VOCABULARY BUILDER QUIZ 12

A

1 d; 2 c; 3 a; 4 f; 5 e; 6 b

B

1 coverage; 4 operation;
2 identified; 5 initially;
3 introduced; 6 expect

C

1 T; 2 F; 3 F; 4 T; 5 F; 6 T;
7 F; 8 T

D

1 fares; 4 rush;
2 irrational fear; 5 species
3 landlord;

UNIT 13

VOCABULARY Films

A

¹SCIENCE FICTION
²HISTORICAL DRAMA
³ACTION
⁴THRILLER
⁵COMEDY
⁶MARTIAL ARTS

B

1 horror; 4 predictable;
2 special effects; 5 martial arts;
3 past; 6 romantic

C

1 A; 2 C; 3 A; 4 B; 5 A; 6 B;
7 B; 8 C

LISTENING

A

1 c; 2 a; 3 b

C

1 C; 2 A; 3 B; 4 C; 5 B; 6 A

D

1 T; 2 F; 3 F; 4 T; 5 T; 6 F

DEVELOPING CONVERSATIONS Supposed to

A

1 d; 2 a; 3 e; 4 f; 5 b; 6 c

B

1 What are you doing; 5 amazing;
2 Would you like; 6 Why don't you;
3 is supposed to; 7 are supposed to;
4 really talented; 8 do you fancy

GRAMMAR -ed / -ing adjectives

A

1 bored; 5 disappointing;
2 interesting; 6 annoying;
3 excited; 7 tiring;
4 shocked; 8 confused

B

1 annoying;	4 disgusting;
2 surprised;	5 boring;
3 worried;	6 amazing

VOCABULARY Music, art and books

A

1 instruments;	9 landscape;
2 rehearse;	10 paintings;
3 composer;	11 auction;
4 albums;	12 authors;
5 voice;	13 novel;
6 portrait photographer;	14 published;
7 sculptures;	15 letter;
8 exhibition;	16 biographies

GRAMMAR Present perfect continuous

A

1 for; 2 for; 3 since; 4 since; 5 for; 6 for

B

1 been acting, starred;
2 directed, been working;
3 started, has held;
4 has been playing, has had;
5 known, have been going;
6 become, published

C

1 has been playing;	3 has recorded;	5 has been
2 has gained;	4 has worked;	touring

READING

A

1 B; 2 C; 3 A

B

1 B; 2 A; 3 B,C; 4 A; 5 B,C; 6 C

C

adjective	verb
moving	move
exciting	excite
disappointing	disappoint
amazing	amaze
shocking	shock
surprising	surprise
upsetting	upset

VOCABULARY Compound nouns

A

film industry, music business, police officer, screenwriter, pop star, special effects

B

1 pop star;	3 special effects;
2 screenwriter;	4 film industry

C

1 special effects;	4 film industry;
2 music business;	5 pop star;
3 police officer;	6 screenwriter

PRONUNCIATION -ed

A

/ɪd/	/d/
excited	bored
disappointed	tired
interested	starred
treated	amazed
directed	played
recorded	surprised

DEVELOPING WRITING Blog entry – a book review

A

1 moving; 2 interested; 3 surprising

B

1 c; 2 a; 3 b

VOCABULARY BUILDER QUIZ 13

A

1 in;	3 of;	5 with
2 for;	4 between;	

B

1 composers;	4 explosion;	7 wealthy;
2 social;	5 addiction;	8 conductor
3 unpredictable;	6 director;	

C

1 rehearsing;	3 biography;	5 corrupt;
2 weird;	4 generate;	6 concert

D

1 e; 2 a; 3 f; 4 b; 5 d; 6 c

UNIT 14

GRAMMAR Relative clauses

A

1 where you can get fit;
2 who prepares food in a restaurant;
3 which cleans carpets;
4 who make things from wood;
5 where you can watch the latest movies;
6 which helps you to get dry;
7 where people race horses;
8 which hold water;

B

1 who;	3 who;	5 who;	7 who;
2 where;	4 when;	6 where;	8 when

C

1 which;	3 who;	5 which
2 which;	4 who ;	

Vocabulary

```
 1C  L  O  T  H
 2B  I  N
 3D  U  V  E  T
 4N  A  I  L
 5P  A  N
         6G  A  R  A  G  E
 7T  H  R  E  A  D
         8T  O  R  C  H
 9I  R  O  N
10H  A  M  M  E  R
```

B

1 mop and bucket, a; 3 dustpan and brush, d;
2 needle and thread, c; 4 hammer and nails, b

Developing conversations

A

1 A: Can I borrow a hairdryer? B: There's one on the bathroom wall.
2 A: Where do you keep the plasters? B: There's a first aid kit in the kitchen cupboard.
3 A: Have you got any snacks? B: Yes, there are some in the fridge.
4 A: Have you got a needle and thread? B: There's a sewing box on the shelf.
5 A: Can I make a drink?
   B: Yes, the coffee is on the shelf.
6 A: Have you got today's paper?
   B: It's on the table by the TV.

B

1 next;   3 at;   5 under; 7 on;
2 in;   4 on;   6 in;   8 in

Listening

A

The following should be ticked:
Clean carpets in lobby; Clean marble floor in dining room; Wipe mirrors; Put up picture

B & C

1 A vacuum cleaner   Under the stairs
2 A mop and a bucket   In the cupboard behind the reception area
3 A cloth   In the drawer in the staff room
4 A hammer and some nails   In the cellar

D
A torch

Vocabulary Containers

A

1 shampoo;   4 butter;   7 crisps;
2 bread;   5 cheese;   8 eggs
3 fish;   6 sausages;

B

1 e;   2 c;   3 b;   4 d;   5 a;   6 f

Reading

A

b

B

1 In an empty shop in Oxford Street, London;
2 10;
3 7,227;
4 *Break Down*;
5 consumer society;
6 his cat;
7 He felt an incredible sense of freedom;
8 He has become one of the most respected artists in the UK.

C

1 T;   2 F;   3 F;   4 F;   5 T;   6 F

D

1 Why do you think that?
2 It was so wasteful!
3 I think he made a good point.
4 We all have too many possessions these days.
5 But he could have given them to charity.
6 You're always going shopping.

Grammar *must, mustn't, don't have to*

A

1 c;   2 b;   3 a

B

1 You must;   6 You must;
2 You mustn't;   7 You don't have to;
3 You must;   8 You don't have to;
4 You mustn't;   9 You mustn't;
5 You don't have to; 10 You mustn't

Grammar Verbs with two objects

A

1 for;   3 to;   5 to;   7 to;
2 to;   4 for;   6 to;   8 for

B

1 He gave me the books.
2 I bought a cup of coffee for you.
3 He poured me a glass of milk.
4 I sent a postcard to you.
5 She made me a sandwich.
6 He read the report to them.
7 They lent us their car.
8 We cooked them dinner.

Pronunciation

A

1 class;   6 could;
2 ban;   7 ban;
3 bin;   8 pad;
4 pair;   9 goal;
5 gold;   10 pouring

Listening

A

1 T;   2 T;   3 F;   4 T;   5 T;   6 F

WRITING

A

a 3   b 4   c 1   d 2

Vocabulary Builder Quiz 14

A

1 rid;   3 forecast;   5 turned;
2 break;   4 going;   6 warming

B

1 T; 2 F; 3 F; 4 T; 5 T; 6 F; 7 F

C

1 reduction	3 attractive	5 efficient
2 confused	4 dispose	6 recycling

D

1 clue;	3 sink;	5 neighbour;
2 petrol;	4 soap;	6 racing

UNIT 15

VOCABULARY The economy and quality of life

A

```
C  O  T  D  E  R  U  K  A  E  W  N  P  U
X  Y  O  O  A  O  N  I  D  Q  W  X  Y  L
W  C  L  C  B  T  E  S  C  E  T  N  T  E
T  N  L  X  T  I  M  E  O  F  F  P  I  V
A  E  U  I  Y  N  P  K  S  A  L  A  R  Y
S  R  I  E  N  A  W  L  Z  T  M  H  J  U
Z  R  T  F  I  Q  O  V  O  I  C  E  C  T
Q  U  A  L  I  T  Y  O  F  L  I  F  E  R
S  C  M  A  K  L  M  B  L  Y  A  R  S  O
T  R  I  T  E  U  E  M  I  R  C  H  B  P
Y  P  L  I  C  I  N  Z  V  Q  D  U  O  S
P  W  C  O  I  W  T  P  I  Y  F  G  J  N
U  L  O  N  S  T  R  O  N  G  G  O  W  A
Q  I  M  A  V  E  R  A  G  E  R  S  A  T
```

B

1 unemployment;	4 quality of life;	7 inflation;
2 pace of life;	5 climate change;	8 salary
3 job security;	6 weak;	

LISTENING

A

1 Yes, she does.
2 It's doing better than before.
3 She and Miguel want to get married, and she wants him to try living in Prague for a while so that he can understand her culture.

B

1 higher;	3 cheaper;	5 higher;
2 lower;	4 expensive;	6 happier

C

1, 3, 4, 6

GRAMMAR Time phrases and tense

A

1 e; 2 f; 3 a; 4 b; 5 g; 6 h;
7 d; 8 c

B

1 The government used to spend more on education in the past.
2 Yesterday they opened a new shopping centre on the ring road.
3 She's going to start a new job in advertising next week.
4 He's had three jobs in the last two years.
5 The economy is improving at the moment.
6 She's had three loans from the bank in the last five years.

C

1 Unemployment has risen over the last few months.
2 The average salary used to be higher when I was at school.
3 Inflation has fallen since last year.
4 The price of petrol has risen again in the last few weeks.
5 The cost of living is falling at the moment, and prices are lower.
6 I think the economy will improve next year.

DEVELOPING CONVERSATIONS Comparing prices

A

1 cheaper;	4 cheaper;
2 cheaper than (it is);	5 the same;
3 more expensive;	6 slightly lower

B

1 they cost €300,000 in Faroland.
2 it costs €20,000 in Celtonia.
3 whereas it costs €1 in Celtonia.
4 whereas they cost €1,000 in Faroland.

READING

A

1 an Economics teacher at university
2 the Grameen Bank.
3 the Nobel Peace prize.

B

1 F; 2 T; 3 T; 4 T; 5 F; 6 T;
7 T; 8 F

C

1 interest;	3 micro-credit;	5 borrowed;
2 lend;	4 pay back;	6 loan

VOCABULARY Money verbs

A

1 owed;	3 won;	5 left;
2 borrowed;	4 gave;	6 save

B

1 credit card;	3 back;	5 attention;	7 interest;
2 bill;	4 to do it;	6 paid;	8 loan

LISTENING

A

1 paying bills online;	3 at first he is worried, then he
2 easy;	likes it

B

1 c; 2 a; 3 b; 4 a; 5 b; 6 b;
7 c; 8 a

PRONUNCIATION

A

/aɪ/ b**i**ll; /əʊ/ **ow**l; /aʊ/ thr**ou**gh; /eɪ/ s**ai**d

GRAMMAR Present tenses in future time clauses

A

1 I'll pay back the money I owe you as soon as **I'm able to/ I can.**
2 Call me after **you transfer** the money. OK?
3 **I'll lend** you the money until you get paid.
5 When I find a job, **I'm going to/I'll** open a savings account.
7 As soon as **I get** confirmation of payment, I'll let you know.
8 When **I have** enough money, I'll buy a new car.

B

1 when;	3 until;	5 after;
2 as soon as;	4 before;	6 as soon as

C

1 will cancel;	4 recovers;	7 take out, check;
2 have;	5 won't invest, falls;	8 finish, will come
3 won't fall;	6 win, will take;	

VOCABULARY Dealing with banks

A

1 take out;	4 charge;	7 transfer;
2 cancel;	5 make;	8 change
3 open;	6 pay;	

B

1 I will transfer some money to him/my brother.
2 I will pay some money into my account.
3 I will charge them some money/a fee for the translation.
4 I will take out a mortgage.
5 I will open an account.
6 I will cancel my credit card.

DEVELOPING WRITING
Email – giving information and advice

A

1 cost of living;	3 cost;	5 expenses;
2 pay;	4 charges;	6 spend

B

£170: rent/accommodation per week
£13: lunches in the university canteen
£210–220: minimum total spending per week

C

1 c; 2 a; 3 b

D

Example answer:
From: Marita Bland
To: Paco Mendoza
Subject: re: social life in Lisbon
Dear Paco,
You asked about the social life in Lisbon. Lisbon is a very exciting, lively city, but it is quite expensive, so as a student here, you'll need to budget carefully.
There are ways that you can save some money. The college student centre offers free films and parties, and discount prices at the bar. Also, the local cinema and theatre offer student discounts, and entry to the art gallery is free. However, some sports facilities are expensive. The cheapest is probably the swimming pool. Also, restaurants are usually expensive here, but don't worry, my mum's a good cook!
We look forward to welcoming you here. Don't hesitate to write again if you have any more questions.
Best wishes,
Marita

VOCABULARY BUILDER QUIZ 15

A

1 T; 2 T; 3 F; 4 T; 5 F

B

1 It's an old motorbike, so it **isn't worth** much.
2 Our **insurance policy** covers fire and flooding.
3 It cost us €10,000 to **repair the damage** to the house.
4 In times of recession, people want more **job security**.
5 She decided to **buy shares** in the company.

C

1 loan;	3 suspect;	5 charity
2 popularity;	4 currency;	

D

1 c;   2 e;   3 d;   4 b;   5 a

E

1 up;	3 down;	5 into
2 down;	4 out;	

UNIT 16
VOCABULARY

A

1 reception;	4 end-of-term;	7 house-warming;
2 launch;	5 office;	8 dinner
3 surprise;	6 leaving;	

B

1 b;   2 f;   3 e;   4 c;   5 a;   6 d

C

1 host;	4 general;
2 comfortable and convenient;	5 full;
3 backward;	6 past

DEVELOPING CONVERSATIONS Linked questions

A

1 Did you have a good time?
2 What time did you leave?
3 And what was the venue like?
4 Was there anything to eat?
5 Or did you hang out with your friends?
6 Was anyone I know there?
7 Is he the person you went to school with?
8 What's he like?

LISTENING

A

d

B

Kind of party	21st birthday
Atmosphere	Fun and noisy
Venue	Converted warehouse
Food	Cold buffet
Music	DJ
End time	3.00 – 4.00 am

C

1 What kind of party is it going to be?
2 What sort of venue do you want?
3 Have you got any suggestions?
4 Can you think of anywhere else?
5 And are you going to serve any food?
6 What kind of music would you like?
7 What time do you want the party to finish?

PRONUNCIATION

A

1 With lots of people? ↗
2 Oh, yes, at least a hundred. ↘
3 How about a cold buffet? ↘
4 Yeah, a cold buffet's good. ↘
5 Shall we say three to four in the morning? ↗
6 Yeah, that's great. ↘

B

1 Where did you go last night? ↘
2 Did you see what she was wearing? ↗
3 Why were you so rude to him? ↘
4 Have you been here before? ↗
5 How many people here do you know? ↘
6 Are you going to eat something? ↗
7 Who's that man in the sunglasses near the bar? ↘
8 Do you have the time? ↗

Vocabulary

A

```
        ¹O C C U P A T I O N
        ²E M P I R E
        ³R E V O L U T I O N
⁴E X E C U T I O N
        ⁵B A T T L E S
        ⁶C R O W N E D
        ⁷M O N A R C H
              ⁸R E P U B L I C
```

B

1 independence;   3 colony;   5 decade;
2 defeated;   4 founded;   6 vote

C

1 Civil;   3 ruled;   5 Kingdom;
2 royal;   4 parliament;   6 Union

Reading

A

3

B

500	*The first settlers arrived.*
1778	*Captain Cook visited the islands.*
1779	*Captain Cook was killed.*
1805	*King Kamehameha established a monarchy*
1820	*Christian missionaries arrived.*
1893	*American businessmen seized power in a revolution.*
1898	*Hawaii became a territory of the USA.*
1941	*Japan attacked Pearl Harbor.*
1959	*Hawaii became the 50th state of the USA.*
1961	*Barack Obama was born.*

Grammar Prepositions and nouns / -ing forms

A

1 After *winning* the election, the President introduced a series of reforms.
2 Everything depends on *being* honest about the situation.
3 We are all opposed *to* raising taxes.
4 This problem was caused *by* cutting costs.
5 He was banned from *leaving* the country.
6 We are not involved in *importing* products from the USA.
7 Before *entering* parliament, he was a successful businessman.
8 These decisions led *to* the current crisis.

B

1 from;   2 in;   3 of;   4 for;   5 to;   6 in

C

1 dating;   5 ignoring;   9 farming;
2 involving;   6 lasting;   10 taking
3 received;   7 becoming;
4 voting;   8 buying;

Writing

A

The Normans sailed across the English Channel.
The Normans established a camp.
The Normans and the English fought a battle.
King Harold was killed.
William marched to London.
William was crowned king.

B

1 1066 is the year that the Normans invaded Britain.
2 William was the first in a line of kings and queens which includes Queen Elizabeth II.
4 Meanwhile = at the same time as

Listening

1 T;   2 F;   3 F;   4 F;   5 F;   6 T

Grammar Verb patterns

A

1 I forgot to post the letter. I remember telling her to go home early.
2 He spent two weeks doing nothing. She decided to review all the work.
3 They hated going to the theatre. They persuaded us to play tennis.
4 I'd like to help my parents with their business. I don't feel like watching TV this evening.
5 She loved taking her brother to school. She asked me to help with her assignment.
6 Her new boss offered to help her sort out the accounts. The new job stopped her spending so much time at home.

B

1 Yes. I hate taking the bus.
2 No. I stopped smoking last year.
3 I'd like to go to Hawaii.
4 No, thanks. I feel like watching TV at home.
5 Because I forgot to pay my bill.
6 I remember seeing my brother's face.
7 I spent a year working for my father's business.
8 Yes. I managed to speak to her yesterday.

Vocabulary Builder Quiz 16

A

1 settled;   4 side;
2 accused;   5 dates;
3 connection;   6 ruined

B

1 warm;   4 opposed;
2 independent;   5 converted;
3 significant;   6 impression

C

1 F;   2 T;   3 F;   4 F;   5 T;   6 T;   7 T

D

1 colony;   4 rule;
2 decade;   5 bowl;
3 empire;   6 agriculture

CD1		
TRACK	**ITEM**	
1	titles	
2	1.1	1 Babur Wahidi
3		2 Joe Albright
4		3 Carrie Hutton
5	1.2	
6	1.3	
7	1.4	
8	2.1	
9	2.2	
10	3.1	Part 1
11	3.2	Part 2
12	3.3	
13	3.4	
14	4.1	Part 1
15	4.2	Part 2
16	4.3	
17	4.4	
18	4.5	
19	4.6	
20	5.1	
21	5.2	
22	6.1	
23	7.1	Conversation 1
24		Conversation 2
25	7.2	Part 1
26	7.3	Part 2
27	7.4	
28	7.5	
29	8.1	
30	8.2	
31	8.3	
32	8.4	Part 1
33	8.5	Part 2
34	9.1	
35	9.2	
36	10.1	
37	10.2	
38	11.1	Speaker 1
39		Speaker 2
40		Speaker 3
41		Speaker 4
42	11.2	Conversation 1
43		Conversation 2
44		Conversation 3
45	11.3	
46	11.4	
47	12.1	
48	12.2	
49	12.3	
50	13.1	
51	13.2	
52	14.1	

CD1		
TRACK	**ITEM**	
53	14.2	
54	14.3	
55	15.1	
56	15.2	
57	15.3	
58	16.1	
59	16.2	
60	16.3	
61	16.4	